SUSAN M. BRAIDI
Assistant Professor, West Virginia University, USA

The Acquisition of Second-Language Syntax

A member of the Hodder Headline

LONDON · NEW YORK

D1387191

First published in Great Britain in 1999 by
Arnold, a member of the Hodder Headline Group,
338 Euston Road, London NW1 3BH

http://www.arnoldpublishers.com

Co-published in the United States of America by
Oxford University Press Inc.,
198 Madison Avenue, New York, NY 10016

© 1999 Susan M. Braidi

The advice and information in this book are believed to be true and accurate at the date of going to
press, but neither the author nor the publisher can accept any legal responsibility or liability for any
errors or omissions.

British Library Cataloguing in Publication Data
A catalogue entry for this book is available from the British Library

Library of Congress Cataloging-in-Publication Data
Braidi, Susan, 1954–
    The acquisition of second-language syntax / Susan Braidi.
        p.   cm.
    Includes bibliographical references (p.   ) and index.
    ISBN 0–340–64592–X. — ISBN 0–340–64591–1 (pbk.)
    1. Second language acquisition.   2. Grammar, Comparative and
general—Syntax.   3. Principles and parameters (Linguistics)
4. Universals (Linguistics)   I. Title.
P118.2.B7   1998
418′.007—dc21   98-8220
                                                      CIP

ISBN 0 340 64592 X (hb)
ISBN 0 340 64591 1 (pb)

1 2 3 4 5 6 7 8 9 10

Production Editor: Rada Radojicic
Production Controller: Helen Whitehorn
Cover Design: Terry Griffiths

Composition by Phoenix Photosetting, Chatham, Kent
Printed and bound in Great Britain by MPG Books, Bodmin, Cornwall

What do you think about this book? Or any other Arnold title? Please send your comments to
feedback.arnold@hodder.co.uk

Table of contents

This book is dedicated to
Louise A. and Andrew P. Braidi
and
Michael Mackert

Preface

Why this book? An informal survey that I conducted revealed that prospective second-language (L2) teachers' interests in L2 acquisition of syntax centred on three main issues: (1) the ease or difficulty with which structural forms are acquired as reflected in the order of acquisition, (2) the relationship between the acquisition of structural forms and their functions, and (3) the possible implications for instruction – i.e. instructional methods that will make the acquisition process more successful for L2 learners.

The implicit questions underlying these interests are 'How and why does L2 grammatical development proceed as it does?' and 'What can I do about it in the classroom?' Although most L2 research is ultimately directed towards answering the first question, it is often difficult for students to see how the research articles that they read relate to the whole puzzle of L2 acquisition. Since many students may also be practically motivated, not only do they want to understand how the information all fits together; they also want to know how they, as prospective L2 teachers, can use this information to inform their decisions about teaching.

One reason that applied-linguistics students have such difficulty integrating the material is the many different perspectives that L2 researchers take in examining L2 grammatical development. In addition, researchers working in different research paradigms ask different types of questions about the L2-acquisition process. Without an understanding of the assumptions which shape those questions, the numerous research findings seem to form a less-than-coherent picture. The goal of this book, then, is to outline and explain the questions asked within different research paradigms, to examine the results found in each approach, and to evaluate the contributions of each to our understanding of L2 acquisition of syntax and to possible implications for L2 instruction.

Acknowledgements

I would like to acknowledge a number of students and colleagues for various types of assistance: discussing ideas, verifying language examples, sending manuscripts, reading drafts, drawing computer graphics, and compiling bibliographic entries. Without the help of the following people, this book would not have been possible: Karen Adams, Maria Amores, Marta Barreales, Dawn Bates, Jennifer Burkart, Rose Chang, Tracy Dingess, Pam Erramuzpe, Ahmed Fakhri, Letticia Galindo, Andrea Graham, S.J. Hannahs, Deborah Janson, Yuko Koga, Paul Lux, Michael Mackert, Frank Medley, Takeko Minami, Jennie Nelson, Kota Ohata, Helene Ossipov, Bethyl Pearson, Manfred Pienemann, Charlene Polio, Michael Reider, Jennifer Ritter, David Roth, Johan Seynnaeve, Anne Vainikka, Julie Van Ooyen, Juliann Vitullo, Wendy Wilkins, and Sharon Wilkinson. I would like to thank the editors at Arnold for all of their assistance: Naomi Meredith, Christina Wipf-Perry, Rada Radojicic, and Hilary Walford. I would also like to acknowledge that this work was funded in part by a research grant from the Department of English at Arizona State University, by a Faculty-Grant-In-Aid from Arizona State University, and by the Direct Document Project at Hayden Library of Arizona State University.

The author and the publisher would like to thank Gunter Narr Verlag for permission to reproduce an extract from Wode, Henning: Learning a Second Language (1981).

Special thanks go to M².

Susan M. Braidi
2 April 1998

Abbreviations

CAH	contrastive analysis hypothesis
COS	Canonical Order Strategy
DO	direct object
DP	determiner phrase
GB	Government and Binding
GEN	genitive
HK	information assumed known to the hearer
IFS	Initialisation/Finalisation Strategy
IL	interlanguage
IO	indirect object
IP	inflection phrase
L1	first language
L2	second language
2L1	bilingual L1 speakers
MDH	Markedness Differential Hypothesis
MUP	Morphological Uniformity Principle
NL	native language
NPAH	Noun Phrase Accessibility Hierarchy
OCOMP	object of a comparative
OP	object of a preposition
PLD	primary linguistic data
SCS	Subordinate Clause Strategy
SLI	specific language impairment
SR	specific referent
SUB	subject
TL	target language
Tp	topic
UG	Universal Grammar

1

Introduction

1.1 Introduction

Since the 1970s there has been a proliferation of research examining second-language (L2) acquisition in general and L2 acquisition of grammar in particular. Not only is the amount of research impressive, but the broad range of approaches taken and the number of structures examined add to the diverse nature of this area of research. The result of this research is threefold: (1) information about which structures L2 learners acquire with ease or with difficulty, (2) explanations of how and why grammatical development proceeds as it does, and (3) ensuing questions about how all of this information fits together. If we consider L2-acquisition research as a large, unfinished jigsaw puzzle (Gass 1989b), research pertaining to L2 grammatical development constitutes one section of that puzzle, with each approach contributing one or more pieces to the puzzle. The question addressed in this book is 'What does L2 grammatical research contribute to our understanding of the L2-acquisition puzzle?' With a broad range of approaches comes diverse usage of terminology, so let us first turn to some issues of terminology.

1.2 What is grammar?

When one asks naïve native speakers, 'What is grammar?', the responses may range anywhere from notions of prescriptive grammar rules taught in school, such as 'Don't strand prepositions at the end of the sentence' and 'It is incorrect to use the word *ain't*', to notions of descriptive grammar rules such as 'Mark the past tense of regular verbs with *-ed*.' A similarly broad range of definitions is evident in the study of L2 acquisition of grammar, since researchers in the field have taken a variety of perspectives on the scope of what constitutes the acquisition of grammar.

In its broadest sense, the term *grammar* is generally accepted to incorporate different levels of structure of language, including phonology, morphology, syntax, and semantics. Grammar, as defined by Richards, Platt, and Platt (1992: 161), is:

a description of the structure of a language and the way in which linguistic units such as words and phrases are combined to produce sentences in the language. It usually takes into account the meanings and functions these sentences have in the overall system of the language.

A narrower view of grammar, on the other hand, limits itself to the domain of *syntax*, the rules which govern the arrangement of words in the formation of sentences in a language. Research of L2 grammatical development has ranged between the broad view of grammar, as it relates sentence-level structures to grammatical functions within the discourse, and the narrower view, which focuses on the sentence level. Both of these approaches have foundations in theoretical linguistics.

L2 research in the generative tradition has taken the narrow view of grammatical development. In his characterization of the ideal speaker, Chomsky (1965) has distinguished between grammatical competence, or (non-conscious) knowledge of language, and performance, or actual use of language. This distinction serves to remove the knowledge of grammatical rules from how one applies those rules in any given situation under the conditions found in language use, such as memory limitations or distractions. This competence/performance dichotomy has formed the basis of the generative approach to linguistics, which focuses on grammatical competence as the subject of enquiry. In the formulation of a generative grammar, linguists have attempted to 'characterize the knowledge of the language that provides the basis for actual use of language' by the ideal speaker-hearer in a homogeneous speech-community (Chomsky 1965: 9). For instance, one area of investigation looks at the grammatical principles which determine the proper placement of adverbs in English sentences with the ungrammatical forms marked with an asterisk (*):

(1.1)
  (a) Sally watches television often.
  (b) *Sally watches often television.

L2 researchers working within this generative approach have focused their attention on the L2 learner's development of competence at the level of syntax.

Functional approaches to language, as exemplified by the work of Givón (1984a, 1990), have rejected the competence/performance distinction which separates grammatical knowledge from language use in favour of approaches that link grammatical form to grammatical function. It is argued that grammatical form cannot be understood in isolation of its function. As Givón maintains (1984a: 29), 'By insisting on the joint study of function and the typology of structures which code it, one opens the door to a serious investigation of how – and ultimately why – particular structures perform their assigned functions'. Functional approaches, then, focus on the speaker's use of language in a social context (the discourse), the functions that the language fulfils, and the grammatical structures that encode those functions. For example, researchers have examined L2 learner usage of full noun phrases and pronouns to mark different discourse functions such as introducing a topic in the discourse (1.2a) versus continuing the topic in the discourse (1.2b):

(1.2)
  (a) *That man, he* is my neighbour.
  (b) *He* works at the hospital.

Within a functional framework, research in L2 grammatical development has examined ways in which the relationship between grammatical form and function interacts in the acquisition process. The focus of enquiry in the study of L2 grammatical development, then, ranges from the study of strictly syntactic phenomena to the production and function of syntactic structures in discourse.

Another issue of terminology involves the notions of rules. For most people the words 'grammar rules' conjure up images of learning language in a classroom setting; the grammar rules learned in class, however, are but one type of grammar rule. Within the study of L2 acquisition of grammar, we can distinguish four types of grammar rule (cf. Rutherford and Sharwood Smith 1988). In the wake of work in generative grammar, the first type is exemplified by the rules derived from generative linguistic theory.[1] The linguists' grammar rules can be seen as the constraints and principles that linguists propose as a description of native-speaker competence. The linguists' rules are not to be confused with the actual rules which constitute the native speaker's competence. Although we cannot specify the actual forms of the rules in a native speaker's competence, we can see the results of those rules as demonstrated by a native speaker's judgements of which sentences belong to the native language (grammatical sentences) and which sentences do not (ungrammatical sentences). This second type of rule, which forms part of the native speaker's mental representation of the language, will be referred to as native-speaker competence rules.[2] This distinction is important in that it emphasizes the fact that the rules formulated within a linguistic theory are a hypothetical model of what a native speaker 'knows' about the native language.

As a basis for understanding the rule types relevant to L2 acquisition, it is essential first to discuss an additional distinction. Some researchers in L2 acquisition (Krashen 1981; Schwartz 1986, 1993; cf. Gregg 1984, 1988) have distinguished between two different types of L2 linguistic knowledge. One type of linguistic knowledge is comparable to native-speaker competence – that is, the non-native speaker's interlanguage (IL) competence that results from the learner's grammar building based on the linguistic input, or primary linguistic data (PLD). Primary linguistic data refer to any utterances of the L2 in the learner's environment; for instance, utterances with different examples of plural nouns in English ('I have cats;' 'Mary likes apples'; 'Buses make too much noise') constitute the primary linguistic data from which the learner may acquire a rule for marking plurality on English nouns. This type of knowledge, referred to by Krashen as 'acquired' knowledge, is differentiated from linguistic knowledge that comes from learning explicit information about the structure of a language (for example, 'To form the plural of English nouns, add an -*s* or -*es*'). Therefore, the distinction is made between acquiring the language from input comparable to the type of input that children receive during first-language (L1) acquisition, primary linguistic data, and learning the language by memorizing explicit rules about the language. Crucial to this distinction is the claim that only primary linguistic data can be used by the learner to construct an interlanguage competence. Other information about the language will form part of the learner's 'learned linguistic knowledge' (Schwartz 1993: 150), comparable to the learner's encyclopaedic knowledge consisting of facts about topics other than language.[3]

With this proposed distinction in mind, we return to the two remaining types of grammar rule. Pedagogical rules, such as the explicit rule for marking English plural nouns stated above, form the third type of rule. Pedagogical rules are formulated by linguists, applied linguists, textbook writers, or teachers and are explicitly taught in instructed L2 acquisition.[4] These rules are incorporated into the learner's knowledge of the structure of the L2 in some way, either only as 'learned linguistic knowledge' or eventually as part of the learner's constructed IL competence. The final type of grammar rule has already been alluded to previously: the rules that the L2 learner actively constructs during the L2-acquisition process. The latter will be referred to as the learner's IL competence rules. As with native-speaker competence rules, we can only infer the form of IL rules based on the L2 learner's performance on production tasks (e.g. free conversation, grammaticality judgements, or grammatical exercises).

These four types of grammar rule are illustrated here with reference to wh-question formation in English. Consider the formation of the question *What is Terry reading?* Different linguistic theories offer differing accounts of question formation. Within a generative grammar approach (Chomsky 1981, 1986b), for instance, it is assumed that the underlying form of the question is *Terry is reading what?* The wh-word *what* and the auxiliary verb *is* are then fronted to different initial positions in the sentence (the details of this approach will be discussed in a subsequent chapter). Whenever any element is fronted, it leaves behind a co-indexed trace (t_i, t_j, etc.) in its original position in the underlying form. The following is a representation of the question with the two co-indexed traces inserted to represent the fronted wh-word and auxiliary:

(1.3)   What$_i$ is$_j$ Terry t_j reading t_i ?

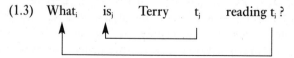

The model is proposed to represent a native English speaker's grammatical intuitions of which sentences are grammatical formulations of questions. Although the actual forms of the rules of the native speaker's competence cannot be specified, the effects of their application can be seen in the following grammaticality judgements, again with the ungrammatical forms marked with an asterisk:

(1.4)
- (a) What is Terry reading?
- (b) *What Terry is reading?
- (c) *Is Terry reading what?
- (d) *Is what Terry reading?

As the judgements show, a native speaker of English will accept questions with fronting of both the wh-word representing the direct object and the auxiliary (1.4a). Fronting of only one of those elements is judged as ungrammatical (1.4b, c). Fronting these elements to the wrong positions is also deemed unacceptable (1.4d).

Examples of possible pedagogical rules that are written to guide L2 learners to the correct form of English wh-questions incorporate both the notions of wh-fronting and subject–auxiliary inversion:

(1.5)
- (a) 'Yes/No Questions with *Be*: To make a yes/no question with the verb *be*, put the correct form of the verb *be* in front of the subject. Put a question mark (?) at the end of the question.' (Badalamenti and Henner-Stanchina 1993: 13)

- (b) '*Wh*-Questions with *Be*: To form *Wh*-questions with *be*, use a *Wh*-question word followed by the correct form of the verb *be*. Use *Wh*-questions to ask for specific information.' (Badalamenti and Henner-Stanchina 1993: 23)

- (c) 'Yes/No Questions in the Present Progressive: To make a question in the present progressive, move the verb *be* in front of the subject.' (Badalamenti and Henner-Stanchina 1993: 202)

As stated above, the extent to which such pedagogical rules are influential in the development of IL grammatical competence is an issue of debate.

An L2 learner's IL competence rules represent part of the learner's IL competence at a given point in time. Therefore, at different stages of development, learners exhibit different grammaticality judgements and produce various forms of wh-questions based on the different IL competence rules that they have formulated. The sample question, *What is Terry reading?*, has been adapted to developmental stages proposed for simple and embedded wh-questions indicated below by roman numerals (Cancino *et al.* 1978: 230):

(1.6)

(I) *Undifferentiation:* learner does not distinguish between simple and embedded questions.

(a) Uninverted wh-questions: both simple and embedded wh-questions are uninverted.
What Terry is reading?
I know what Terry is reading.

(b) Variable inversion: simple wh-questions are sometimes inverted, sometimes not.
What is Terry reading?
What Terry is reading?

(c) Generalization: increasing inversion in wh-questions and inversion being extended to embedded questions.
What is Terry reading?
I know what is Terry reading.

(II) *Differentiation:* learner distinguishes between simple and embedded wh-questions with inversion in simple wh-questions and uninversion in embedded wh-questions.
What is Terry reading?
I know what Terry is reading.

It is proposed that L2 learners will pass through these stages of development for wh-questions and will exhibit IL production and grammaticality judgements consistent with these stages.

In contrast to the competence-based generative approach, functional approaches to language focus on the functions of linguistic forms by also taking into account discourse and pragmatics. Functional analyses typically include how information is presented, identified, and maintained in the discourse as well as what the expectations and goals of the interlocutors are (Givón 1984a; Klein and Perdue 1992b). The proposed functions (e.g. presenting and tracing referents, indicating presupposed knowledge, signalling background and foreground information (Givón 1984a)) may be encoded by a number of grammatical devices, and different languages allow for different encoding mechanisms. For example, the presentation of an entity in the discourse in English may be achieved by the use of a proper noun (*John* stole the umbrella), or a common noun with an indefinite article (*A man* stole the umbrella) or with a deictic marker (*This* man stole the umbrella), depending on the context. I shall refer to these encoding mechanisms as grammar encoding rules to identify them as discourse based, as opposed to the grammatical rules and the pedagogical rules discussed above.

As with IL competence rules, IL grammar encoding rules developed by the L2 learner may differ in form from those of the native speaker. That is, while the native English speaker encodes noun reference in one way (e.g. by using the definite article *the* to mark nouns which have specific referents that are assumed to be known to the hearer), the L2 learner may encode nominal reference differently. As shown by Huebner (1983), his subject originally marked the reference of nouns with *da* (i.e. *the*) to include specific referents that were known to the hearer and that were not the topic. How, then, do IL grammar encoding rules differ from IL competence rules? The major difference is theoretical. IL competence rules are based on the notion that language competence is distinct from language use. IL grammar encoding rules, on the other hand, are based on the notion that grammatical forms develop from communicative function; that is, learners develop particular grammatical forms in their IL to fit their communicative needs in the L2. Because of these theoretical differences, the L2 researcher's linguistic description of and explanation for the L2 learner language system will also differ based on the conventions of the particular linguistic theory.

There is one additional factor to be considered which is related to our discussion of rules. The native speaker competence rules and the IL competence rules both exemplify a speaker's mental representation of his/her linguistic competence. Models of L2 acquisition based on descriptive models of such linguistic knowledge have been termed 'competence models' (Bialystok 1990a; Spolsky 1989). L2 acquisition, however, also involves the processing of linguistic information; models which include 'descriptions of methods of storage and means of accessing those rules' are seen as processing models (Bialystok 1990a: 637). Therefore, not only is one's mental representation of linguistic knowledge a relevant factor in L2 acquisition, but the effect of linguistic processing on L2 development must also be taken into account.

There are several reasons for distinguishing these types of rules. First, L2-acquisition research makes specific reference to these various rule types. In addition, L2 researchers working in different paradigms are examining the development of a learner's IL rules based on different types of linguistic models: competence-based, discourse-based, and processing-based models. As a result, research findings may be intricately related to the particular formulation of the linguistic rules on which the research is based (White 1991b). Finally, since L2 acquisition occurs in instructed settings and natural settings, it is necessary to account for the effects of pedagogical rules in addition to those of discourse/pragmatic functions in the developmental process.

1.3 What is acquisition?

The issue of L2 acquisition of grammar becomes even more complicated when we consider the term *language acquisition*. What does it mean to say that a structure has been acquired by a given learner or even by a group of learners? Again, diverse answers to this question can be found in the L2-acquisition research. Much of the L2-acquisition research that was modelled on research examining the L1 acquisition of morphemes adopted the convention that a structure was acquired when it occurred three times in a row in an obligatory context at a rate of 90 per cent (Cazden 1968). There are a number of problems, however, with this definition (Hatch 1978a). One problem has to do with limiting the definition to obligatory contexts; that is, by considering the learner's suppliance of the structure only in obligatory contexts, we ignore any occurrence of the structure in other, perhaps incorrect, contexts. In addition, it is often difficult to define what an obligatory context is. In the question *What is Terry reading?*, it is fairly straightforward to identify obligatory contexts for the occurrence of the auxiliary *is* in combination with the inflectional verbal morpheme *-ing* marking progressive aspect or for subject–auxiliary inversion in a wh-question. The obligatory contexts for other structures are less evident. Certain languages, such as Italian and Spanish, allow for two different word orders in declarative sentences, as seen in the Italian example below:

(1.7)
   (a) I   bambini mangiano le mele.
       The children are eating the apples.

   (b) Mangiano le mele   i   bambini.
       Are eating the apples the children.

The difference in word orders signifies a difference in emphasis, with the emphasis placed on the sentence-final position. However, how does one accurately determine the obligatory contexts for emphasis even if discourse is taken into account?

In addition to the issues involving obligatory contexts, the morpheme-acquisition studies of the 1970s raised the question of acquisition order versus accuracy order (Larsen-Freeman 1975). In a longitudinal study of a learner's acquisition, it is possible to determine the order in which given morphemes appear in the learner's grammar, since samples of the learner's production are taken at various points in the acquisition process. On the other hand, in cross-sectional studies of groups of learners at a single point in time, we can establish the level of accuracy with which those learners use those morphemes only at that given time. We cannot claim, however, that the accuracy order at a given time reflects the acquisitional order across time.

An alternative has been to define the acquisition of a structure as the point at which it emerges in the learner's IL. For example, Meisel, Clahsen, and Pienemann (1981) posit different stages of development for German word order which are determined by the emergence of a rule characterizing each given stage (e.g. subject–verb inversion). At that point, the learner is said to have entered the new stage of grammatical development, even though the rules from the previous stage may not yet have been mastered in all possible contexts. Thus, this approach eliminates the problem of defining the point at which a learner has reached the target-language norm. It does not, however, eliminate the issue of obligatory versus nonobligatory contexts; that is, since this approach allows for variation within a given stage, the possible contexts must still be identified in order to depict that variation accurately.

Acquisition has also been viewed from a 'dynamic', form–function approach, which focuses both on the structural form and on the function of that form in the learner's IL system. In a longitudinal study of a single L2 learner, Huebner (1983) shows that the subject's acquisition of the definite- and indefinite-article system in English cannot be determined simply from the occurrence of these forms in obligatory contexts. For example, from a strictly formal analysis, the subject of his study seems to acquire the definite article in obligatory contexts relatively quickly. However, by analysing the subject's use of the article *da* (*the*) in obligatory, optional, and ungrammatical contexts, a number of shifts in the function of *da* are revealed. Huebner argues, then, that not only is it necessary to examine the occurrence of the structure in all possible contexts, but it is also necessary to examine the functions for which the structure is being used.

Other researchers have utilized statistical measures to determine whether or not a given structure has been acquired (e.g. White 1988). By including both an experimental group of L2 learners and a control group of native speakers, one is able to measure the difference in performance between the learners and the native speakers. If the L2 group performance is not significantly different from the L1 control group as measured statistically, then the L2 group is said to have acquired the L2 structure.

As seen above, the L2 researcher's definitions of both *grammar* and *acquisition* influence not only how L2 grammatical development is viewed, but, more basically, what constitutes the focus of enquiry – that is, the L2 grammar itself. In order to be able to include in this book the broad range of studies that examine L2 grammatical development, I adopt here a broad definition of grammar to include not only rules that apply at the sentence level, but also rules of discourse that may constrain or influence the actual form that the grammar takes. The subsequent usage of the terms *grammar* and *syntax* will reflect respectively the broad and narrow definitions.

1.4 Historical perspectives on second-language grammar development

The current approaches to L2 grammatical research reflect reassessment and development of earlier approaches. In order to understand the current trends in L2 research of grammatical development more completely, it is first necessary to consider this research within its historical context. Research in the field has at different times focused on different aspects of language development, from a focus on particular structures to the examination of different stages and processes of acquisition, each determined by differing underlying assumptions guiding the research. The three major approaches to L2 acquisition that have led to the current state of acquisition studies are contrastive analysis, error analysis, and IL analysis.

The focus of L2-acquisition studies from the 1950s to the 1970s was influenced by both structural linguistics and behavioural psychology. Structural linguistics was mainly concerned with the description of patterns of structures within a language system. Therefore, emphasis was placed on the identification and distribution of linguistic structures – sounds, words, and sentences – in a given language. The influence of structural linguistics is seen clearly in the contrastive-analysis approach to L2 development, and particularly in the work of Fries (1945) and Lado (1957). The contrastive-analysis hypothesis stated that, by comparing and contrasting the structures of the native language with those of the target language, one could predict which target-language structures would cause difficulties for the L2 learner. As Lado (1957: p. vii) wrote in his preface to *Linguistics across cultures*:

> The plan of the book rests on the assumption that we can predict and describe the patterns that will cause difficulty in learning, and those that will not cause difficulty, by comparing systematically the language and culture to be learned with the native language and culture of the student.

Lado further claimed that learners tended to transfer both the forms and the meanings and the distribution of forms and meanings from their native language to the target language (1957: 2). Therefore, learners would have difficulties with some aspects of the target language and not with others. The underlying assumption was that, owing both to this tendency to transfer native-language forms and meanings and to the differences evidenced between the two languages, learners would have difficulty with structures that differed and would find structures that were similar to their native languages less difficult.

From the perspective of behavioural psychology, language acquisition was seen as a process of habit formation in which a stimulus triggered a particular response, which in turn was strengthened by continued reinforcement. The influence of behaviourist methods as applied to language teaching was manifested in the Audio-Lingual Method, in which isolated language patterns were drilled until the learner had acquired the new language habits. By also taking contrastive analysis into account, one could concentrate on those patterns predicted to cause difficulty.

By the late 1960s and early 1970s, the contrastive-analysis approach to language development had come under attack for reasons related to the frameworks of both structural linguistics and behavioural psychology. Wardhaugh (1970), in arguing against the value of contrastive analysis, distinguished two versions of the contrastive-analysis hypothesis, a strong and a weak version. The strong version assumed that it was

> possible to contrast the system of one language – the grammar, phonology, and lexicon – with the system of a second language in order to *predict* those

difficulties which a speaker of the second language will have in learning the first language and to construct teaching material to help him learn that language. (Wardhaugh 1970: 124).

Wardhaugh (1970: 125) pointed out, however, that linguistic theory was unable to meet the demands of the strong version because there were no comprehensive linguistic theories formulated that dealt adequately enough with syntax, semantics, and phonology to allow for the type of analysis needed. The weak version of the hypothesis claimed that one could use the linguistic knowledge provided by a contrastive analysis to account for the difficulties that L2 learners were observed to experience. The weak version, therefore, gave up the predictive claims of the strong version while maintaining the assumption that difficulties experienced by language learners could be traced back to structural differences between the native and the target languages.[5]

Corder (1967), in his influential paper on learner errors, noted two problems with contrastive analysis: that contrastive analysis simply confirmed what teachers already knew because teachers were familiar with the errors predicted by contrastive analysis and, more importantly, that many of the errors that learners made were not predicted by contrastive analysis. Thus, the predictive effectiveness of contrastive analysis was again called into question. Corder also highlighted another flaw of contrastive analysis – namely, that its focus was on teaching rather than on learning. Learners' errors would gain a new significance if the focus of research were on the learning process. Following Chomsky's (1965) notions of linguistic competence and performance, Corder maintained that a learner's errors revealed the nature of his/her underlying linguistic knowledge, or *transitional competence*. These errors, as contrasted with unsystematic mistakes of performance, 'provide evidence of the system of the language that he is using (i.e. has learned) at a particular point . . .' (Corder 1967: 167). Learners' errors came to be viewed as an indication of the learning process rather than as evidence of bad language habits and thus became the new focus of L2-acquisition research.

In addition to the criticism concerning the underlying assumptions and the teaching focus of contrastive analysis, researchers began to find that learners of different native languages made similar errors, a fact that was not predicted and that could not be accounted for by the contrastive-analysis approach. In a series of studies examining children's L2 acquisition of grammatical structures (e.g. wh-question formation and word order) and of grammatical morphemes (e.g. past tense and possessive) in English,[6] Dulay and Burt (1972, 1973, 1974a, b) found evidence that child learners from different native-language backgrounds (Spanish, Chinese, Japanese, and Norwegian) made errors that were 'strikingly similar' (1974b: 37). They proposed that these L2 learners were utilizing a process of 'creative construction' defined as:

the process in which children gradually reconstruct rules for speech they hear, guided by universal innate mechanisms which cause them to formulate certain types of hypotheses about the language system being acquired, until the mismatch between what they are exposed to and what they produce is resolved. (Dulay and Burt 1974b: 37)

Therefore, the impact of the native language on the acquisition of these grammatical structures seemed far less influential than did the natural process of creative construction. Similar findings with adult learners of English as a second language reported by Bailey, Madden, and Krashen (1974) had led to the claim that children and adults used common strategies in the L2-acquisition process and that there was a natural order of acquisition for these grammatical functors. Although a thorough discussion of the findings and the difficulties of the morpheme-acquisition studies is beyond the scope of this book (see J.D. Brown 1983; Hatch 1983; Larsen-Freeman 1975, 1976; Larsen-Freeman and Long 1991; Rosansky 1976), suffice it to say that the creative-construction hypothesis helped to shift the focus of L2 research away from native-language interference towards the learner's developmental processes.

Corder's argument for the significance of learner's errors and the new focus on learner's strategies and processes resulted in the rise of error analysis as an approach to dealing with L2 acquisitional data. The underlying tenets of this approach, as outlined by Schachter (1974: 206–7), were as follows:

The main assumption is that error analysis will reveal to the investigator just what difficulties the learners in fact have, that difficulties in the target language will show up as errors in production. The second assumption is that the frequency of occurrence of specific errors will give evidence of their relative difficulty.

Richards (1974) identified three types of errors made by learners: interference errors, caused by the structure of the native language (L1 Spanish speakers of L2 English: *(I) no speak English*); intra-lingual errors, originating in the structure of the target language itself (dummy *do* for question formation in L2 English: *Did he talked*), and developmental errors, reflecting the strategies employed to acquire the target language (*is* as a present tense marker in L2 English: *She is speaks Japanese*).

Error analysis was not without problems, however. Schachter and Celce-Murcia (1977) argued that it was not enough to analyse errors in isolation. A more complete picture of the grammar that the learner was constructing was possible only by analysing both the errors made and the instances in which the structure was used correctly. In addition, once an error had been identified, classification of the identified error was not so straightforward. For example, the following errors made by Chinese learners of English (taken from Schachter and Celce-Murcia 1977: 445) could be analysed as either intra-lingual or interference errors:

(1.8)
  (a) There are so many Taiwan people * live around the lake.
  (b) ... and there is a mountain * separate two lakes.

As examples of intra-lingual errors, these errors were analysed as errors in English subject relative clauses in which the learners had failed to include the relative pronouns *who*, *that*, or *which*. Schachter and Celce-Murcia argued that an equally plausible alternative analysis was that the Chinese speakers were attempting to construct a topic–comment structure in which the topic was first established (e.g. *Taiwan people*), and the comment about the topic followed (e.g. *(they) live around the lake*). The topic–comment analysis would constitute an interference error caused by the structure of Chinese, the native language. Finally, although error analysis attempted to account for the nature and frequency of learner errors, it could not account for non-errors. That is, learners avoided producing structures that were difficult for them, resulting in no or few errors (Kleinmann 1977; Schachter 1974). Thus, error analysis neglected to identify avoidance of difficult structures as a strategy in L2 acquisition.

Despite differences in these two approaches, contrastive analysis and error analysis shared one basic underlying assumption: the view that the learner's developing system was in some way flawed because it did not conform with the rules of the target language. From the perspective of contrastive analysis, learners' errors reflected bad language habits influenced by the native language. From an error-analysis perspective, errors were determined based on the target-language norm without recognition of the role that such ill-formed structures had in the learner's transitional system. The IL approach, the third approach to L2 acquisition, shifted the focus to the learner's developing grammar as a systematic grammar in its own right.

Selinker (1972) described the L2 learner's grammatical system as an 'interlanguage' – that is, 'a separate linguistic system based on the observable output which results from a learner's attempted production of a TL [target language] norm' (p. 214).[7] This new focus on IL led researchers to examine how the learner's developing grammar functioned as a separate system. Selinker outlined five central processes that contributed to the form of a learner's IL: language transfer, transfer of training, strategies of L2 learning, strategies of L2 communication, and overgeneralization of target-language linguistic material. Adjemian (1976) further developed the notion of IL by arguing that IL systems were natural languages, and as natural languages they were constrained by a system of linguistic rules exhibiting internal consistency, 'which results in the production of particular structures on a more or less regular basis' (p. 307). At the same time, ILs differed from other natural languages because they were in a state of flux and thus permeable, a characteristic that allowed the IL system to be penetrated by native-language rules or forms and to distort target-language rules or forms in attempts to communicate. Although the IL system became the focus of research, Bley-Vroman (1983) cautioned that research that analysed data with 'concepts defined relative to the target language' (p. 1) was based on a 'comparative fallacy'. That is, the continued comparison with the target-language norm obscured the internal logic of the IL system.

As we shall see, current approaches to L2 acquisition incorporate characteristics of all of these three trends, but with some changes in perspective. IL grammars have been accepted as language systems with their own rules, which may differ from both the native language and the target-language rules. The variation found in IL grammars is due to a variety of factors, including structure, task, or interlocutor, among others. Furthermore, researchers recognize an influential role for the native language in the formulation of IL grammars. While contrastive analysis was originally based on the contrast between the surface structures of the native language and the target language, current approaches compare and contrast the underlying, abstract constraints on language rules in order to make predictions about the course of L2 development (Flynn 1987a). The notion of creative construction has been similarly reformulated; for example, the hypothesis of Universal Grammar as the innate mechanism that guides both L1 and L2 acquisition has set the direction for one approach to L2 grammatical development research. Finally, other research (Clahsen 1980; Pienemann 1984) has examined different stages of acquisition, reminiscent of the claims made for a natural order of acquisition for particular grammatical structures. As the area of L2 acquisition develops, researchers continue to reformulate and refine earlier hypotheses and notions and to incorporate new and enlightening discoveries.

1.5 The plan of the book

Although I have claimed that there are several approaches taken in the investigation of L2 acquisition, in reality, the different approaches are not always so distinct from one another. For example, studies based on the notion of language transfer focus on the role of the L1 in L2 acquisition by asking questions pertaining to which elements of the L1 can be transferred to the L2 and which elements actually are transferred (Gass and Selinker 1992). Similarly, the role of the L1 figures in research in the generative framework based on Universal Grammar. Within this framework, it is suggested that the L1 parameter setting will probably be adopted in the learner's L2 grammar if the L1 and the L2 both accept null subject pronouns (i.e. have the same setting for the pro-drop parameter). In other cases, research studies may take the same theoretical approach, but may focus on different aspects of the acquisition process – for instance, a functional approach to the processing of sentences (Gass 1987) as compared to a functional approach to the development of basic learner language (Klein and Perdue 1992b). It is, therefore, not such a straightforward task to identify distinct approaches and to classify particular research studies based on these approaches. This difficulty reflects the nature of

L2 acquisition as well, since the process involves a number of factors: the role of the L1, the strategies that L2 learners adopt in the acquisition process, the effect of the linguistic properties of the L1 and of the L2, and the cognitive processes involved in acquisition, comprehension, and production, to name just a few.

A coherent picture of L2 grammatical research is built by integrating this information in two different steps. First I address the different approaches taken to L2 grammatical development. As stated previously, I am here adopting a broad definition of grammatical development to include approaches concerning sentence-level syntax, those incorporating discourse constraints on the acquisition of syntax, and approaches dealing with processing constraints. In this step, I examine the contributions of researchers working in each approach to our understanding of L2 grammar acquisition and use. In the next step, I explore issues and notions that occur across different research paradigms (e.g. distinct views of how the L1 prior knowledge affects L2 grammar development, different perspectives on the emergence of learner stages, and diverse explanations for the acquisition of particular grammatical structures). By showing the interactions between the syntactic, processing, and functional/discourse levels and by highlighting the continuity of issues across approaches, I demonstrate how the diverse strands of L2 grammatical research complement each other.

In order to make a vast amount of information accessible, the development of each chapter will include three sections. The introductory section to each framework is guided by the following questions: What are the theoretical foundations of this approach? What assumptions are made within this approach? What structures are studied and why? The second section will address the following questions: What questions are asked within this paradigm? Why are those questions asked? The goal of this section is to synthesize the research findings by discussing how the particular structures are studied and what the research findings are. Finally, the findings are evaluated in terms of the goals and assumptions of the framework. In this manner, I examine the following approaches to the acquisition of grammar: L1 and L2 interrelations, Universal Grammar, typological universals, processing approaches, and functional approaches. My two criteria for discussing research in a particular chapter are the theoretical background of the research and the main focus of the work (e.g. competence, stages of acquisition, sentence processing).

Chapter 2, concerning L1 and L2 interrelations, makes the connection between earlier contrastive-analysis and morpheme-acquisition studies and more recent work examining L2 grammatical development. As Gass and Selinker (1992: 6) note, it is possible to view L2 acquisition as involving both processes of utilizing L1 knowledge and processes of hypothesis testing in the creation of an IL grammar. Thus, in more recent L2 research, the two central focuses of the earlier work, L1 influences and acquisitional/developmental stages, are expanded to include additional structures and more refined explanations. In this transitional chapter I review work that investigates L1 and L2 interrelations and that does not fit easily into the theoretical framework of other approaches.

The Universal Grammar approach explores the relationship between linguistic universals and L2 acquisition. This approach is based on Chomsky's (1981) notion of Universal Grammar (UG), an innate language structure consisting of a set of linguistic constraints that determine the forms that human language can take. UG is proposed to guide the child's L1 acquisition through interaction with the child's linguistic environment. The UG approach to L2 acquisition examines whether or not this innate language faculty remains operative in L2 acquisition, and it explores the effects of UG on the L2-acquisition process. Much recent work in this paradigm also investigates the relationship between UG, instruction, and grammatical development. This approach is discussed in Chapter 3.

Chapter 4 focuses on typological universal research in L2 acquisition. Typological studies in general examine the linguistic universals that account for the variability in human languages by focusing on the range of variation found in human languages and by exploring the limits of that variation. The typological approach to L2 acquisition examines the relationship between those typological universals and L2 acquisition to discover what role if any typological universals play in the acquisition process – that is, do these universals also operate on non-primary languages. Additional research in this paradigm looks at the effects of instruction on linguistic universals in L2 grammatical development.

Chapter 5 reviews the varied approaches taken to language processing and the role of processing in L2 acquisition of syntax. Several processing models have been proposed and applied to L2-acquisition research. For example, researchers have looked at the Competition Model proposed by Bates and MacWhinney (1981, 1982) to determine the types of competing linguistic cues (e.g. word order, animacy, pragmatics) that L2 learners utilize in L2 comprehension (Gass 1987; Harrington 1987). Additionally, information processing models have been proposed to 'describe the form and content of mental representations, the nature of their development, and the processes that operate upon those representations' (Bialystok 1990b). These models, as applied to L2 acquisition, attempt to account for ways in which linguistic information is analysed, represented, restructured, and produced (Bialystok and Sharwood Smith 1985; McLaughlin 1987, 1990; Sharwood Smith 1986). Yet other approaches treat the relationship between speech-processing constraints and stages of L2 syntactic development (Clahsen 1980, 1984; Pienemann 1984, 1989, 1997) as well as notions of input processing and language acquisition (VanPatten and Cadierno 1993b). It has been argued that a distinction must be made, however, between processing constraints and strategies for comprehension of L2 input and processing constraints and strategies for L2 production (White 1991a).

Functional approaches, as discussed in Chapter 6, take a broader perspective on L2 grammatical development with a focus on the relationship between grammatical forms and the meanings and/or functions they encode. Perdue and Klein (1992a), for instance, report on L2 learners' development of a 'basic variety', which the researchers characterize as a particular way in which learners structure 'their utterances which seems to represent a natural equilibrium between the various phrasal, semantic and pragmatic constraints' (p. 311). In a functional/discourse approach, various syntactic structures (e.g. noun phrases, word order, subordinate clauses, verbal morphology) are examined as they develop in relation to their functions. One example is the way in which pronouns develop in relation to their function of reference maintenance in a narrative discourse. Perdue and Klein (1992c: 265) find that '1. singular appears before plural, 2. nominative appears before oblique, 3. pronouns referring to humans appear before pronouns referring to inanimates, and 4. deictic NPs are generally used before pronouns'. Within a functional/discourse approach, discourse, semantics, syntax, and morphology are seen not as isolated aspects of grammar, but rather as factors that interact and influence the course of L2 grammatical development.

In the concluding chapter, I discuss the contributions of each approach. In order to illustrate the differences between the diverse approaches in a concrete way, in the first section of the chapter I explore the insights that each approach brings to the analysis of one particular syntactic structure: noun forms including nouns, lexical pronouns, zero pronouns, reflexive pronouns, and pronoun copies. Finally, based on this analysis and on the previous chapters, I evaluate how the research findings of all of these approaches can be integrated, and I discuss the implications of this research for teaching. My goal is to incorporate the many different pieces of the grammar puzzle into a more coherent, useful picture.

Notes

1. Recent developments in generative linguistics have moved from a more traditional notion of language-particular and construction-particular rules (e.g. the rule for English question formation) to notions of universal principles that constrain all languages (e.g. the relationships between verbs and their complements (X-bar theory)) and language-particular manifestations of universal principles (e.g. English complements, which follow the verb, versus Japanese complements, which precede the verb) (Chomsky and Lasnik 1995).

2. Although this discussion has been based on the generative notion of *competence* and the linguistic rules posited to represent NS competence, an analogy of these first two types of grammar rule can be made to other

linguistic approaches. For example, the typological approach to language universals aims to discover the range of variation between languages and the limits on that variation (Comrie 1981). Proposed typological universals – i.e. the limitations on variation – represent linguists' hypotheses of universal constraints on language that form part of human linguistic knowledge.

3. This distinction has been criticized in the literature because of the difficulty distinguishing between the two types of knowledge in a practical way and because of the strict restriction on what types of input can become part of the IL competence (McLaughlin 1987).

4. Westney (1994) discusses various perspectives on pedagogical rules. See also the other discussions of pedagogical grammar in Odlin (1994).

5. The two versions of the contrastive analysis hypothesis (CAH) may also be referred to as CA *a priori* for the predictive or strong version and CA *a posteriori* for the weak version (Schachter 1974: 205).

6. The grammatical functors examined in the child and adult L2 studies included pronoun case, articles, singular copula, present progressive -ing, plural, singular auxiliary, past regular, past irregular, long plural, possessive, and third person singular. This work followed research in L1 acquisition of grammatical morphemes by Roger Brown (1973) and de Villiers and de Villiers (1973).

7. Nemser (1971) described learner systems as 'approximative systems'.

2

First-language and second-language interrelations

2.1 Introduction

The rejection of the contrastive-analysis and error-analysis approaches to L2 acquisition in favour of an interlanguage (IL) approach led to a re-examination of the complex interrelations between the L1 and the L2 during the course of L2 acquisition. Instead of viewing contrastive analysis and error analysis as a dichotomy, an IL approach encompasses the realization that the influences of prior linguistic knowledge may be intricately connected to the processes that determine acquisitional stages and to the various forms that those acquisitional stages ultimately take. In the wake of this renewed interest in the interrelations between the L1 and the L2, two different types of research emerged in the 1970s and 1980s: the description of stages of acquisition and alternative views of transfer. These two trends in L2-acquisition research are especially important because, as we shall see, these approaches affect subsequent research within different paradigms in a variety of ways.

2.2 Theoretical responses to contrastive analysis and error analysis

The reasons for focusing on stages of L2 acquisition were both theoretical and practical. As already noted, L2 research had begun to show evidence of similar developmental sequences in child L2 acquisition for language learners of English from different L1 backgrounds (Dulay and Burt 1974b; Ravem 1974), leading researchers to propose that language learners utilize common processing strategies to organize and produce the L2. These findings highlighted the fact that L2 acquisition involved processes that were similar to those utilized in L1 acquisition. Researchers began to investigate this 'L1=L2' hypothesis by examining stages of acquisition for different grammatical structures with learners of various ages and L1s in order to scrutinize the similarities and differences between L1 and L2 acquisition more carefully. Similarities found between L1 and L2 acquisition would help to reveal the universal properties of language-acquisition processes (Wode 1980, 1981,

1984), while differences between learners with different L1 backgrounds would help to distinguish between the effects of the L1 (Schumann 1979; Wode 1980) and the effects of other factors such as age or affective variables. One practical application of such research would be to sequence instructional materials to the identified stages of acquisition (Ioup 1983; Pienemann 1984).

In addition to the focus on L1 and L2 acquisitional similarities and differences, the research focus on stages of acquisition can also be understood within the context of IL research. Although Selinker's term *interlanguage* has been generally adopted in the field, it must be noted that the current notions of IL are not identical to Selinker's notion of IL as originally defined. Since the L2-acquisition work in the 1960s and 1970s (Adjemian 1976; Corder 1967; Nemser 1971; Selinker 1972), IL has come to be understood as a series of grammars developed by the language learner at different points in the L2-acquisition process. At a given time, an IL grammar is systematic, permeable, transitional, and discrete.

IL grammars are systematic in that they exhibit internal consistency – that is, IL grammars are rule governed. As a result, at a given time L2 learners can make judgements as to what is or is not grammatical based on their current IL grammar systems. The IL is a system in its own right with forms that are not part of either the L1 or the L2. However, although ILs are systematic, like other natural languages, they also exhibit a degree of permeability. Adjemian (1976) has argued that the permeable nature of ILs allows for the adoption of an L1 rule in the IL grammar as well as for the overgeneralization of an IL rule in L2 contexts in which this rule is inappropriate. As an example of the first case, German-speaking L2 learners of English may mark negation after the main verb (*I go not to school*), reflecting the post-verbal negation structure of the German L1 (*Ich gehe nicht in die Schule*). In the second case, English-speaking L2 learners of Spanish may overgeneralize the usage of the present progressive to indicate a future event, an inappropriate context for this structure in Spanish (**Estoy saliendo mañana* ('I am leaving tomorrow') for *Voy a salir mañana*).

ILs are transitional because they can change over time. However, Selinker (1992: 225) has argued that the lack of continued L2 development, or fossilization, is possible in subsystems of the IL from the very beginning stages of L2 acquisition. Therefore, although ILs can change, fossilization is 'possible and common'. Nemser (1971), on the other hand, has characterized IL changes as closer and closer approximations of the target language. A workable notion of IL must, therefore, account for both of these facts: that ILs are transitional because they do exhibit changes and that some subsystems may fossilize while others may develop in ways that more closely approximate the target-language norms.

Finally, IL grammars are discrete in the sense that there are definable differences between one IL grammar and subsequent ILs – that is, that there are discernible stages. Evidence of such stages is seen in what has been referred to as 'U-shaped behavior' (Bowerman 1982; Kellerman 1985). L2 learners may exhibit an error-free linguistic behaviour at one stage which is then replaced by a deviant form in the next stage and which then returns as error-free behaviour in the third stage (thus, the 'U'). As Selinker (1992) points out, logically one cannot talk about such 'U-shaped behavior,' or 'backsliding', in cases where there is no discernible difference between one stage and the next.

Within this context of L2 research, one can understand the growing interest in stages of L2 acquisition – as a means both to explore the similarities between L1 and L2 acquisition and to study the development of ILs as a series of learner grammars.

2.3 Questions explored

● How are different stages of second-language acquisition determined?
● What are the syntactic characteristics of different stages of second-language acquisition?

2.3.1 HOW ARE DIFFERENT STAGES OF SECOND-LANGUAGE ACQUISITION DETERMINED?

A primary goal of the acquisitional-stages research was to characterize the syntactic structures and the structural changes at each stage of development. While this may seem a fairly straightforward undertaking, the operational issues involved in describing and determining developmental stages are in no way simple. As Cancino, Rosansky, and Schumann (1978: 209) point out, the traditional notion of writing 'grammars' of languages of native speakers is based on a 'presumably static' grammatical system. Since ILs are dynamic rather than static systems, such a grammar would not be suitable. This dynamic quality of ILs causes two additional description problems: (1) differentiating between one stage and the next when there are cases of overlapping structures in both stages, and (2) accounting for individual learner variation within stages (Cancino *et al.* 1978; Wode 1981).

Different solutions to these problems have been explored. One approach is to determine the stages of acquisition based on the frequency of occurrence of structures. In the case of negation (Cancino *et al.* 1978; Schumann 1979), for example, each device used to mark negation is first catalogued:

(2.1)
   (a) *no* + Verb   (*no V*)
   (b) *don't* + Verb   (*don't V*)
   (c) auxiliary-negation (*aux-neg*)
   (d) analysed *don't*   (*don't*)

Then, the proportion of each device to the total number of negatives used at a given time is calculated. For example, a learner may produce the following proportion of negative utterances during one taping session:

(2.2)

(a)	*no V*	31%
(b)	*don't V*	46%
(c)	*aux–neg*	23%
(d)	analysed *don't*	0%
		100%

In this case, the stage of acquisition is characterized by the learner's predominant use of *don't V* (46 per cent), while, at the same time, the learner is still using the earlier predominant form *no V* to a lesser degree, and also to a lesser degree the newly emerging *aux–neg* form (Cancino *et al.* 1978). Therefore, while particular stages of development are determined by the use of the most often used structure at a given time (*don't V*), overlapping structures and learner variation are accounted for, since simultaneously used structures are also recorded. The changing predominance of one form over another is tracked longitudinally.

Another resolution to these problems proposed by Wode (1978b) is first to catalogue the various devices used for a given structure in the chronological order of occurrence (e.g. *no* V, *no* Verb Phrase (VP), Subject Verb *no/not* X).[1] Next, 'the point of (most likely) first non-imitative use' is determined as the emergence of the new structure. The devices are then characterized into chronological stages based on common features. For example, one stage of negation is characterized as externally marked negation because in all instances the negative morpheme *no* is in initial position and is therefore considered external to the word or phrase that is being negated, as seen in the following structures (Wode 1981: 98):

(2.3)

(a)	no ADJ	no cold
(b)	no V	no sleep
(c)	no N(P)	no bread
(d)	no VP	no catch it

Wode (1981: 68) argues that the acquisition of an item, so designated by the first emergence of the item, must be distinguished from its productive usage. The first emergence is determined by 'carefully considering frequency of occurrence, error types, morphological diversity of a given structure, and the like . . .' (Wode 1978b: 42). The stages of acquisition are therefore characterized by the chronological emergence of particular structures; whereas individual variability is accommodated, since old forms may still be in use until the newly acquired form becomes more productive.

Meisel, Clahsen, and Pienemann (1981) propose a somewhat different solution. They argue that language acquisition is not a strictly linear process. As a result, not every change in a learner's production necessarily represents a move to a new developmental stage. In their proposal, L2 acquisition is a sequence of strictly ordered developmental stages in which some structural features represent developmental changes while others represent variation within a single stage. The variation within a given stage is a result of the learner's choice of communication strategies.

Meisel *et al.* explore the question of exactly which structural features determine different developmental stages in their examination of the L2 acquisition of German word order. The proposed criteria for identifying developmental features depend in part on the assumption that grammatical rules are acquired in a strict order and that the acquisition of one rule implies the acquisition of an earlier rule:

(2.4) $Rule_3 \supset Rule_2 \supset Rule_1$

With regard to rules in such an implicational order, if a learner produces grammatical structures consistent with $Rule_3$, it is assumed that the learner has also acquired $Rule_2$ and $Rule_1$. If the learner has acquired $Rule_2$, it is assumed that the learner has also acquired $Rule_1$, but not $Rule_3$. However, learners are considered to have reached a new stage of development even though they have not yet mastered the previous rule in all of its possible contexts. In other words, structures consistent with $Rule_2$ may appear as evidence that the learner has moved into the next stage of development while the learner has not yet acquired $Rule_1$ in all of its obligatory contexts.

For example, Meisel *et al.* (1981) propose four stages of acquisition of German word order (designated below with roman numerals) based on the application of three rules in both matrix (or main) and embedded clauses (given below with examples):

(2.5)
   (I) *None of the three rules has been acquired.*

   (II) *The particle rule has been acquired:* the particle rule moves non-inflected verbs and particles to sentence-final position in matrix clauses.

   (a) Non-inflected verb
      Ich habe ein Buch *gekauft*
      I   have a   book bought

   (b) Particle
      Maria schrieb die Addresse *auf*
      Maria wrote the address down

   (III) *The inversion rule and the particle rule have been acquired:* the inversion rule inverts the subject with the inflected verb.

   (a) After an interrogative pronoun (e.g. wann)
      Wann *gehst du* in den Stadtpark?
      when go   you to the city park

(IV) *The V→end rule, the inversion rule, and the particle rule have been acquired*: the V→end rule moves inflected verbs to sentence-final position in embedded clauses.

(a) After a subordinating conjunction (e.g. als)
Ihr   Hund bellte, als   sie nach Hause *kam*
Her   dog   barked when she to   home came

As in the procedures above, Meisel *et al.* (1981) catalogue all instances of the structures related to the three rules. They then examine all of the structural contexts which require the application of a particular rule. The proportion of occurrence of each structure to the total number of obligatory contexts is then calculated. For any given structure, the learner may be scored for (1) the percentage of occurrence of the structure in the obligatory context (1–100 per cent), (2) the occurrence of the obligatory context without the application of the rule (0 per cent), or (3) the lack of the obligatory context (X). For example, a hypothetical learner who has the following production in the obligatory contexts for the particle and inversion rules is said to have reached stage III because she/he is able to apply the inversion rule in some contexts (IIIa) while not yet having mastered the particle rule in all contexts:

(2.6)
(II) particle-rule obligatory contexts
(a) particle   58%
(b) modal + main verb   X
(c) aux + past participle   59%
(d) particle + verb   X
(e) aux + particle + past participle   0%

(III) inversion-rule obligatory contexts
(a) subject–verb inversion   29%
(b) after a wh-pronoun   X
(c) after a preposed adverbial   0%
(d) after a topicalized NP   X
(e) after a topicalized embedded clause   X

Because of the implicational ordering of the particle, inversion, and V→end rules, the learner must have acquired the particle rule in stage II before moving on to stage III. This 'multidimensional model' allows for both strictly ordered developmental stages determined by particular developmental features – the three rules – and variation related to structural contexts within stages.

As we can see from the above discussion, the notion of what determines a new stage in L2 development has included the most frequent structure used at a given time, the first non-imitative use of a structure, and the emergence of developmental features as opposed to variational features. But, what must a developmental-stages approach to L2 acquisition account for? Minimally, this type of approach should identify the changes in the IL grammatical system, identify an order of stages, identify the variation within a given stage, and identify and explain the differences between learners. In addition to a description of stages, one might also look for explanations for the order of the developmental stages, for the proposed stages for learners of all L1s, for the variation between learners, and for the difference between what learners can do versus what they actually do as evidenced in their performance in different tasks. We shall see that this early research reveals basic stages of development in diverse contexts with a fairly limited number of subjects. A complete review of all of the research in each of these areas is beyond the scope of this work. Here we examine but a few examples from the 1970s and 1980s. With these caveats in mind, we now turn to different stages of acquisition for various structures.

2.3.2 WHAT ARE THE SYNTACTIC CHARACTERISTICS OF DIFFERENT STAGES OF SECOND-LANGUAGE ACQUISITION?

One of the questions that emerged in the 1970s and 1980s was 'What are the characteristics that constitute the different stages of L2 acquisition for different syntactic structures?' In order to address this question, researchers examined the L2 acquisition of negation, interrogatives, word order, embedded clauses, and pronouns.

2.3.2.1 Negation

We begin here with negation. Cancino *et al.* (1978: 229) propose the following stages (designated here with roman numerals) as evidenced in the L2 acquisition of English of native Spanish speakers:

(2.7)

(I)	*no V*	I no understand
(II)	*don't V*	He don't like it
(III)	*aux–neg*	You can't tell her
(IV)	analysed *don't*;	He doesn't spin
	disappearance of *no V*	

A closer examination of the example data offered reveals the following different verb types at stages I–III:

(2.8)

(I) *no V*
(a)	auxiliary verb	I no can see
(b)	main verb	You no walk on this
(c)	copula	But no is mine is my brother

(II) *don't V*
(a)	auxiliary verb	I don't can explain
(b)	main verb	I don't hear

(III) *aux-neg*
  (a) auxiliary *be*   Somebody is not coming in
  (b) auxiliary *can*   You can't tell her
  (c) copula   It's not danger

In this characterization, the *V* in stage I can be either an auxiliary, a main verb, or a copula, whereas with the *don't V* constructions in stage II, only examples of auxiliaries and main verbs are given. In stage III, *be* occurs both as a copula and as an auxiliary (Cancino *et al.* 1978: 210–11). In addition to verb types, the form of the negation also changes. From the simple use of *no* in stage I, the negative marker changes to unanalysed *don't* in stage II. Unanalysed *don't* refers to the use of *don't* as a single lexical item without the recognition that it is comprised of two morphemes: *do* + *not*. This can be determined by the fact that the form always occurs as *don't*. It does not occur as separate morphemes (*do, does,* or *did* plus *not*), nor is it inflected for number (*doesn't*) or tense (*didn't*). Stauble (1978) finds a similar series of stages, again with native speakers of Spanish acquiring English. Her stages expand on those of Cancino *et al.* by including additional structures in stage I – the use of *no* + phrases other than V – and the dominant use of unanalysed *don't/doesn't* + *V* in stage II. Her characterization of the stages also includes the increase or decrease of structure usage within the various stages.

Wode (1981), in reporting the L2 acquisition of negation for four German-speaking children, describes a more detailed series of stages, which includes, like Stauble's (1978), the marking of negation in verbless utterances with adjectives and nouns in addition to a separate treatment of the copula *be*. In addition, Wode includes a more basic stage which consists of simply *no* in reference to a previous utterance in the discourse. The stages are characterized as follows (adapted from Wode 1981: 98–108):

(2.9)
  (I) *Anaphoric negation with no*, in which the negator refers back to a previous utterance rather than to the items co-occurring in the construction.
  no, X   no, Tiff
  X, no

  (II) *External non-anaphoric negation*, in which the negative refers to co-occurring constructions, and the negative occurs in initial position.
    (a) no ADJ   no cold
        no V   no sleep
        no N(P)   no bread
    (b) no VP   no catch it

  (III) *Internal be-negation*, in which the negative is placed within the structure of the sentence following the copula and the progressive *be*.
    X (be) no Y   that's no right
    X (be) not Y   you not dummy

(IV) *Internal full verb negation and imperative don't*, which includes post-verbal, pre-verbal, and post-auxiliary negation, as well as imperatives with *don't*.

post-verbal *no/not*

S V no/not X	everybody catch no the fish
S V Pron not (X)	you got me not out
S V not/no N	you have a not fish

pre-verbal *no/not*

S no/not VP	you not shut up

post-auxiliary *no/not*

S can no/not/n't VP	you can no have it
	he cannot hit the ball

post-verbal imperative *not*

V (Pron) not (X)	hit it not over the fence

imperative *don't*

don't VP	don't broke

(V) *Suppletive don't/didn't and sentence-internal don't/didn't*, which includes two types of non-imperative *don't/didn't*.

suppletive *don't/didn't*

don't	no, don't
S don't/didn't	no, you don't

sentence internal *don't/didn't*

S don't/didn't VP	I didn't see
S don't/didn't Aux VP	I didn't can closed it

pre-nominal *nothing*

SV nothing N	I got nothing shoe

negative *any*

SV any N	I saw any wheels

Wode's stages of negation follow the same general progression as that of Cancino *et al.* and Stauble: from the use of *no* V/*no* phrase in stage II to aux + neg/unanalysed *don't* in stages III and IV. Wode notes that the data do not support an analysed interpretation of *don't/didn't* as *do* + negation, since the learners produce utterances such as '*Where did Bärbel didn't put your shoes?*' and '*Do you don't know that?*' at the same time as other utterances in stage V. In addition, although Wode lists non-imperative *don't* in the stage following aux + neg rather than preceding it as seen in the previous stages listed above, the first occurrences of non-imperative *don't* in fact precede or occur simultaneously with aux + neg. This highlights some of the difficulties with the actual analysis of such variable data into discrete developmental stages.[2]

One major difference is evident, however. Wode's German-speaking subjects alternate freely between pre-verbal and post-verbal negation in stage IV, a strategy which the Spanish-speaking subjects do not use. It is proposed that this variation is due to the negation structure of the L1, a point to which we return below. Thus, the stages of acquisition for English negation seen in these three studies support a general movement from external to internal negation as well as a progression from unanalysed to analysed *don't* (see also Hyltenstam 1977; Schumann 1979).

2.3.2.2 Interrogatives

In determining the stages of acquisition for questions, it is valuable first to establish what needs to be acquired. In order to do that we must differentiate the various aspects of question formation. For example, questions have different semantic functions: to elicit a *yes* or *no* answer; to elicit information such as time, place, cause, or participants (wh-questions); or to elicit the selection of alternative choices. In addition to the semantic function, languages utilize a combination of diverse formal devices to mark questions, as seen below (adapted from Wode 1978b: 41–2):

(2.10)

   (a) *intonation questions*, which are distinguished from non-questions solely through intonation;

   (b) *pronominal questions*, which are marked as questions with a free morpheme, i.e. an interrogative pronoun such as *who* or *what* in English or *wer* or *was* in German;

   (c) *particle questions*, in which the interrogative constituent is marked by a bound morpheme, i.e. an interrogative particle, such as Bulgarian *-li* or Finnish *-ko* and *-kö*; and

   (d) *inversion or word-order questions*, which differ from non-questions by word-order permutation.

English, for example, uses intonation, pronominal, and inversion questions; Chinese, on the other hand, utilizes intonation, pronominal, and particle questions (Li and Thompson 1990). And languages combine/manifest these devices in different ways. As Wode further points out, while English and German both utilize inversion questions, German allows inversion of auxiliary and main verbs whereas English allows inversion only with auxiliary verbs or the copula, not with main verbs. Finally, the acquisition of questions is also influenced by the acquisition of the specific lexical items – for example, the different interrogative pronouns in English: *who*, *what*, *when*, etc. (Butterworth and Hatch 1978; Ellis 1984; Wode 1978b).

Recall from Chapter 1 that Cancino *et al.* (1978) outline two basic stages of question acquisition for their child, adolescent, and adult Spanish-speaking learners of English: stage I, in which learners do not differentiate between simple and embedded questions, and stage II, in which learners utilize inversion only in simple wh-questions and not in embedded wh-questions. In stage I, learners progress from a general lack of inversion to variable inversion and then to the generalization of inversion in simple questions to embedded questions. Several studies examine child L2 acquisition of English interrogatives by native German, Norwegian, Chinese, and Spanish speakers (Butterworth and Hatch 1978; Huang and Hatch 1978; Ravem 1974; Wode 1978b). The majority of these children (from age 3; 9 to 13) are acquiring English in a naturalistic setting with little, if any, specific language instruction (30 minutes a week for the 13-year-old). The results of the child L2 studies support these general stages and provide a more detailed account of the progression from undifferentiation of simple and embedded questions to differentiation.

Wode (1978b) first identified separate stages of acquisition for yes/no and wh-questions and then classified the major stages for overall question development. The stages exemplified here generally follow Wode's overall stages. Excluded from Wode's stages is a preliminary stage of simple intonation questions. Citing the inconclusive nature of the available data, he questions the legitimacy of an intonation stage as a precursor to the development of either yes/no or wh-questions. However, according to Huang and Hatch (1978), their child subject Paul produces intonation questions as his first productive, non-imitative questions, although it is not clear from the available data whether these utterances are yes/no or wh-questions. Since Paul's intonation questions are much simpler in structure than those exemplified in Wode's later non-inverted stage, a preliminary stage has been added here to Wode's stages.[3]

The studies do not offer evidence of complete development to the target-language norm, nor do they all begin at the same stage of development. A further complication is that each study does not deal with the same types of questions – that is, yes/no questions, simple wh-questions, and embedded wh-questions. However, the chronological order of emergence of structures is consistent, while exhibiting some degree of learner variation. The compilation of examples here are taken from Huang and Hatch (1978), Ravem (1974), and Wode (1978b) and are identified by the authors' initials, HH, R, and W respectively.[4]

(2.11)
    (I) intonation questions

(a) demonstrative	noun	This+++slipper?	(HH)
(b) noun	noun	Ball+++doggie?	(HH)
(c) noun	V	Fish+++see?	(HH)

    (II) wh-questions with copula

(a) wh cop X	What is that?	(R)
	Henning, what is it	
	fishing pole?	(W)
	Where's Kenny?	(HH)
	Where's pen?	(HH)

(III) non-inverted yes/no and wh-questions with all verb types

(a) wh	S	V	(X)	What you want it?	(W)
(b) wh	S	Ving	(X)	What you doing, Craig?	(W)
(c) wh	S's	Ving		What he's doing?	(R)
(d) wh	S	aux	Ving	What she is doing?	(R)
(e) S	V	(X)		You see my little football?	(W)
(f) S	aux	(X)		You can see that?	(W)
(g) S	cop	(X)		no example given	(W)

(IV) inversion with copula, auxiliaries, and main verbs in yes/no and wh-questions

(a) cop	S	(X)		It's (=is) my fishing pole in the water?	(W)
(b) aux	S	(X)		Please, can I have a piece of drink?	(W)
				Can K have some juice?	(HH)
(c) V	S	(X)		Catch Johnny fish today?	(W)
(d) wh	V	S	(X)	Why drink we tea and coffee?	(R)
(e) wh	aux	S	Ving	What is he doing?	(R)

(V) *do*-support with main verbs in wh-questions

| (a) wh | *do* | S | V | (X) | How do you clean them? | (W) |
| (b) wh | *do* | S | Ving | (X) | What do you doing to-yesterday? | (R) |

(VI) *do*-support with main verbs in yes–no questions

| (a) *do* | S | V | (X) | Henning, did you catch anything? | (W) |

This sequence of proposed stages is not problem free, however. While Wode (1978b) states that the wh-questions with the copula *be* in stage II evidenced target-like inversion 'from the very beginning', Cancino *et al.* (1978) question whether these structures really do involve inversion. They posit two possible reasons for the target-like inversion found in similar structures produced by their subjects: direct translation from Spanish or wh + copula as unanalysed chunks. Huang and Hatch (1978: 129) also note that their subject heard so many questions with 'what's (X)?' and 'where's (X)?' that 'the 's was not the copula but part of the interrogative word'.

The complex nature of questions is evident not only in the stages as outlined, but also in the variation evidenced in a single data-gathering session. For example, the following structures are found by Ravem (1974) in one session for his son Rune:

(2.12)

(a) wh	S	V	(X)	What you did in Rothbury?
(b) wh	S	Ving	(X)	Why the baby crying?
(c) wh	S's	Ving	(X)	What he's doing?
(d) wh	aux	S	Ving	What is he doing?
(e) wh	V	S	(X)	Why drink we tea and coffee?
(f) wh	do-S	V	(X)	When dyou went there?
(g) wh	do-S	Ving	(X)	What dyou reading to-yesterday?

We can see that Rune's questions include inversion of auxiliaries and main verbs (2.12d and e) at the same time as the lack of inversion (2.12c) and the omission of the obligatory auxiliary (*do* in 2.12a and *is* in 2.12b). What is more interesting is the first emergence of *do*. *Do* occurs attached to the subject in what appears to be an unanalysed *do*-Subject form before the use of *do* is productive (2.12f and 2.12g). As in the case of unanalysed *don't* seen in the acquisition of negation, these forms are not actual cases of *do*-support in English but rather precursors to it. Three weeks later, in the subsequent sessions, both *do* and *did* occur separately from the subject *you*, but it is obvious that Rune is still working out the restrictions on *do*-support:

(2.13)
- (a) What did you talk to them? (say/talk about)
- (b) What do you doing to-yesterday?
- (c) What did you do to-yesterday?
- (d) When you go to bed?

One last indication of the complexity of English questions is seen in an additional final stage demonstrated in Wode's data, that is, *do*- support with auxiliaries and/or the copula:

(2.14)

(a) *do*	cop	(V ...)
(b) *do*	aux	(V ...)
(c) wh	*do*	cop	(V ...)

Although the stages immediately preceding this one (V and VI in (2.11)) appear to represent target-like usage of English, these learners are obviously still working out the mechanics of *do*-support in relation to other verb forms.

To recap here, the general developmental stages for questions are as follows:

(2.15)
- (I) intonation questions
- (II) wh-questions with copula
- (III) non-inverted yes/no and wh-questions with all verb types
- (IV) inversion with copula, auxiliaries, and main verbs in yes/no and wh-questions
- (V) *do*-support with main verbs in wh-questions
- (VI) *do*-support with main verbs in yes/no questions

These general stages follow a progression from intonation questions to non-inverted questions to inverted questions and ultimately to inverted questions with *do*-support – all stages with some degree of individual learner variation.

2.3.2.3 Word order

Stages of acquisition of different sentence types have been studied in both child and adult L2 acquisition. Felix (1977) has found that English-speaking child learners of German begin with sentence imitation and two-word utterances consisting of a single phrase (i.e. a partial noun phrase or an adjective phrase) before developing multi-word utterances consisting of several phrases. This finding is corroborated by Pienemann (1980) for Italian-speaking children learning German. Felix (1977: 151–2) outlines the stages as follows:

(2.16)
    (I) two-word utterances
    (a) Adj + N
        grüne   Baum
        'green tree'
    (b) Adv + Adj
        ganz   gross
        'very big'

    (II) copular sentences
    (a) Demonstrative + Copula + NP
        das   ist   ein Wind
        'that is a wind'
    (b) Demonstrative + Ø Copula + NP
        dies   ein Haus
        'this a house'
    (c) Demonstrative + Copula + Adj
        das   ist   grün
        'that is green'
    (d) Demonstrative + Copula + PP
        das   ist   for du
        'that is for you'

    (III) auxiliary sentences
    (a) S + Aux + NP
        ich   kann   das
        'I can (do) that'
    (b) S + Aux + Adv
        du   kann   hier
        'you can (play) here'

(IV) main verb sentences

   (a) S   + V + NP
       ich   essen Banane
       'I eat banana'

   (b) S   + V + Adv
       du   bleib   hier
       'you stay here'

Several comparisons to other studies are possible. At stage I, for example, Huang and Hatch (1978) also show evidence of an initial two-word stage. In these two-word utterances, they note a pause between the two words, and equal stress as well as falling intonation on each word: 'This+++kite', 'Yeah, that+++bus'. These characteristics help to identify these utterances as non-imitative, self-generated utterances. Felix's stage II development of sentences with the copula exhibits a lesser degree of variation than that found in Butterworth and Hatch (1978), who provide evidence of free variation between three distinct copular patterns for their 13-year-old Spanish-speaking subject:

(2.17)

(a)	Cop	NP		Is man
	Cop	Adj		Is nice
	Cop	Locative		Is here
(b)	NP	NP		He champion
	NP	Adj		Me thin
	NP	Locative		She over there
(c)	NP	Cop	NP	This is map
	NP	Cop	Adj	Wood is good
	NP	Cop	Locative	He is in ocean

This free variation between forms persisted throughout the thirteen weeks of taping. Although copula deletion occurred regularly at this stage for Felix's learners as well, subjects were always in the form of pronouns, and the subjects were not omitted, as in Butterworth and Hatch's data. Both studies suggest that the prepositional and/or locative forms emerge later than the NP and Adj structures.

Comparing these stages of acquisition of sentence types with Huang's (1971, as cited in Felix (1977)) study, Felix notes that the Aux structures in stage III as seen in (2.16) emerge much sooner with his learners of German than for Paul, Huang's Taiwanese learner of English – that is, Paul produced Aux + V structures after producing SVO, SV, imperative, and *want* + V structures. Felix accounts for this difference based on the formal differences between auxiliaries in German and English. Pienemann's (1980: 49) Italian-speaking learners of German acquire their verbs in a 'stable sequence: 1. verb, 2. copula, 3. auxiliary, 4. modal'. As seen in (2.18), one subject, Concetta, produces Aux structures at a much later stage in her acquisition of multi-constituent sentence structures (adapted from Pienemann 1980: 46):[5]

(2.18)

(a) NP	V		
(b) NP	V	PP	
(c) NP	V	NP	
(d) NP	CopP	NP	
(e) NP	V	PP	PP
(f) NP	V	NP	PP
(g) *NP	AUX	V	NP NP
	MOD		PP PP

While pointing out that there is considerable variation within particular stages for each learner, Pienemann explains Concetta's late production of auxiliaries as a strategy for avoiding a context that requires the application of the inversion rule (that is, complex verb constructions with auxiliaries or modals) before that rule has been acquired (as in (2.5 III)). And, in fact, the structure in (2.18g) is ungrammatical in the target language. The early occurrence of adverbials as in (2.18b) for all three learners is accounted for by the 'high communicative effectiveness of adverbials' (Pienemann 1980: 47).

The stages of development exemplified above for learners of German and English show some variation in both the order of the stages (acquisition of the auxiliary) and their degree of stability (copula structures).

For the L2 acquisition of German word order beyond the affirmative sentences given above, Meisel *et al.* (1981) suggest that the stages of acquisition follow a sequence related to the acquisition and application of the three rules explained above: the particle, inversion, and V→end rules. Assuming that L2 learners of German begin with a canonical SVO word order, Pienemann (1980, 1984) outlines the four stages of acquisition which reflect L2 child learners' permutations of that canonical order (see 2.19 I–IV). The fifth and final stage in (2.19) is adapted from Meisel *et al.* (1981: 124):

(2.19)

    (I) *Canonical SVO word order:* none of the three rules has been acquired.

    (a) Die   Kinder   spielen mim   ball
        the   children   play   with the   ball

    (II) *Adverb preposing:* the inversion rule required with adverb preposing is not applied.

    (a) *Da   kinder   spielen
        there   children   play

    (b) Standard German
        Da   spielen   kinder
        there   play   children

    (III) *Particle shift:* the particle rule is applied by moving non-inflected verb to sentence-final position.

(a) Alle kinder   muβ   die pause   *machen*
    all children   must   the break   do/make

(IV) *Inversion:* the inversion rule is applied in addition to the particle rule by inverting the subject with the inflected verb.

(a) Dann   *hat*   *sie*   wieder   die Knoch   gebringt
    then   has   she   again   the bone   bringed

(V) *V→end:* the V→end rule is applied by moving the inflected verb to sentence-final position in embedded clauses.

(a) Ich   kaufe   diesen   Tabak,   *wenn*   ich   nach Hause   *gehe*
    I   buy   this   tobacco, when   I   home   go

Note that these examples represent a somewhat simplified version of the stages of acquiring German word order because each rule has more than the single context illustrated here in which it must be applied. Meisel *et al.* (1981), then, utilize the position of the verb as an indication of the learner's stage of development, while each learner's movement through the stage is determined by the type of strategies the learner employs. For instance, a learner who uses a strategy of simplification may be at stage IV but may not produce all of the contexts for inversion and may also delete obligatory structures such as subjects and copulas, resulting in a simplified variety of German. Another learner may only be at stage III but may produce the rules in more of the obligatory contexts with fewer deletions, thus exhibiting a more complex and target-like IL grammar. Meisel *et al.* (1981) discuss learners who fit both of these descriptions. These researchers thus argue for a series of stages of development which represent obvious restructuring of the IL grammatical system (the addition of a rule) and which also accommodate the learners' diverse approaches to the acquisition process (for example, the utilization of simplification, communication, and avoidance strategies).

The research on word-order developmental stages is somewhat incomplete. We have evidence of child learners of English and German and of adult learners of German, two L2s with rather strictly determined word orders. Additional research on developmental stages of word order of L2s with more flexible word orders would offer a more complete picture of this aspect of L2 acquisition of syntax.

2.3.2.4 Embedded clauses

At the time of this interest in developmental stages for negation, questions, and word order, L2 researchers also began to explore acquisitional stages for embedded clauses and pronominals. However, the evidence for acquisitional stages of embedded clauses and pronominals was much more limited and was focused on difficulty orders as opposed to longitudinal acquisitional stages. We will see two examples of this approach to L2 acquisition as related to embedded clauses and pronominal structures.

One of the most widely studied structures in L2 acquisition is the relative clause – for example, *This car, which we bought last month, was sold at an auction.* In order to determine a 'natural difficulty ordering for the stages of relative clause acquisition', Ioup and Kruse (1977) elicited grammaticality judgements on relative clauses which varied on two dimensions: (1) whether the head noun is a subject (*SS* or *SO*) or an object (*OS* or *OO*) of the main clause, and (2) whether the relative pronoun functions as a subject (*SS* or *OS*) or an object (*SO* or *OO*) within the relative clause. In the following sentences, taken from Ioup and Kruse (1977: 167), the head nouns and the relative pronouns are underlined; the functions of the head nouns and of the relative pronouns – i.e. *which* – are indicated below.

(2.20)
    (a) SS   The *dish which* fell on the floor broke in half.
                  S   S
    (b) SO   The *sweater which* I found on the bus belongs to
                  S   O
           Susie.
    (c) OS   The little girl is looking for the *cat which* ran away.
                                        O   S
    (d) OO   The boys are reading the *books which* they borrowed from the
           library.   O   O

Those sentences with right branching clauses – that is, with object head nouns (OS and OO as in (2.20c and d)) – were easier for the Arabic-, Chinese-, Japanese-, Persian-, and Spanish-speaking learners of English than were the sentences with centre embedding – that is, with subject head nouns (SS and SO). These findings are corroborated for child, adolescent, and adult learners of English by Schumann (1980).

While Ioup and Kruse utilize a cross-sectional grammaticality judgement task, Schumann reports on production data collected longitudinally for five Spanish-speaking subjects and at a single time for two Italian-speaking subjects. Therefore, rather than indicating ordered stages of acquisition, the results of these studies represent an order of difficulty – that is, indicating a comparison of which clauses are less/more difficult to produce than others. For Ioup and Kruse's learners, those structures with the least errors (OS and OO) are the least difficult. Schumann equates high frequency in production with ease, resulting in OO and OS structures as the most frequent and preferred.

Finally, Ioup (1983) has further investigated the difficulty order of complex sentence types by examining Arabic speakers' production of both tensed and nontensed embedded clauses in English. She includes adverbial clauses (beginning with *while, because, when,* and *if*), tensed sentential complements (with *that, why,* and *whether*), relative clauses (SS, OO, and OS), infinitive complements, participle phrases, and gerund complements. In general, the tensed clauses (adverbial clauses, tensed sentential complements, and relative clauses) contained fewer errors than did the nontensed clauses (infinitive complements, participle phrases, and gerund complements). The rank order of difficulty was as follows:

(2.21)
1. adverbial clauses
2. tensed sentential complements
3. relative clauses
4. infinitive complements
5. participle phrases
6. gerund complements

These few studies demonstrate that there is some predictable degree of difficulty of given embedded-clause types. However, without longitudinal data, no claims for ordered stages of development similar to those for negation, questions, and word order can be made. We will return once again to relative clauses in the research guided by alternative paradigms.

2.3.2.5 Pronouns

The stages of acquisition for pronouns have received little attention in this early L2 literature, although, as we shall see, pronouns figure prominently in the L2 research in other frameworks. The articles discussed below present a set of hypothetical stages of acquisition of object pronouns based on difficulty order and then test those stages longitudinally.

Pronominal anaphora in these studies refers to instances in which a noun phrase that has been introduced into the discourse is replaced by a pronominal form.[6] In the sentence *The children saw the movie, and they liked it*, the pronouns *they* and *it* replace the noun phrases *the children* and *the movie*, respectively. In instances of zero anaphora, the position of the noun-phrase referent is left empty, as in *The movie that the children saw Ø was playing downtown*. Gundel and Tarone (1983: 282–4) outline the following constraints on pronominal anaphor usage: the noun-phrase referent of the pronoun must have been introduced and focused on in the discourse; pronouns cannot corefer to a following full noun phrase in certain structures; languages differ in allowing pronoun or zero anaphora; languages differ in the information encoded in the pronoun (gender, person, social relationship); languages differ in the positions of the pronoun and the full noun phrase relative to the verb.

In their study of the L1 influence on the L2 acquisition of pronominal and zero anaphora, Gundel and Tarone (1983: 291) examined the acquisition of pronominal and zero anaphora of Spanish and Chinese learners of English and English-speaking learners of French. Of special interest was the performance of the learners with regard to object anaphora. Of the languages involved in the study, English, Spanish, and French require pronominal anaphora in object positions, while Mandarin Chinese allows for both pronominal and zero anaphora in these positions (p. 285).

(2.22)

    (a) English   John saw *him/*Ø*.

    (b) French   Jean *l'/*Ø* a vu.
                        'John saw him.'

    (c) Spanish   Juan *lo/*Ø* vió.
                        'John saw him.'

    (d) Chinese   wo bu xihuan *Ø/ta*.
                        'I don't like (it).'

Gundel and Tarone found a complex interaction between the L1 restrictions on object pronominals and the learners' L2 performance. Based on their results of this study, they posit three learner hypotheses for the acquisition of direct object pronouns (p. 291):

(2.23)

    (a) The L2 will have object pronouns in the same position as in the L1.

    (b) The L2 has no pronoun forms in object context at all, resulting in zero anaphora.

    (c) The L2 does have object pronouns, but in a different position from that in the L1.

These hypotheses result in the following three stages for English-speaking learners of French, as seen in examples from Gundel and Tarone (1983: 292, emphasis and translations added).

(2.24)

    (I) S V pro   *il   n'est   pas   prend *le*
                            he   neg-is   neg   take   it
                            'He doesn't take it'.

    (II) S V Ø   *je   n'ai   pas   voir   Ø
                            I   neg-have neg   to see Ø
                            'I didn't see Ø'.

    (III) S pro V   . . . mais   je   *l'*aime
                       . . . but   I   him/her/it-love.
                       '. . . but I love her/him/it'.

Gundel, Stenson, and Tarone (1984) subsequently tested these stages with English-speaking children learning French in a Canadian immersion programme. The children were tested at the end of Grades 1 and 2. Two of the six children were also tested at the end of Grade 5 (age 11). Although the group scores did not confirm the hypothesized stages at Grades 1 and 2 as seen in (2.25), scores for the two extended learners show tendencies consistent with the hypothesized stages; that is, the stage I pattern becomes less frequent, while the stage II and stage III patterns increase in frequency of occurrence (in (2.25)). The following percentages indicate the usage of the three structures exemplified in the stages above.

(2.25)	Grade 1	Grade 2
All learners		
(I) S V pro	26%	12%
(II) S V O	69%	85%
(III) S pro V	5%	3%

(2.26)	Grade 1	Grade 2	Grade 5
Extended learner B			
(I) S V pro	63%	50%	12.5%
(II) S V O	37%	50%	12.5%
(III) S pro V	0%	0%	75.0%
Extended learner T:			
(I) S V pro	33%	100%	17%
(II) S V O	50%	0%	50%
(III) S pro V	17%	0%	33%

As the authors state, these results are only suggestive of possible stages of acquisition for direct object pronouns. Gundel, Stenson and Tarone (1984) also report on a follow-up study with adult learners of French which reveals no evidence of the stage I S V pro pattern but more extensive use of the full noun phrase where a pronoun would be more appropriate. That is, the adult learners use an S V NP pattern in 45 per cent of the contexts where a pronoun could, and in some cases should, be used, as in '*Le garçon voit un balle* [*sic*], *et il prend le balle, et il joue avec le balle* . . .' (p. 221) (the child sees *the ball*, and he takes *the ball*, and he plays with *the ball* . . .). They suggest that this pattern of NP usage may be a result of avoidance of the required pronominal form.

This section has outlined several developmental stages for various structures for different types of learners. While some common developmental stages do emerge – for example, for negation and question formation – the overall picture for developmental stages is inconclusive owing in part to the limited number of languages examined. The differences that are evidenced (e.g. negative placement for Spanish and German learners of English, declarative sentences with auxiliaries for German or Chinese learners of English, or variation in supplying the copula in obligatory contexts) point to L1 influences or individual learner differences. We turn now to the issue of transfer.

2.4 First-language influences: transfer

One special aspect of L2 acquisition is the fact that the L2 learner, having already acquired the L1, is not a novice language learner. The role of the L1 (or L2 or L3) in subsequent language acquisition has engendered considerable investigation from a variety of theoretical perspectives. Here we first consider the notion of transfer and the issues surrounding it (that is, definitions, manifestations, identification, and conditions), before addressing the interaction between transfer and the developmental stages examined above.

Recall from Chapter 1 that the notion of transfer derives from the application of behaviourist psychology and structural linguistics to language teaching. Lado (1957: 2) claimed that, by making a comparison of the structures of the L1 and the L2, teachers could determine the L2 learners' 'real learning problems'. The underlying assumption was that in L2 acquisition the learner would transfer to the L2 the L1 elements that were similar. Structures could be similar in three ways: they could be signalled by the same formal device, have the same meaning, or have a similar distribution in the language system (Lado 1957: 66). Lado illustrated this comparison between structures with yes/no question formation with *be* in English and in Spanish (adapted from Lado 1957: 68–74):

(2.27)
    (a) English: Is he a farmer?
        Form
            (i) a form of the verb *be* preceding the subject;
            (ii) agreement between the third person singular subject, *he*, and the verb, *is*;
            (iii) a falling high–low intonation which does not differ from statement intonation.
        Meaning: to elicit verbal responses of the yes/no type.
        Distribution: restricted to the verb *be* and optionally to *have* (other main verbs require the presence of *do*).

    (b) Spanish: *Es   un   campesino?*
              is   a   farmer?
        Form
          (i) a form of the verb *ser* (be);
          (ii) no presence of a separate word for *he*;
          (iii) a rising intonation sequence from mid to high or a rise to extra high and a drop to mid or low, which differs from statement intonation.
        Meaning: to elicit verbal responses of the yes/no type.
        Distribution: the pattern applies to all verbs.

According to Lado, the learning difficulties would be predictable from the differences. Therefore, the Spanish learner of English would have difficulty with supplying the subject pronoun, using subject–verb inversion to signal a question, using a high–low intonation pattern, and restricting this pattern to the verbs *be* and *have*. An English learner of Spanish was predicted to have difficulty omitting the subject pronoun and using a contrastive intonation pattern to signal the difference between a question and a statement. It was believed that these predictions could be made based solely on the detailed comparison of the two languages in question.

While most language professionals – theorists and practitioners alike – will attest to the fact that the L1 does play some role in L2 acquisition, the extent to which a learner's L1 affects the L2 acquisition process has been an ongoing debate since the rise of error analysis and creative construction in the 1960s and 1970s, and the issues in the debate have changed somewhat over the years (Gass 1988b; Martohardjono and Flynn 1995).

The use of the term *transfer* itself became an issue for several reasons. Lado (1957: 58) stated that 'The student tends to transfer the sentence forms, modification devices, the number, gender, and case patterns of his native language.' As seen in (2.27), Lado saw transfer as the use of overt L1 grammatical structures in the L2 – in other words, transferred language habits. With this characterization of transfer in mind, some researchers felt that the term *transfer* was too closely connected to the behaviourist theoretical framework. Corder (1983: 86), for instance, argued that 'the danger of using such technical terms closely associated with particular theories is that they may perhaps quite unconsciously constrain one's freedom of thinking about the particular topic'. It was also argued that the term *transfer* was too narrow because it did not allow for all of the different phenomena evidenced in the L2 acquisition data (e.g. transfer, avoidance, and borrowing), nor did it apply to related phenomena, such as L1 or L2 language loss (Corder 1983; Sharwood Smith and Kellerman 1986). Sharwood Smith and Kellerman (1986) suggested the term 'cross-linguistic influences' as a broader, more encompassing term.

These terminological disputes underscore the second issue – the nature of transfer. In other words, what is transfer? Transfer has been characterized as a learning and/or communication strategy (Kellerman 1978), a process of superimposing L1 structures on the L2 structures (Gass 1983), a filter on the learner's input (Andersen 1983), and a constraint on the learner's formulation of hypotheses (Schachter 1983). A more general view of transfer, such as that offered in Odlin's working definition, subsumes the notions of strategy, process, filter, and constraint: 'Transfer is the influence resulting from similarities and differences between the target language and any other language that has been previously (and perhaps imperfectly) acquired' (Odlin 1989: 27). A broader definition such as this serves to include a number of L1 influences that were not originally considered in Lado's narrow definition, including, but not limited to, delayed rule restructuring (Zobl 1980a), avoidance of particular structures (Kleinmann 1977; Schachter, 1974), use of L1 typological organization and overproduction of structures (Schachter and Rutherford

1979), and resetting of abstract grammatical constraints (Flynn 1984, 1987a; White 1985a, b; see also Gass 1988b). This broad range of L1 effects demonstrates that the influence of the L1 is indeed as pervasive and as subtle as Corder (1983) predicted.

Although it has generally come to be accepted that L1 influence manifests itself in these subtle and complex ways, how then is transfer identified? This issue has been somewhat problematic. In contradiction to Lado's structure-by-structure predictive approach, Felix (1980: 94) noted that 'The crucial problem is that we do not possess any well-established criteria by which it can be decided in a unique and principled way which ungrammatical utterances are demonstrably instances of language transfer.' In other words, is everything that looks like transfer indeed transfer and how can we tell the difference? Schachter and Celce-Murcia (1977) agree that many errors may be ambiguous – that is, they may be the result of transfer or, alternatively, an example of a developmental error which reflects the characteristics of the language-acquisition process (Richards 1974).

This situation is clearly exemplified by Felix (1980) with a comparison of Spanish, German, and L1 English learners of English who all produce similar errors. A Spanish learner of English produces sentences with the copula *be* which omit the subject pronoun required in English:

(2.28)
   (a) is man
   (b) is boat

Based on the structure of the L1, these errors are considered the result of the transfer of Spanish subjectless sentences into English (Butterworth and Hatch 1978). However, two English learners of L2 German similarly produce subjectless sentences in German, although neither language allows the omission of the subject pronoun in independent clauses (Felix 1980):

(2.29)
   (a) ist nicht meine   (is not mine)
   (b) ist Guys Ball   (is Guy's ball)
   (c) ist gleich weg   (is soon away)

Felix notes that such subjectless sentences are also evident in the L1 acquisition of English and might just as easily be the result of language development rather than of transfer. Therefore, do the data indicate transfer for the Spanish learner of English, but not for the English learner of German? These data highlight the fact that L2 acquisition includes the influences both of the L1 and of acquisition processes. Schachter (1974) has also pointed out that identifying transfer of syntax is more difficult than transfer in an area such as phonology, because learners can more easily paraphrase or simply avoid difficult syntactic structures whereas difficult sounds are not easy to avoid. How then is transfer identified? Simply put: with care – and with the awareness that the identification of transfer is not as clear-cut as originally proposed. For instance, while research has shown that L1 transfer may manifest itself in a variety of ways, research has also shown that there are a myriad of other influences involved in the course of L2 acquisition in addition to the L1 that need to be taken into account in the analysis of learner data. A final, important consideration is the fact that Lado was comparing and contrasting surface syntactic structures; he was not concerned with abstract linguistic constraints. This consideration figures prominently in more recent versions of transfer in L2 acquisition to be examined in subsequent chapters.

2.5 Questions explored

- What is transferable and why?
- How does first-language knowledge interact with the developing second-language knowledge at different stages of acquisition?

2.5.1 WHAT IS TRANSFERABLE AND WHY?

Recall that the downfall of contrastive analysis occurred precisely because it was unable accurately to predict which structures would transfer and which would not. Similarity between L1 and L2 structures did not necessarily facilitate the acquisition of those structures, nor did L1/L2 differences necessarily inhibit acquisition. As can be expected, a broader definition of transfer leads to a wider range of questions. For example, in delayed rule restructuring can we predict which rules will be delayed and which ones will not? Similarly, can we predict which structures will be avoided and, conversely, which structures will be overproduced?

Kellerman (1978, 1979, 1983) addressed some of these concerns when he posed the question 'What is transferable?' in relation to L2 acquisition of vocabulary, and successfully argued that 'not everything that *looks* transferable *is* transferable' (Kellerman 1983: 113). His work with L1 Dutch learners of L2 German and L2 English revealed that L2 learners transferred L1 structures that they 'perceived' as transferable. He suggested that L2 learners' notions of transferability were based partially on their 'perception of language distance' between the L1 and the L2 (or the learner's 'psychotypology' (1983: 114)), and partially on their perceptions of the nature of a particular structure. Structures that were perceived as 'infrequent, irregular, semantically or structurally opaque, or in any other way exceptional, what we could in other words call "psycholinguistically marked"' (p. 117) would be less likely to be transferred than those structures that were considered less psycholinguistically marked. From this perspective, transferability depends on the learner's perception of the L1 and the L2 structures, regardless of the similarity and/or differences between the two languages. For example, in judging the transferability of Dutch idioms with the verb *breken* (to break), L1 Dutch learners of L2 English were asked to judge the transferability of sentences in Dutch, all of which had acceptable English equivalents, as seen in the examples below (adapted from Kellerman 1978: 68–9).

(2.30)

(a) Zij   brak   zijn   hart
    She   break-past his   heart
    'She   broke   his   heart.'

(b) Na   't   ongeluk is hij 'n gebroken man geworden
    After the accident is he   a   broken   man become
    'After the accident he became a broken man.'

(c) Zijn val   werd   door 'n boom gebroken
    His   fall become-past by   a   tree broken
    'His fall was broken by the tree.'

The learners did not allow for the transfer of the idiom *to break a fall* because the meaning was seen as marked, while they did allow for the transfer of *to break a heart* and to a lesser degree *a broken man*.

While Kellerman's view of transferability focused on the role of the learner, Zobl (1980b) emphasized the role of the L2 linguistic system itself, noting that some linguistic structures seemed more transferable than others, based in part on linguistic congruity between the L1 and the L2 and on the linguistic ambiguity or instability of the L2 structure. For instance, verb type had an effect on transfer. In the yes/no questions of L1 German learners of L2 English, the learners did not transfer the L1 rule of subject–base verb inversion to verbs marked for progressive aspect (*V-ing*), although these verbs occurred in declarative sentences elsewhere in the IL data. This would result in forms such as that in (2.31a) but not as that in (2.31b).

(2.31)

(a) *Go you to school?*   for *Do you go to school?*
(b) *Going you to school?*   for *Are you going to school?*

Zobl also noted a difference between yes/no questions and wh-questions regarding transfer: subject–base verb inversion lasted two to three months longer in yes/no questions than in wh-questions. Zobl (1983) further argued that, in order to make adequate predictions about the transferability of L1 structures in the acquisition of particular L2 structures, independent evidence was needed that the L2 structure was 'inherently ambiguous, unstable, opaque' (1983: 105).

Eckman (1977) also related aspects of the linguistic systems to the interaction between the L1, the L2, and learner difficulty with particular structures. In his Markedness Differential Hypothesis (MDH), Eckman essentially argues that L2 structures that are different from L1 structures and that are not more linguistically marked than the L1 structures will not be difficult for the learner. Whether or not these 'easier' structures are actually more transferable is an empirical question which we deal with more extensively in Chapter 4.

2.5.2 HOW DOES FIRST-LANGUAGE KNOWLEDGE INTERACT WITH THE DEVELOPING SECOND-LANGUAGE KNOWLEDGE AT DIFFERENT STAGES OF ACQUISITION?

The final influence on transferability is the actual developmental stage of the learner (Wode, 1978a, 1981; Zobl 1980a, b), which brings us back to one of our original points. That is, while contrastive analysis and creative construction were seen as two opposing theories of L2 acquisition, researchers have pointed out that L2 acquisition can include both processes of transfer from the learner's previous language knowledge and at the same time processes of creative hypothesis testing (Andersen 1984; Gass and Selinker 1983; Kellerman 1984; Wode 1986). Let us turn now to the interaction between specific developmental stages and the L1 influence.

Wode (1981) claims that a particular developmental stage may create the prerequisites that allow learners to transfer their L1 rules into their IL grammars. For example, English and German have the same structure in relation to the copula and the negative – that is, copula + negative. Once learners have reached the stage in which they place the negative in relation to the copula as in (2.9 III), they note that the structures are the same in the L1 (German) and in the L2 (English). In the subsequent stage of development (2.9 IV), the learners vary freely between pre- and post-verbal negation, with the L1 structure – post-verbal negation – winning out. Wode hypothesizes that post-verbal negation is favoured because the L2 learners have formulated the notion of similarity between the structures of the L1 and the L2 based on the copula, thus allowing for transfer of L1 structures into the IL grammar (see also Schumann 1979).

According to Zobl, this notion of similarity also plays a role in constraints on transfer as evidenced in the different stages of acquisition of English questions by L1 French speakers. Zobl (1980a, b) argues that, while the use of a dummy auxiliary as in *Is the breakfast is good?* is common in both L1 and L2 acquisition of English questions, French speakers utilize this structure much more frequently than do other learners of English. Once French learners have acquired pronoun subject–auxiliary inversion in questions, they note the similarity between English and French questions (as in 2.32a and c).

(2.32)

    (a) He is a tourist.   Is he a tourist?

    (b) Mark is a tourist.   Is Mark a tourist?

    (c) Il est touriste.   Est-il touriste?

    (d) Marc est touriste.   *Est Marc touriste?

    (e) Marc est-il   touriste?

        Mark is-he (a) tourist?

    (f) Est-ce que Marc est   touriste?

        Is-it   that Mark is (a) tourist?

At this point they transfer the French restriction against noun subject–auxiliary inversion (2.32d) into their English ILs, resulting in dummy auxiliary structures which are 'overwhelmingly confined' to noun subjects as opposed to pronoun subjects.

While perceived similarity between the L1 and the L2 may influence the form that a subsequent developmental stage takes, it may also prolong the length of a developmental stage. This phenomenon has been observed in the acquisition of English negation by Spanish and Italian speakers who remain in the *no + Verb* stage of development longer than do speakers of other L1s such as Japanese (Agnello 1977; Schumann 1978; Zobl 1980a).

A final interaction between developmental stages and L1 transfer can be seen in the constraints on hypothesis testing made by learners. Gundel and Tarone (1983) proposed that the structure of the L1 would influence the hypotheses made by the L2 learners. That is, once learners discover that the French L2 does not have post-verbal pronominal objects as does the English L1, they will hypothesize that zero anaphora is allowed – i.e. no objects as opposed to pre-verbal pronominal objects. Gundel, Stenson, and Tarone (1984) find suggestive results that learners do in fact allow for zero anaphora following a stage in which the IL pronominal structure mirrors that of the L1.

The interaction then of developmental stages and transfer phenomena includes the developmental stage as a prerequisite for the transfer of an L1 rule, the prolonged developmental stage due to the similarity to the L1 structure, and the form of a developmental stage as a result of L1-constrained hypothesis testing.

2.6 Conclusion

This chapter has offered an extensive review of early L2 research dealing with stages of acquisition and with the effects of the L1 on L2 acquisition in general and on the stages of acquisition in particular. Wode's proposal that the examination of developmental stages could reveal both universal properties of acquisition and a clearer indication of L1 influences has been only partially realized. With the increased interest in both generative and typological universals, the search for universals of L2 acquisition has taken a different theoretical turn.

So too has the perspective on L1 influences. Once researchers began to extend the notion of transfer from Lado's restricted notion of structural transfer to other levels of analysis, it has become clear that transfer is a very complex phenomenon. These studies lay the theoretical foundation for subsequent work in L2 acquisition in which the extended notion of transfer is utilized in the analysis of data within different theoretical frameworks (e.g. Flynn 1987a, b; Gass 1979; Hyltenstam 1984; White 1985b, 1990–1). With the proposals of Universal Grammar and typological universals, L2 researchers have begun to reconfigure the notions of what is transferable and why.

Notes

1. In these characterizations of the negation structures, the following conventions are used: S = subject, V = verb, VP = verb phrase, AP = adjective phrase, X and Y = variables that can be replaced by different structures, ( ) = optionality, neg = a variable negation marker, Pron = pronoun, and Cop = copula.
2. Wode (1981) discusses in detail the problems with the chronological priority of occurrences of *don't*. The first emergence of *don't* occurs in the chunk 'I don't know' for all subjects. This usage precedes both the initial emergence of *don't* in other phrases and the use of auxiliary + negation.
3. Butterworth and Hatch (1978) also discuss evidence for intonation questions in addition to other interrogative structures (formulaic wh-questions and non-inverted wh-questions) for Ricardo. However, the occurrence of these structures at different stages is not specified.
4. To maintain consistency within this text, I have used the terms 'wh-question' and 'main verb' in place of Wode's terms 'information question' and 'full verb.'
5. CopP here represents copula phrase and replaces Pienemann's KopP.
6. This is a broad use of the term anaphora. A more narrow use of anaphora makes the distinction between anaphora (reference backward to a preceding entity), cataphora (reference forward to a following entity) and exophora (reference to an entity in the extralinguistic context).

3

Universal Grammar

3.1 Introduction

With the development of the notion of Universal Grammar (UG) within the generative theory of Government and Binding (Chomsky 1981) came a renewed interest in the application of generative theory to L2 acquisition (Newmeyer 1983; White 1987a, b). This interest was in part strengthened by the formulation of specific principles and parameters that could be tested empirically and that accounted for cross-linguistic variation, an important issue in L2 acquisition. Interest was also generated by similar research in the application of UG to L1 acquisition. Still other researchers found applications to L2 classroom instruction in the UG paradigm.

Chomsky's later theoretical revisions (*Barriers* (1986a) and the *Minimalist Program* in 1992) have modified the theoretical explanation for many of the principles and parameters on which much of the L2 research is based. These revisions have therefore changed the questions that need to be asked in L2 research. As White (1995) points out, keeping abreast of the changes in a developing theory is both advantageous and problematic. While a changing theory offers new perspectives on language-acquisition data, it also presents practical challenges to the researcher in formulating questions and testing those questions.

In this chapter we first introduce the various principles and parameters of UG that have been investigated in L2 acquisition, illustrate how the different parameter settings are manifested in language, and discuss some of the relevant theoretical shifts. The second section of the chapter examines some of the questions that have been investigated in L2-acquisition research in more detail. This research focuses on the issues of UG accessibility in L2 acquisition, L1 transfer and parameter resetting, and input. Because of the extensive amount of research in this paradigm, it is necessary for students to understand this work in order to understand L2 acquisition of grammar. At the same time, it is important to understand how the assumptions underlying the research in the UG paradigm differ from those of other approaches, and how earlier theoretical concepts have been reformulated within the UG approach.

3.2 Universal Grammar principles and parameters

UG has been developed as part of Chomsky's Government and Binding (GB) Theory (1981), which is a theory that aims to account for native-speaker knowledge of language and, in part, for the acquisition of that knowledge (Chomsky 1986b). UG is the innate component which functions as the 'language acquisition device'. It consists of an abstract set of principles and parameters which serve to define the core aspects of all natural languages. The child in the L1 linguistic environment comes equipped with UG. The L1 linguistic input to the child interacts with UG to establish the core grammar of the child's L1, as schematized in (3.1). The child in the Japanese linguistic environment comes into contact with the Japanese language and selects the parameter setting (schematized as a or b) that matches the linguistic input for each UG parameter (schematized as X, Y, or Z). The child in the English linguistic environment similarly sets the parameters of the L1 core grammar to match the L1 English input. Some aspects of Japanese core grammar may be the same as English (for example, Parameter setting Xa), while others may

(3.1)

(a) Japanese linguistic environment

    Child with UG

    Core grammar of Japanese

Input ⟶ Parameter X
        Setting a or b Xa,
        Parameter Y
        Setting a or b Ya,
        Parameter Z
        Setting a or b Zb,
        . . .   . . .
        + Japanese Input ⟶

(b) English linguistic environment

    Child with UG

    Core grammar of English

Input ⟶ Parameter X
        Setting a or b Xa,
        Parameter Y
        Setting a or b Yb,
        Parameter Z
        Setting a or b Za,
        . . .   . . .
        + English Input ⟶

differ (Parameter setting *Ya* versus *Yb*). For example, the Japanese child will hear sentences with a subject–object–verb word order and will select the word-order setting accordingly. The English child will hear sentences with a subject–verb–object word order and will thus set the word order.

The principles and parameters of UG distinguish the variations of only certain structures found in human language – that is, those making up the core grammar of individual languages. Other more language-specific structures – such as those resulting from historical change or borrowing, for example, English past tense forms *talked* versus *went* – are not governed by UG principles and parameters and thus make up part of the peripheral grammar of individual languages.

In order for a given parameter to be set, it must be triggered by some structural feature in the input. In L1 acquisition, it is assumed that the necessary triggers are available in positive input to the child – that is, in examples of the language (Chomsky 1981; Lightfoot 1989, 1991; cf. Gibson and Wexler 1994). It is further assumed that negative evidence which directs the learners' attention to the ungrammatical nature of their utterances – correction – does not significantly contribute to L1 acquisition.[1] In the case of L1 acquisition, then, positive input alone is considered sufficient for triggering the setting of UG parameters. A parameter setting is considered the default or unmarked setting if it is the assumed correct initial setting. L1 learners will change the value of this setting only if there is sufficient evidence in the input to prompt a change. Therefore, for the L1 Japanese learners in (3.1), they retain the unmarked *Ya* value because they receive no input to the contrary. The L1 English learner begins with the unmarked *Ya* setting and, upon receiving the necessary input, changes the unmarked setting to the marked *Yb* setting. The core grammar that results from all L1 parameter setting is considered unmarked, or easier to learn, and the peripheral grammar is considered marked, or more difficult to learn.

In L2 acquisition, parameter setting is not so straightforward. It is hypothesized that L2 learners either have direct access to the default UG setting with which L1 learners come equipped or that they must reset the L1 setting to the L2 setting where the L1 and L2 settings differ, as in the example Parameter settings *Ya* and *Yb* seen above. With direct access to the UG default setting, L2 acquisition would proceed like L1 acquisition. If L2 parameter resetting is necessary, the notion of markedness comes into play. For example, for L2 learners who must reset their marked L1 setting – English *Yb* – to an unmarked L2 setting – Japanese *Ya* – parameter resetting should be relatively easy. However, parameter resetting from an unmarked L1 setting to a marked L2 should be more difficult. The prediction, then, for L2 acquisition is that unmarked parameter settings will be acquired with less difficulty than will marked settings.

In order to explore the issue of parameter setting, we must first examine the proposed principles and parameters more closely. It is not possible, however, to address all aspects of UG, of GB Theory, and of the Minimalist Program in detail here. Readers are referred to the primary literature noted in the bibliography.[2]

GB Theory assumes that there are different components of grammar, roughly corresponding to the lexicon, the syntax, the phonology, and the semantics. These components relate to different levels of representation of the grammar: the Lexicon, Deep Structure (D-structure) and Surface Structure (S-structure) of the syntax, Phonetic Form (PF) and Logical Form (LF) (adapted from Chomsky and Lasnik 1995):

(3.2)

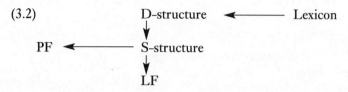

At the level of D-structure, the underlying sentence structure is generated and the appropriate lexical items are inserted into the sentence structure in accordance with various restrictions, such as restrictions on verbs (transitive versus intransitive verbs: *Mary saw, Mary saw the movie, John jogged; verbs allowing noun-phrase complements versus verbs allowing clausal complements: John believed the story, *John thought the story, John thought (that) the story was fascinating) or on nouns (animate versus inanimate nouns: The dog ate the cake, *The cake ate). The D-structure is then transformed (hence the earlier term 'transformational' grammar) into the S-structure by a general movement rule, Move α (Move alpha), that moves different items – for example, wh-words.

(3.3)
    (a) wh-questions
        D-structure: [John will invite whom]
        S-structure: [whom$_i$ [will [John invite t$_i$]]]³

At the levels of PF and LF, the final forms of the sentences are checked to make sure that they conform to the phonetic and logical meaning constraints of the language. The principles and parameters of UG correspond to different levels of the grammar.⁴

The principles and parameters of UG are distinct from the types of grammar rule discussed in the previous chapter. They are abstract; therefore, they can be generalized to a variety of grammatical structures. In addition, they can be seen as a binary system in which a language has either a plus (+) or minus (–) setting for a given parameter (such as the *a* and *b* choices given above), and the setting of the parameter results in a cluster of characteristics. A specific example of this is the pro-drop parameter as it was originally proposed (Chomsky 1981; Rizzi 1982). A positive setting for the pro–drop parameter, such as in Spanish, results in the following cluster of structural characteristics: null subject pronouns, subject–verb inversion in declarative sentences, and also extraction of subjects from embedded clauses with overt complementizers (e.g. the subject *who* extracted from the embedded clause with the complementizer *that* in (3.4)). Note that this abstract parameter relates a cluster of structures that on the surface seem unrelated.

(3.4)
  (a) null subject pronouns
      Ø   viene
      [He] comes.
      'He comes.'

  (b) subject–verb inversion in declarative sentences
      Viene Juan.
      Comes Juan.
      'Juan comes.'

  (c) *that–trace* effects[5]
      Quién dijiste   que llegó?
      Who   did you say   that arrived?
      'Who did you say arrived?'

A negative setting for the pro-drop parameter results in a non-pro-drop language, such as English, in which this cluster of structures is ungrammatical. While this analysis of the pro-drop parameter has been revised somewhat, it has formed the basis of much L2 research.

The pro-drop parameter, as with other principles and parameters of UG, has evolved so that much of the data remains the same, but the predictions and hypotheses differ. Current analyses of the pro-drop parameter focus not on the clustering of the structures seen in (3.4) but rather on the relationship between inflectional markings on the verbs, the existence of null subjects and objects, and the existence of expletives such as *it* and *there* in English (Hermon and Yoon 1989; Huang 1984; Jaeggli and Hyams 1988). Languages that allow pro-drop are said to exhibit uniform verbal inflectional paradigms (the Morphological Uniformity Principle (MUP) of Jaeggli and Safir (1989)). That is, a morphologically uniform language has either all verb forms inflected for person and number, as in Italian and Spanish, or only underived inflectional forms, as in Chinese, exemplified in (3.5). In any 'mixed' language, which has both derived and underived forms, such as those found in English (I, you, we, you, they *say*; and he, she, it *says*), pro-drop will not be allowed, or, technically speaking, will not be 'licensed'.

(3.5)
  (a) Uniform marking of all verb forms
      Spanish   *hablar* to speak
      habl*o*   I speak
      habl*as*   you (informal) speak
      habl*a*   he, she, it, you (formal) speaks
      habl*amos*   we speak

habl*ais*   you (informal) speak
habl*an*   they, you (formal) speak

(b) Uniform non-marking of all verb forms
Chinese   *xihuan*   like

The second aspect of the pro-drop parameter involves the mechanisms by which the identity of the dropped or *zero* pronoun is recovered. 'Identification' is possible by 'rich' morphological marking, as seen in Spanish, or by identification with a topic, as in languages like Chinese (examples adapted from Huang 1984):

(3.6)
(a) Zhangsan Kanjian Lisi le ma?
'Did Zhangsan see Lisi?'
Ø kanjian ta le.
'[He] saw him.'

(b) Zhongguo, difang hen da. (Ø), renkou hen duo. (Ø), tudi hen feiwo. (Ø), qihou ye hen hao. (Ø), women dou hen xihuan.
'(As for) China, (its) land area is very large. (Its) population is very big. (Its) land is very fertile. We all like (it).'

The discourse topics *Zhangsan* and *China* serve as the referents of the dropped pronouns and thus 'identify' the zero pronouns. Therefore, in order to exhibit pro-drop, a language must both license pro-drop by morphological uniformity and identify the dropped pronoun in some way.

Another component of UG is X-bar theory, which constrains the word-order relations in phrases such as noun phrases (NP), adjective phrases (AP), verb phrases (VP), and prepositional phrases (PP). Each phrase consists of a head, a complement, and a specifier. For example, the English NP *a description of the picture* is headed by the noun *description*. Its complement is the PP *of the picture*, and its specifier is the indefinite article *a*. These phrasal components form a hierarchical phrase structure in which the head (N) comprises the lowest level; the head plus its complement form the next higher level (N' or N-bar), and the N' plus its specifier comprise the highest level (N'' or N double-bar), as seen in (3.7):

(3.7)

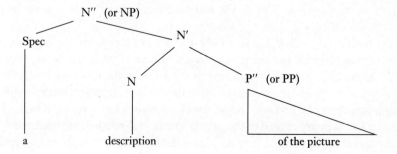

X-bar theory is the abstract formulation of this hierarchical phrase structure which applies to all phrases, NP, AP, VP, and PP:

(3.8)
  (a) X   = head
  (b) X′   = head (X)   +   complement
  (c) X″   (or XP)   = specifier   +   X′

In traditional grammar there is a distinction between content words and function words. In X-bar theory, a similar distinction is made between lexical categories (verbs, nouns, adjectives, and prepositions), and functional categories, which correspond to grammatical morphemes, such as auxiliaries, determiners, complementizers, tense markers, and agreement markers. Examples of each category in English are as follows: auxiliaries (can, will, should), determiners (the, a, this, etc.), complementizers (that, whether, if), tense markers (-ed), and agreement markers (nominative case *she* versus accusative case *her*).

X-bar theory applies to functional category phrases as well as to lexical category phrases. For instance, sentences, or independent clauses, must have a tensed verb; they are, therefore, characterized as being marked by tensed, or inflected, verbs. The functional category, Inflection, or INFL, is seen as the head of the sentence, or INFL Phrase (IP). Following X-bar theory, IPs are projected as follows with a specifier (the subject NP) and a complement (the predicate VP):

(3.9)

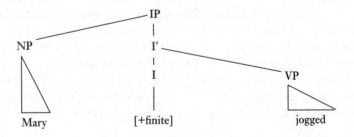

In this way, the principles of X-bar theory relate to all kinds of phrases – lexical category phrases, such as NP and VP, and functional category phrases, such as IP.

More recent proposals (Chomsky 1992; Pollock 1989) separate the functional category Inflection still further into different categories for tense features (the functional category Tense, TP) and agreement features (the functional category Agreement, AgrP). The separation of these functional categories interacts with other parameters in UG – for example, the characteristics of agreement in AgrP in a given language are related to the pro-drop and verb movement parameters.[6]

Languages differ with respect to the order of heads, complements, and specifiers within a phrase and are categorized by the order of the head and its complement (Chomsky 1988; cf. Kayne 1994).[7] For example, in Japanese, verbal complements – for example, direct and indirect objects – precede the head verb, that is, occurring to the left of the verb; thus, Japanese is categorized as a head-last language, as seen in (3.10a). Spanish (3.10b), as a head-first language, has verbal complements following the head verb:

(3.10)

(a) Yuko-wa $[_{VP}$ $[_{V'}$ baiorin-o $[_V$ hikimasu$]]]$
    Yuko-topic   violin-object   plays
    S   O   V

(b) Ernesto $[_{VP}$ $[_{V'}$ $[_V$ toca$]$ el violín$]]$
    Ernesto   plays   the violin
    S   V   O

Head-last languages are also referred to as 'left-branching' languages, because the phrase-structure trees are drawn to branch towards the left. Similarly, head-first languages are referred to as 'right-branching' (as seen in (3.7) and (3.9)). Examples of utterances such as those in (3.10a and b) in the linguistic input serve to set the Head Parameter in Japanese to head-last and in Spanish to head-first.

UG also constrains the meaning relationships between nouns and other nominal constructions such as pronouns (*you, she, he,* or *we*) and anaphors such as the reflexives *himself, themselves,* or *herself.* This component of UG, known as Binding Theory, specifies the syntactic domains within which nominal constructions are allowed to refer to each other. Several examples will serve to illustrate the relevant relationships. The proper nouns, pronouns, and anaphors seen in (3.11) are subscripted with indices which indicate the coreference relationships between these constructions. For example, the reflexive anaphor *himself* refers back to the antecedent $John_j$ in (3.11a) but (incorrectly) to Tom_i in (3.11b).

(3.11)

(a) $[Tom_i$ thinks $[$that $[John_j$ hurt $himself_j]]]$

(b) *$[Tom_i$ thinks $[$that $[John_j$ hurt $himself_i]]]$

(c) *$[Mary_i$ saw $her_i]$

(d) $[Mary_i$ saw $her_j]$

(e) $[Jane_i$ said $[$that $[Sally_j$ got a new job$]]]$

(f) $[Jane_i$ said $[$that $[she_i$ got a new job$]]]$

(g) $[Jane_i$ said $[$that $[she_j$ got a new job$]]]$

Consider a tensed clause – *John hurt himself* or *Mary saw her* – as the relevant structural domain (or governing category) for coreference in English.[8] The difference in grammaticality between (3.11a) and (3.11b) demonstrates that a reflexive anaphor (*himself*) must corefer – be bound to an antecedent – within its immediate or local tensed clause to result in a grammatical sentence in English, as in (3.11a), in which *himself* is bound to the local NP antecedent *John*. *Himself* cannot be bound to *Tom*, which is outside the local tensed clause, resulting in the ungrammatical sentence in (3.11b). Conversely, a pronoun must not be bound in its governing category, as shown in the ungrammatical (3.11c) as opposed to the grammatical (3.11d); *her* cannot be bound to the local NP *Mary*, as in (3.11c), but must be free within the governing category, resulting in the correct coreference in (3.11d): *her* refers to someone other than *Mary*. The pronouns in (3.11f) and (3.11g) are similarly free in their governing categories; they refer to an entity outside the local tensed clause *she got a new job*; either *Jane* as in (3.11f) or someone else (3.11g). Thus, Binding Theory results in distinct coreference properties for nouns, pronouns, and anaphors, with English anaphors bound within the local governing category and English pronouns free within the local governing category.[9]

The parametric differences exhibited between languages relate to the different syntactic domains in which binding is possible or impossible for nouns, pronouns, and anaphors (Wexler and Manzini 1987). For example, while coreference for reflexive anaphors in English is constrained to within a tensed clause, in Chinese, long-distance binding across a clause boundary is permitted, as in the following example (from Cole *et al.* 1990):

> (3.12) [Zhangsan$_i$ renwei [Lisi$_j$ zhidao [Wangwu$_k$ xihuan ziji$_i$]]]
>   Zhangsan$_i$ thinks   Lisi$_j$ knows   Wangwu$_k$ like   self$_i$
>   'Zhangsani thinks that Lisi$_j$ knows that Wangwui likes himself$_j$.'

As a result of long-distance binding, any of the nouns *Zhangsan$_i$*, *Lisi$_j$*, or *Wangwu$_k$* can be possible antecedents of the reflexive *ziji$_i$* (-self). Binding domains range from English-like languages, representative of the most restrictive domain, and Chinese-like languages, representative of the widest binding domain.

Languages differ in another way with respect to binding – that is, the syntactic function of the antecedent. For example, the antecedent of a reflexive in English may be the subject of the clause, as in the relationship between the reflexive *himself* and its antecedent *John* in *John$_i$ hurt himself$_i$*, or the antecedent may have another syntactic function in the sentence, such as the direct object of the verb (e.g. *Bill* in *John$_i$ asked Bill$_j$ about himself$_j$*). Other languages, such as Japanese, require that the antecedent be the subject of the clause. The selection of the proper antecedent based on its syntactic function has been proposed as an additional parametric variation related to binding, the Proper Antecedent Parameter (Wexler and Manzini 1987).

Alternative analyses of coreference have combined both the characteristics of local versus long-distance binding with the restrictions on subject antecedents. For example, the difference in the morphological structure of reflexives has been proposed as the determining factor in binding (Battistella 1989; Katada 1991; Pica 1991). That is, mono-morphemic reflexives such as the single morpheme *ziji* for 'self' in Chinese allow long-distance binding but require subject antecedents. Conversely, the compound reflexives with two morphemes, such as *him* + *self* in English, require local binding but allow different types of antecedents.[10] Thus, we see that Binding Theory constrains nominal reference in a number of ways: type of nominal (noun, pronoun, reflexive pronoun), type of syntactic domain (local versus long distance), syntactic function of antecedents (subject versus object), and the internal morphological structure of the nominal (one morpheme versus more than one).

The verb movement parameter (Pollock 1989) accounts for language variation in the word order of verbs, adverbs, verbal complements, and negation as a result of how verbs get marked with inflectional morphology. Consider the following examples of adverb placement in French and English (from White 1991a):

(3.13)
   (a) Jean boit   son café   rapidement.
        John drinks his   coffee quickly.

   (b) Prudemment Jean   a ouvert la   porte.
        Carefully   John   opened the   door.

   (c) *Marie souvent   regarde la télévision.
        Mary   often   watches television.

   (d) Marie   regarde souvent la télévision.
        *Mary watches often   television.

While adverb placement in sentence-final (3.13a) and sentence-initial (3.13b) positions is grammatical in both French and English, the permitted sentence-internal word order between the verb and the adverb clearly differs in French and English, as evidenced in the ungrammatical sentences in (3.13c) and (3.13d). The verb movement parameter requires that all tensed verbs in French be raised into the INFL position in order to be marked for tense and aspect, as schematized in (3.14).

(3.14) Verb raising

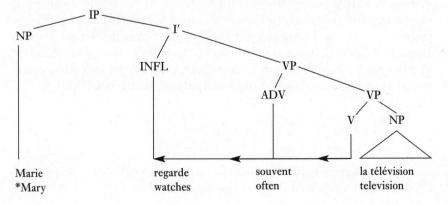

English, on the other hand, prohibits verb raising (except for *have* and *be*) and thus does not allow the verb–adverb–object word order exemplified in (3.13d). As with the original analysis of the pro-drop parameter, the verb movement parameter affects a cluster of structures: adverb placement (as in (3.13)), negation, and question formation (adapted from White 1992a):

(3.15)
    (a) Jean n'aime pas Marie.
        *John likes   not Mary.
        'John doesn't like Mary.'

    (b) Aime-t-elle Jean?
        *Likes she   John?
        'Does she like John?'

The cluster analysis predicts that languages that allow raising, like French, will have negation after the main verb (3.15a) and will allow inversion of the subject and the main verb in questions (3.15b). Languages like English that do not allow verb raising must resort to other mechanisms for negation and subject–verb inversion; English inserts the 'dummy' auxiliary *do*.

    Finally, Subjacency is a UG principle that constrains movement in two ways: (1) the distance that an extracted element, such as a wh-question word, can move (across phrase and clause boundaries), and (2) the types of structures out of which an element may be extracted (embedded wh-questions, relative clauses, and complement clauses). For instance, in English, Subjacency determines the difference in grammaticality between the following questions: the grammatical *What did Mary say that Jane believed that John saw?* (with extraction of a wh-word, *what*, out of a verbal complement clause: *Jane believed [that [John saw what]]*) versus the ungrammatical *What did Mary believe the claim that John saw?* (with extraction of *what* out of a complex NP: *the claim [that [John saw what]]*) (examples from White 1985a). The difference in grammaticality is due to the type and number of syntactic boundaries that are crossed. The syntactic boundaries in question mark the boundaries of different types of syntactic structures: for example, clause boundaries (IP), complementizer boundaries (CP, which includes a complementizer such as *that* and a clause), noun-phrase boundaries (NP), and prepositional-phrase boundaries (PP)). The parametric differences between languages relate to the types of boundaries that count as barriers to movement for each language. Differences can be found, for instance, between wh-question extraction in French and English (examples adapted from White 1985a):

(3.16)
    (a) Combien [$_{IP}$ as tu vu [$_{NP}$ —— [$_{PP}$ de personnes?]]]
        *'How many did you see (of) people?'

    (b) De quel livre [$_{IP}$ connais-tu [$_{NP}$ la fin [$_{PP}$ ——?]]]
        *'Of which book do you know the ending?'

(c) *Qui [$_{IP}$ croit–il [$_{NP}$ l'histoire [$_{CP}$ que tu as vu ——?]]]
  *'Who does he believe the story that you saw?'

While French allows for the extraction of the wh-word, *combien*, out of these structures, English does not allow this type of extraction. Therefore, the barriers to movement in the French structures differ from those in the comparable English structures.[11] In the earlier GB formulation of Subjacency, particular boundaries were determined to block movement for individual languages. For example, CP, NP, and PP were considered the critical boundaries for French, whereas the critical boundaries for English were IP, CP, NP, and PP. A more recent analysis of Subjacency (Chomsky 1986a) makes the critical boundaries related to particular structures within a language rather than relevant to all structures concerning those boundaries in the language. As a result, not all IP boundaries are barriers to movement in English; only some of them are. Under this analysis, Subjacency is structure-specific within a given language.

It is clear from this overview of UG that these principles and parameters affect a wide range of grammatical structures, including many of the same structures seen in Chapter 2: negation, word order, interrogatives, embedded clauses, and pronouns. It is also evident, however, that research in a UG approach to L2 acquisition presents quite a different view of these structures; the principles and parameters are complex in nature and are interrelated. In this approach the questions asked in earlier research are reformulated in the light of this theoretical perspective. One must remember, as noted above, that UG relates only to aspects of core grammar and not to many other grammatical structures of interest in L2 acquisition.

One additional characteristic of UG requires our attention. Because of the complex and abstract nature of UG principles and parameters, it is argued that the linguistic knowledge that a native speaker acquires is not sufficiently evident in the input to the learner; the input is therefore seen as impoverished. As an illustration of this phenomenon, consider what the learner must discover from the input about the restrictions on wh-questions seen in (3.17) (several examples have been adapted from Bley-Vroman *et al.* 1988).[12]

(3.17)
  (a) What did John think Carol wanted her mother to give to the postman?
  (b) *What did Bill believe the claim that Carol had bought?
  (c) Who does John want to see?
  (d) *Who does John say that left?
  (e) What did Bill think that the teacher had said?
  (f) *What did John hear the news that the mayor had said?
  (g) Who did Bill think would win the election?
  (h) *Who did John buy the house that had recommended to him?
  (i) *What does Tim wonder where Nancy has put?
  (j) Which bed does John like to sleep in?
  (k) *What time will Mary arrive before?

The learner must recognize that the length of the wh-question is not necessarily a factor in its grammaticality (3.17a and 3.17c versus 3.17b and 3.17d). While extracted subjects from embedded clauses are sometimes grammatical (the extracted *who* in 3.17c and 3.17g), extracted subjects from other embedded clauses are not (the extracted *who* in 3.17d and 3.17h). Similarly, extracted objects from embedded clauses are sometimes grammatical (the extracted *what* in 3.17e) and sometimes ungrammatical (the extracted *what* in 3.17f and 3.17i). Finally, extraction from some adverbials is grammatical, while extraction from others is not (3.17j versus 3.17k). These restrictions on wh-questions are not readily evident from the L1 input alone, nor are they explicitly taught to L1 learners. The ungrammatical forms simply do not occur. The input to the learner, then, does not provide sufficient information to account for the complex knowledge that is ultimately acquired.[13] The resulting assumption is that UG is not taught to L1 learners; rather, it is innate. Similarly, although L2 learners may be learning the L2 in an instructional setting, the abstract rules that determine the grammaticality – and ungrammaticality – of these question forms are not taught. As in the L1 setting, the ungrammatical forms do not occur.

An additional perspective on input and L2 parameter setting includes the subset–superset relationship resulting from the differences between an L1 parameter setting and the corresponding L2 parameter setting. Once again, let us consider the pro-drop parameter. A +pro-drop language, such as Spanish, allows for two types of sentences: those containing overt subject pronouns (e.g. *Juan* in *Juan viene*) and those containing null subject pronouns (*ø viene*). A –pro-drop language, such as English or French, allows for only a subset of the sentences allowed for in a +pro-drop language – that is, only those sentences containing an overt subject pronoun.

Predictions can be made about the relative difficulty of L2 parameter resetting based on this subset–superset relationship. Speakers of the subset language, in this case L1 English, will require only positive input to reset the pro-drop parameter for L2 Spanish. The positive input consists of sentences with null subject pronouns such as *ø viene*, which are readily available in the L2 input. With this positive input, L1 English speakers can reset the pro-drop parameter to include the superset sentences.

On the other hand, speakers of the superset language, L1 Spanish, will have more difficulty resetting the pro-drop parameter for L2 English. The positive input in L2 English simply indicates that overt subject pronouns are allowed in English (*Mary is sleeping*), and this type of sentence constitutes a subset of the sentences which are already allowed by the L1 Spanish grammar. This positive input, however, does not indicate that sentences with null subject pronouns are ungrammatical in English. As a result, for L2 parameter resetting from a superset language to a subset language to take place, negative evidence marking the ungrammaticality of null subject sentences (**ø is sleeping*) would be required (White 1989), thus making L2 parameter resetting in this situation more difficult.

With this generative approach to L2 acquisition, researchers can make very precise predictions. They can predict the acquisition of related structures, as in the verb movement parameter. They can also predict the likelihood of the transfer of different grammatical structures based on the markedness of the L1 and L2 parameter settings. Finally, they can predict the relationship between specific kinds of input – the structures that will trigger parameter resetting – and L2 acquisition. With these predictions in mind, we turn to the questions that have been examined in L2 acquisition research.

3.3 Questions explored

- Are Universal Grammar principles and parameters accessible in second-language acquisition?
- What is the interaction between the first-language parameter setting and the second-language parameter setting?
- What is the initial state of the second-language grammar in the second-language acquisition process?
- What is the effect of positive and/or negative input on the resetting of Universal Grammar in second-language acquisition?

In the earlier work in the 1960s and 1970s L2 researchers were interested in discovering the similarities and differences between L1 and L2 acquisition. Investigations of L1 and L2 acquisitional stages sought to confirm the 'L1=L2' hypothesis and to explore universal properties of language acquisition. Work within the UG paradigm explores similar issues in terms of UG principles and parameters. In this case, the question has become whether or not the UG principles and parameters that constrain L1 acquisition are accessible to the learner in L2 acquisition. Recent developments have shifted the focus from whether or not UG is accessible, to what the initial state of L2 learners' grammars is – that is, what parts of UG L2 learners bring with them to the L2-acquisition process. Another area of continuing interest in L2 acquisition has been that of transfer. From the perspective of UG, research has focused on the effects of L1 parameter setting on L2 parameter resetting; in other words, does the L1 setting transfer to the L2? Finally, the discussion of parameter resetting has offered a new perspective on L2 instruction. We examine each in turn.

3.3.1 ARE UNIVERSAL GRAMMAR PRINCIPLES AND PARAMETERS ACCESSIBLE IN SECOND-LANGUAGE ACQUISITION?

The question that has been explored most is whether or not UG principles and parameters are accessible to L2 learners. Regarding the accessibility of UG in L2 acquisition, White (1989: 48–9) outlines five logical possibilities:

(3.18)
   (a) UG is accessible in L2 acquisition and functions as it does in L1
       acquisition.
   (b) UG is totally accessible, although L2 learners initially transfer the
       settings of the L1.
   (c) UG is accessible only via the settings of the L1.
   (d) UG is accessible but does not function exactly as it does in L1
       acquisition.
   (e) UG is not accessible in L2 acquisition.

Let us consider these five possibilities with a concrete example. Let us first
assume that the parameter setting that results in a pro-drop language [+pd] is
the initial or default setting for L1 acquisition (Hyams 1992, 1994; cf. Valian
1994).[14] If UG were totally accessible in L2 acquisition as in L1 acquisition, L1
speakers of Spanish (a pro-drop language) and L1 speakers of English (a non-
pro-drop language) would both have the default pro-drop setting as the initial
setting for learning either L2 Chinese [+pd] or L2 French [–pd]. In the L2
acquisition of French, for example, both groups would begin at the default pro-
drop setting and then set the parameter to –pro-drop based on the French
input, as schematized in (3.19a). In the second possibility with access to UG,
the L2 learners do not have access to the initial UG default setting; instead,
they transfer the settings of the L1 (3.19b). Since UG is still accessible, L2
learners can reset the [+pd] setting in Spanish to the [–pd] setting for French.
Without access to UG, schematized in (3.19c), L2 learners have access only to
the L1 settings and thus cannot reset the parameter to an L2 setting that differs
from the L1 setting. The possibilities seen in (3.19d) and (3.19e) both result in
variable success in acquiring pro-drop, due either to other components which
are accessed in addition to UG (for example, abstract learning mechanisms)
(3.19d) or to the total unavailability of UG (3.19e). As a result, pro-drop may or
may not be acquired in the L2.

Research into the accessibility of UG principles and parameters has centred
on four basic areas: binding theory, pro-drop, branching direction, and
subjacency. Here we discuss binding and subjacency.

Binding differences in L2 acquisition have been examined in two ways: (1)
the domain in which an anaphor can be bound – that is, the binding domain or
governing category, and (2) the syntactic function of the antecedent. The
accessibility question as related to binding has focused on the change from the
binding domain of the L1 to the binding domain of the L2. In other words, do
L2 learners still have access to the principles constraining binding, and can they
reset the governing category? The resulting answers to these questions have
been somewhat contradictory. Work by Finer and Broselow (1986) (also
Broselow and Finer 1991; Finer 1991; cf. Thomas 1991) examines the binding
domains of Korean learners of English based on Wexler and Manzini's (1987)
five-point continuum ranging from the most restrictive binding domain as in

(3.19)
    (a) UG is accessible

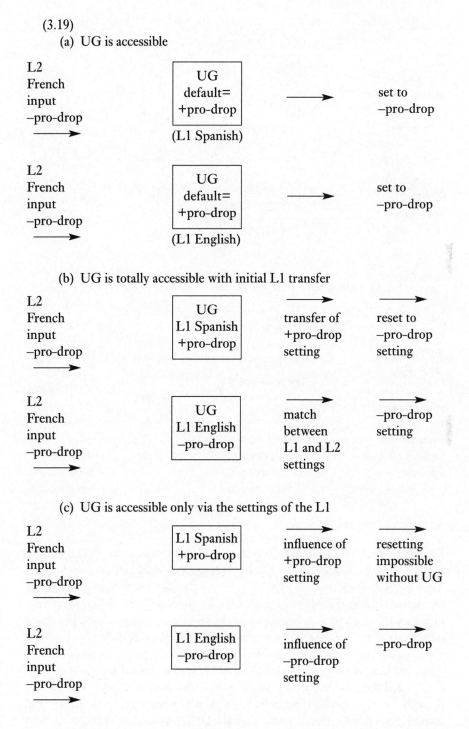

L2
French
input
−pro−drop
⟶

UG
default=
+pro−drop
(L1 Spanish)

⟶

set to
−pro−drop

L2
French
input
−pro−drop
⟶

UG
default=
+pro−drop
(L1 English)

⟶

set to
−pro−drop

    (b) UG is totally accessible with initial L1 transfer

L2
French
input
−pro−drop
⟶

UG
L1 Spanish
+pro−drop

⟶
transfer of
+pro−drop
setting

⟶
reset to
−pro−drop
setting

L2
French
input
−pro−drop
⟶

UG
L1 English
−pro−drop

⟶
match
between
L1 and L2
settings

⟶
−pro−drop
setting

    (c) UG is accessible only via the settings of the L1

L2
French
input
−pro−drop
⟶

L1 Spanish
+pro−drop

⟶
influence of
+pro−drop
setting

⟶
resetting
impossible
without UG

L2
French
input
−pro−drop
⟶

L1 English
−pro−drop

⟶
influence of
−pro−drop
setting

⟶
−pro−drop

(d) UG is accessible but does not function exactly as it does in L1 acquisition

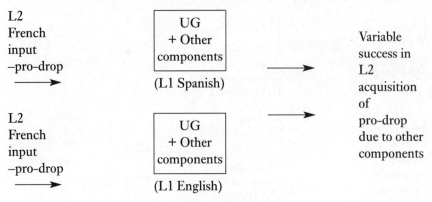

(e) UG is not accessible in L2 acquisition

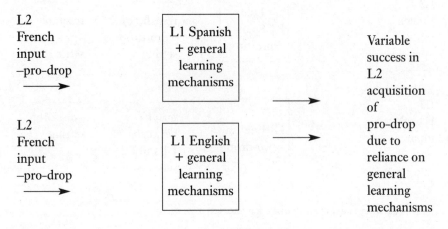

English to the least restrictive domain as evidenced in Korean. While Korean allows for long-distance binding, Korean learners of English do not maintain the least restrictive domain of their L1, nor do they readily adopt the more restrictive binding domain of English; instead, they adopt two different binding domains. They allow for long-distance binding of reflexives in clauses with infinitivals (e.g. the clause containing *to paint* in *Mr Fat$_i$ expects Mr Thin$_j$ to paint himself$_i$*), but prefer local binding in tensed clauses (e.g. *Mr Fat$_i$ believes that Mr Thin$_j$ will paint himself$_j$*). Although these binding domains are inconsistent with the L1 and the L2, they are consistent with those found in natural languages, Russian and Icelandic respectively, and are, therefore, still considered constrained by UG. Findings by Thomas (1989) show that speakers of both Spanish, which restricts reflexive binding to local binding, and Chinese, which allows long-distance binding, allow long-distance binding in English. These findings also support the conclusion that L2 learners do not necessarily transfer the binding domain of their L1s but do arrive at UG-constrained IL grammars. Other research, however, shows evidence of both L1 transfer and UG access (Bennett 1994; Hirakawa 1990; Thomas 1993). Bennett (1994) finds that Serbo-Croatian learners of English transfer long-distance binding from the L1 into the L2 in certain constructions but that the L2 learners are also guided by UG in constructions which do not occur in the L1.

The second aspect of binding involves the selection of the proper antecedent for the anaphor.[15] Recall from the earlier discussion that, in general, anaphors which require local binding allow both subject and non-subject antecedents, as seen in (3.20a), while anaphors which allow long-distance binding require subject antecedents as seen in (3.20b and c) (examples adapted from Hermon 1994 and Thomas 1993).[16]

(3.20)

   (a) Subject and non-subject antecedents in English with *herself*
     Alice$_i$ told Sue$_j$ about herself$_{i/j}$.

   (b) Subject antecedents in Japanese with *zibun* ('self')
     Yamada$_i$ ga Tanaka$_j$ ni zibun$_{i/*j}$ no atarashii kateikyooshi o syookaishita.
     'Yamada$_i$ introduced Tanaka$_j$ to self's$_{i/*j}$ new tutor.'
     Yamada$_i$ ga Tanaka$_j$ ni zibun$_{i/*j}$ no atarashii kateikyooshi o syookaishita to Ohata$_i$ ga omou.
     'Ohata$_i$ thinks that Yamada$_i$ introduced Tanaka$_j$ to self's$_{i/*j}$ new tutor.'

   (c) Subject antecedents in Chinese with *ziji* ('self')
     Zhangsan$_i$ song gei Lisi$_j$ yipian guanyu ziji$_{i/*j}$ de wenzhang.
     'Zhangsan$_i$ gave Lisi$_j$ an article about himself$_{i/*j}$.'
     Wangsan$_i$ shou Zhangsan$_i$ song gei Lisi$_j$ yipian guanyu ziji$_{i/*j}$ de wenzhang.
     'Wangsan$_i$ said that Zhangsan$_i$ gave Lisi$_j$ an article about himself$_{i/*j}$.'

It is argued that, if L2 acquisition is constrained by UG, L2 learners of languages that allow long-distance binding should recognize the constraint on proper antecedents – i.e. that they must be subjects, once they have acquired long-distance binding. Thomas (1995) finds that high-proficiency adult L2 learners of Japanese allow long-distance binding and have acquired the restriction on subject orientation for proper antecedents but that low-proficiency learners who allow for long-distance binding do not show evidence of a subject orientation. While this research, as well as the research discussed above, shows that L2 learners can acquire the proper L2 binding domain, it is unclear whether they link binding domain with constraints on subject orientation, as some theories of UG would predict.

With regard to the five possibilities listed in (3.18), the question of UG accessibility and binding is only partially answered. The mixed evidence of L1 transfer and of UG accessibility (binding domains and proper antecedents) points to a sixth possibility that combines aspects of (3.19b) and (3.19d) – that is, that L2 learners may initially transfer the L1 settings of UG and that, while UG is accessible, it does not function exactly as it does in L1 acquisition. We return to this issue below.

Other researchers argue that UG is either not directly accessible or not accessible at all in L2 acquisition (Bley-Vroman 1989; Clahsen and Muysken 1986, 1989; Schachter 1989b, 1990). Bley-Vroman (1989) argues that L2 acquisition is fundamentally different from L1 acquisition in terms of learners' ultimate language attainment, variation in success, and indeterminate intuitions about the grammaticality of sentences, among other factors (cf. Schwartz 1990). Based on these differences, Bley-Vroman argues that the characteristics of adult L2 acquisition resemble general adult learning of any skill such as learning mathematics or piano rather than resembling UG-guided L1 acquisition. UG, therefore, is not directly accessible in adult L2 acquisition, and the role of UG in L1 acquisition is replaced by the L1 grammar and a 'general abstract problem solving system' (Bley-Vroman 1989: 50). Clahsen and Muysken (1986, 1989) compare the L1 and L2 acquisition of German word order involving verb placement, verb inflection, and verb negation, and they conclude that, while L1 acquisition is guided by UG, L2 learners do not have direct access to UG. They note that in a parameter-setting model of language acquisition, related phenomena occur at the same time, for example, the emergence of verb inflection and the occurrence of tensed verbs in the correct word order – the verb-second position in German. Since, in their analysis of the L2 data, these phenomena do not occur simultaneously and therefore represent two separate acquisitional tasks, the L1 and L2 acquisition processes are claimed to be distinct. While Clahsen and Muysken do acknowledge that L2 learners may have access to UG via the settings of their L1 grammars, they argue in favour of L2 acquisition guided by information processing and general problem-solving principles rather than UG (cf. du Plessis *et al.* 1987; Eubank 1992; Schwartz 1990, 1992).

Findings in favour of L2 learners' access to UG are also mixed with regard to Subjacency (Bley-Vroman *et al.* 1988; Johnson and Newport 1991; Martohardjono and Gair 1993; Schachter 1989b, 1990; White 1985a, 1988; White *et al.* 1992). Working within the Government and Binding framework, Schachter (1989b, 1990) examined the presence of Subjacency effects in the L2 grammar of learners of English from different language backgrounds. The L1s allow wh-word extraction to varying degrees: Dutch, which allows extraction in the same instances as in English; Indonesian, which allows extractions out of sentential subjects, relative clauses, and embedded questions; Chinese, which does not have wh-movement but which exhibits relative-pronoun extraction out of complex NPs and sentential subjects; and Korean, which permits no extraction at all (cf. Martohardjono and Gair 1993). She hypothesized that, if UG principles are accessible to all learners, then even though Subjacency is not manifested in the L1 – e.g. Korean – it should be evident in the learner's judgements of English. If UG is not directly accessible, then it should be evident in the L2 only if it is present in the L1. In support of the latter hypothesis, Schachter found that the native language of the subject had the greatest effect on the subject's ability to detect Subjacency violations; that is, the Dutch subjects exhibit judgements most like those of the native English speakers, and the Korean subjects exhibit little knowledge of Subjacency violations, with the Chinese and Indonesian speakers falling somewhere in the middle (cf. Eubank 1989b).

Studies by Bley-Vroman *et al.* (1988) and White (1985a, 1988) suggest that UG may be accessible, but these results are not conclusive. Bley-Vroman *et al.*, for example, conclude that the performance of their Korean L2 learners of English is significantly better than chance, therefore displaying some access to UG. They nevertheless question why the results in favour of UG effects were not stronger than they were. White's (1988) findings show that some subjects are able to recognize Subjacency violations found in extraction of wh-elements from embedded clauses (e.g. *Which book did John wonder whether Mary had chosen t?*), while others are not.

However, studies based on more recent analyses have shown additional support for UG constraints on movement (Martohardjono and Gair 1993; Uziel 1993; White 1992a, c; White *et al.* 1992). For instance, Eubank (1989b) reanalyses the data of Schachter's Korean subjects from the perspective of Chomsky's Barriers framework (1986a) and suggests that the reactions of this group fall within UG. He cautions, however, that the data of the other language groups would also need to be reanalysed in a similar way. Recall that Subjacency is a constraint on movement. Martohardjono and Gair (1993), following an analysis by Huang (1984), make the distinction between languages that form questions by movement and languages that form questions without movement. They hypothesize that Indonesian learners of English, in accordance with the structure of their L1, may analyse English wh-questions from a non-movement perspective, in which case Subjacency would not be a factor in their L2 question formation. Their results show that intermediate learners who do not show linguistic evidence of a movement analysis do not recognize Subjacency constraints, whereas advanced learners who do show evidence of a movement analysis do recognize Subjacency constraints. Similarly, White *et al.* (1992) find that Malagasy L2 learners of English have knowledge of both grammatical and ungrammatical extractions which cannot be accounted for by other learning principles.

With the changes in the theory, new analyses for both binding and subjacency make it difficult definitively to judge the findings of the earlier studies. However, L2 learners do not seem to exhibit grammars that are not sanctioned by UG. Theoretical shifts notwithstanding, many researchers working within this paradigm today conclude that UG plays an active role in L2 acquisition in conjunction with the L1 grammar and may not function in the same way as in L1 acquisition. The configuration of the relevance of UG, the L1, and other learning factors offers a new area to be explored.

3.3.2 WHAT IS THE INTERACTION BETWEEN THE FIRST-LANGUAGE PARAMETER SETTING AND THE SECOND-LANGUAGE PARAMETER SETTING?

In the previous discussions of contrastive analysis and creative construction, it was noted that proponents of contrastive analysis attributed learners' errors to transfer, while proponents of creative construction attributed learners' errors to universal developmental processes functioning in both L1 and L2 acquisition. With the parameter-setting model, the effects of both L1 experience and universal language acquisition processes could be reconciled (Flynn 1987a, b; White 1986); the parametric constraints are hypothesized to constrain both L1 and L2 acquisition and, in L2 acquisition, to reflect the L1 parameter setting.

Recall from Chapter 2 that there are several issues surrounding transfer. Within the UG model, evidence of transfer may be found in the transfer of the L1 parameter setting to the L2. Also note that the parameter-setting model makes specific predictions as to the nature of the structures that will be transferred; in the case of binding, for example, L1 speakers of languages that allow long-distance binding (e.g. Chinese, Japanese, and Korean) are predicted to transfer this characteristic to L2 languages that do not allow it (e.g. English and Spanish) in addition to the constraints on subject antecedents. One difference between a UG approach to transfer and a contrastive-analysis approach is that the predictions are based on the operation of abstract syntactic principles as opposed to simple surface structures.

Evidence for the transfer of parameter settings is mixed in the UG literature (Eubank 1989a, b; Finer and Broselow 1986; Flynn 1987a, b; Hilles 1986; Liceras 1989; Phinney 1987; Thomas 1989; White 1985b, 1986, 1991a, c). As we have seen above, there is some evidence for the transfer of L1 settings for binding (Bennett 1994; Hirakawa 1990; Thomas 1993), while other studies do not show the expected transfer (Broselow and Finer 1991; Finer 1991; Finer and Broselow 1986). Also, the more recent Subjacency studies show evidence for transfer of the L1 analyses (Martohardjono and Gair 1993; Uziel 1993).

Additional evidence of transfer is found in an early series of studies in which White (1985b, 1986) investigated the three proposed properties of the pro-drop parameter in the L2 acquisition of adult Spanish ([+pd]) and French ([−pd]) L2 learners of English. White's findings show that Spanish speakers exhibit null subjects in the initial stages and improve over time, showing that they can reset the parameter. French speakers, on the other hand, do not accept null subjects as often as do their Spanish-speaking counterparts, and there is less improvement across proficiency levels. These results are expected if the L2 learners are transferring the L1 parameter setting for null subjects. However, White's findings, among others (Lantolf 1990; Liceras 1988, 1989), do not support the notion that all properties of the parameter are triggered simultaneously. This is not surprising, given that current analyses do not link these three structures.

Research of pro-drop based on the morphological uniformity analysis has had similarly mixed findings (Hilles 1991; Lakshmanan 1991). Most of Hilles's (1991) Spanish-speaking learners of English begin with null subjects, but Hilles speculates that, for those learners who show evidence of UG access, the initial null subjects seem to result from the default UG setting rather than from the L1 setting. In a study on Japanese, Spanish, and French children learning English, Lakshmanan (1991) finds transfer of null subjects in the case of the Spanish speaker but not in the case of the Japanese speaker (cf. Hyams and Safir 1991). In an examination of wh-questions and different forms of anaphora (for example, null subjects and pronouns), Martohardjono and Flynn (1995) directly address the difference in predictions that are made by the UG approach and the contrastive-analysis approach. They find that the L2 learners do not exhibit the acquisition difficulties predicted by a comparison of the L1 and L2 surface structures, but the learners do show evidence of difficulties based on a UG analysis.

While the UG approach offers a predictive advantage over contrastive analysis, some of the influences on transferability discussed previously in Chapter 2 may also be relevant here. For example, learners were found to transfer some types of structures more frequently than others. The transfer of null subjects was found to be more common with particular types of pronominal subjects – that is, nonreferential pronouns, the expletives *there* and *it*, were more likely to be omitted by Spanish speakers learning English than were subject pronouns that referred to specific entities, for example, *she*, *he*, or *you* (Lakshmanan 1991; Liceras 1988; Phinney 1986). As seen in Chapter 2, the question of transfer is not a simple matter. This is especially true if the UG constraints and parameter settings do not trigger the simultaneous acquisition of the proposed clusters – e.g. binding domains and constraints on proper antecedents. The analysis of how and when transfer will occur – i.e. what is transferrable and why – needs to be reconsidered given these findings.

3.3.3 WHAT IS THE INITIAL STATE OF THE SECOND-LANGUAGE GRAMMAR IN THE SECOND-LANGUAGE ACQUISITION PROCESS?

It is clear from these studies that transfer does indeed occur to some extent. A slightly different perspective on both transfer and accessibility emerges in the third question: what is the 'extent of the knowledge that forms the initial state of language acquisition' (Hoekstra and Schwartz 1994: 17)? Given the assumption that UG is accessible and is a part of that initial state, researchers have begun to examine the 'extent to which knowledge of the native-language grammar determines subsequent development' (Hoekstra and Schwartz 1994: 17). This perspective on the initial state makes a much stronger claim than the previous views of transfer in which transfer is seen to influence L2 acquisition in some way. The question here is how the structure of the L1 in conjunction with UG actually determines the L2 acquisition process.

Several studies have examined the development of phrase structure in L2 German, English, and French. In any mature L1 grammar, the L2 learner has a full grammar with a full phrase structure system – with both lexical and functional phrases. The initial state question in this case asks 'How much of the L1 phrase structure is transferred to the L2?' Different syntactic and morphological evidence demonstrates whether learners bring their full L1 grammars to the L2 process or whether they bring only part of it. The following are examples of some of the structures seen as evidence for the different functional categories (the French and English examples for determiner phrase (DP) and inflection phrase (IP) are from Grondin and White 1993; Lakshmanan 1993–4, respectively, with emphasis added):[17]

(3.21)

Determiner Phrase (DP)

(a) nominals with determiners
le livre
the book

(b) pronominal possessives
ma maman
my mummy

Inflection Phrase (IP)

(c) productive use of morphological markings for tense and agreement

ça	c'*est*	un cheval
this	it's (3rd person singular present)	a horse
c'	*était*	toute la famille
it	was (3rd person singular past)	all the family

(d) verb raising: negation and adverbs occurring after the verb
moi je veux *pas*
no I want not
'I don't want to.'

ils ont *toujours* un parachute
they have always a parachute
'They always have a parachute.'

(e) auxiliary and modal verbs
Mother *is* cooking supper.
You *can't* tell her.

(f) inversion in yes/no questions
Can we go up there?

Complementizer Phrase (CP)
(g) wh-questions
Wann   macht sie   gewöhnlich ihre   Hausaufgaben?
When   makes she   usually   her   homework
'When does she usually do her homework?'

In their examination of L2 acquisition of German, Vainikka and Young-Scholten (1994, 1998; Young-Scholten and Vainikka 1992) argue that L2 learners initially transfer the VP of their L1: head-final SOV for Korean and Turkish learners of German, head-initial SVO for Romance speakers. They argue further that these L2 learners begin with only the lexical category VP because they lack the following evidence of a functional IP node: modals, auxiliaries, verbal agreement, and verb raising. Vainikka and Young-Scholten conclude that L2 learners transfer only lexical categories so that the initial state does not include all of the L1 syntactic knowledge; UG then comes into play in the distinction between lexical and functional categories. L2 learners then develop functional categories in the L2 based on an interaction between UG and the L2 input.

These findings have been challenged by other researchers who do find evidence of the functional categories DP and IP (Eubank 1994; Grondin and White 1993; Lakshmanan 1993–4; Schwartz and Sprouse 1994). Grondin and White find that English-speaking children learning L2 French show evidence of lexical categories and of the functional categories DP and IP from the beginning stages of acquisition, while the status of the CP is unclear. Other evidence for functional categories in child L2 acquisition comes from Lakshmanan (1993–4). Adult L2 learners are also claimed to have both lexical and functional categories from the beginning stages (Eubank 1994; Schwartz and Sprouse 1994), but it is not altogether clear whether all of the characteristics of the L1 IP are transferred (Eubank 1994).

The studies discussed here in reference to transfer and to the initial state demonstrate that the UG approach offers a principled way to address the issue of transfer. For instance, a UG analysis can predict what will transfer – binding domains, proper antecedents, null subjects, Subjacency constraints, lexical and functional phrases. This approach also offers the analytical tools for distinguishing between cases of transfer and of non-transfer. What is not entirely clear, however, is how to account for the lack of transfer in all cases. Several explanations are possible: the structure is misanalysed; the L1 setting is overridden by direct access to the UG default setting; the study may have missed an earlier stage in which transfer was indeed evident, or the correct analysis of transfer may be obscured by other developmental aspects. Although it is obvious that UG constraints and parameter settings do transfer, issues concerning the conditions on transfer are yet to be resolved.

3.3.4 WHAT IS THE EFFECT OF POSITIVE AND/OR NEGATIVE INPUT ON THE RESETTING OF UNIVERSAL GRAMMAR IN SECOND-LANGUAGE ACQUISITION?

The final question to be addressed here involves the issue of instruction. The theory of UG principles and parameters in a parameter-setting model seems the appropriate theory to test the relationship between grammatical theory and the role of instruction in L2 acquisition for two reasons: (1) the theory predicts that certain structures are related and that the setting of a particular parameter will result in the acquisition of a cluster of structures, and (2) the setting of a parameter is based on simple triggers that are available in the input. Recall that L1 acquisition is believed to proceed on the basis of positive input alone – that is, there is no explicit instruction, and no negative input is necessary. Can L1 parameters be reset to the L2 setting based on positive input alone, or is explicit instruction necessary to reset parameters? One potential problem in L2 acquisition is that the resetting of parameters may involve setting the parameter to a value that may, on the face of it, seem contradictory to the input. For example, adverbials in English can occur in almost any position in the sentence except between the verb and its complement. For a speaker of French, the English input, as seen in (3.22), may seem to indicate that adverbials can occur in any position. The non-occurrence of adverbials between verbs and their complements may not be salient in the input to the French learner of English.

(3.22)
    (a) *Daily*, Mary reads the newspaper.
    (b) Mary *usually* reads the newspaper.
    (c) Mary reads the newspaper *carefully*.
    (d) *Mary reads *carefully* the newspaper.

In a case such as this, negative input – correction – may be necessary in addition to positive input or explicit instruction, but does negative input really make a difference (White 1987a, 1990–1, 1991a, b; cf. Schwartz 1993; Schwartz and Gubala-Ryzak 1992)?

Each of these questions – the role of positive input, negative input, and explicit instruction – is addressed in a series of studies focusing on the word-order variations in French and English resulting from the verb movement parameter. We will examine each issue briefly in turn. The verb movement parameter constrains the order of adverbs, negatives, auxiliaries, main verbs, and complements. As seen in (3.23), French allows the adverb to occur between the verb and its complement, SVAO order, and prohibits the adverb from occurring between the subject and the verb, SAV order; English has the opposite word-order configuration:

(3.23)

(a) SAV French = *SAV
*Marie souvent regarde la télévision.
English = SAV
Mary often watches television.

(b) SVAO French = SVAO
Marie regarde souvent la télévision.
English = *SVAO
*Mary watches often television.

The first question is whether or not explicit instruction and negative input influence the parameter resetting from the French setting, which allows SVAO and prohibits SAV, to the English setting, which prohibits SVAO but allows SAV. White (1991a) found that explicit instruction on adverb placement (including error correction) was effective in teaching learners both to allow SAV orders and to disallow SVAO orders. The group of learners receiving only positive input with no special reference made to adverbs did not learn that the SVAO pattern was ungrammatical in English. However, the beneficial effects of instruction and negative input were only short term; a follow-up study of the same subjects one year later showed that learners were reverting back to the L1 pattern.

Is positive input alone – without explicit instruction or error correction – sufficient to promote the parameter resetting from the French setting to the English setting? Trahey and White (1993) 'flooded' French-speaking learners of L2 English with input containing adverbs. While the input flood did result in an increased use of the grammatical SAV structures, it did not teach learners that the SVAO pattern was ungrammatical in English. Therefore, the parameter was not reset based on a short (two-week), intense input flood of positive input alone. These studies, therefore, show some short-term beneficial effects of explicit instruction and negative input and some limited effects of positive input.

The final question examines the notion of clustered structures: can instruction on one structure of a cluster (for example, wh-question formation), generalize to another, adverb placement? White (1990–1) studied two groups of learners receiving explicit instruction on only one aspect of the verb movement parameter, either adverb placement or question formation. The two groups were later tested on their knowledge of adverb placement. The focus was to see whether the question group, by learning wh-questions with *do* in English, would automatically acquire a related structure in the cluster. The answer, in a word, is 'no'. Both groups show some increase in the acceptance of SAV structures as grammatical, but only the adverb group learned that the SVAO pattern is ungrammatical. Another perspective on the resetting/cluster issue is that the two structures, SAV and SVAO, should not occur simultaneously in the learner IL grammar if the parameter has been reset.

However, learners do go through a stage in which both of these structures are in evidence (White 1991a, c). White suggests that they may have an optional rule of verb movement, which would account for both their interpretation of the data in the light of L1 transfer and the simultaneous SAV and SVAO structures.

This group of studies offers a clear example of how a particular theory of language (UG) and of language acquisition (parameter setting and resetting) can be examined in an instructional setting (explicit instruction and correction or implicit instruction). And, according to White (1990–1), each of these aspects may, in part, be responsible for the outcome of the studies: the analysis of the verb movement parameter may be incorrect, explicit and/or negative input may not be appropriate for resetting parameters (Schwartz 1993), or the time periods and amounts of instruction and 'flooded' input may have been too limited. While the results of these studies are somewhat inconclusive, they do represent a model for examining the parameter-setting theory in the classroom.

3.4 Conclusion

The UG approach offers a rich theoretical basis within which to explore the various issues related to L2 acquisition of syntax. First, it offers a principled approach to L2 acquisition: the linguistic analyses allow for specific predictions – which can be proven true or false – of how language acquisition should proceed. Second, it offers explanations of cross-linguistic variation and predicts how that variation will be manifested in L2 acquisition. Third, it makes testable predictions about the type of input that will enhance language acquisition.

Briefly to summarize the answers to the research questions explored in this area of L2 acquisition, in general, the research findings seem to reflect access to UG in L2 acquisition (UG-constrained binding domains and movement), an initial role of the L1 in parameter resetting (binding domains, pro-drop, verb movement), and some promising effects for instruction. This is not to say, however, that the answers to these questions are clear-cut. As with any evolving theory, the research questions change, and the answers to previous research questions can contribute to that change or can further corroborate the need for those changes. In fact, L2 researchers have often argued that L2-acquisition research can inform linguistic theory in a two-way relationship (Eckman, 1993; Flynn 1988, 1993b; Gass 1984, 1988b; Rutherford, 1988). This may be especially true now that L2 researchers in the UG approach believe, for the most part, that UG is accessible in L2 acquisition.

Take, for example, the question of access to UG in L2 acquisition. One prediction from a parameter-setting model is that, if UG is accessible and L1 parameters are reset, all of the structures constrained by that parameter should be in evidence once the parameter is reset. The L2 research discussed above shows that this is not the case for the earlier formulation of the pro-drop parameter nor for the verb movement parameter. Two reasons suggested for these results are that the parameter has not been reset or that the analysis of the parameter is incorrect. In the case of the pro-drop parameter, the analysis of the pro-drop parameter has indeed changed. A third possibility is that a parameter-setting model may not be the correct one. Perhaps a model which predicts the relationship of structures but allows for development over time is the correct approach – that is, a developmental approach as opposed to an instantaneous parameter-setting approach. This would entail that the analysis of the structures as related may be correct but that the representation of these structures as a parameter that is set at a single instance in time is not. This question has been under debate in acquisitional research (Lust *et al*. 1994b). The changing theory thus allows for new perspectives of the data.

Although the UG approach offers a strong theoretical basis for L2-acquisition research, UG theory has been criticized as a theory of L2 acquisition from two basic perspectives: (1) for its narrow view of L2 acquisition – that is, its focus on grammar to the exclusion of other aspects of the L2 acquisition process (for example, affective variables or sociolinguistic aspects), and (2) for the assumptions on which the theory is based. With regard to the first criticism, Larsen-Freeman and Long (1991: 240) note that one problem with the theory is that it is based on language rather than on language learning. For example, other theories of L2 acquisition – the Multidimensional Model (Meisel *et al*. 1981), to name one – incorporate affective and sociolinguistic influences on language acquisition as well as linguistic influences. However, one could argue that the UG approach does encompass issues involved in language learning, but that these issues are linguistic in nature and are not necessarily the same issues that other theories include nor do they need to be. In addition, several theoretical assumptions of the UG approach have also been questioned: the question of innateness, the poverty of stimulus argument, the diminished role of negative input, and the parameter-setting model versus a developmental model, to name a few. Researchers working in the UG paradigm do assume that UG is innate based in part on the poverty of stimulus argument; however, researchers do debate several of the issues raised by the critics, including the role of negative input in L2 acquisition (Schwartz 1993; Schwartz and Gubala-Ryzak 1992; White 1992b) and the reconciliation of parameter setting with actual acquisitional sequences found in both L1 and L2 acquisition (Lust *et al*. 1994a, b; White 1991a, c).

Newcomers to this theoretical approach may be asking why researchers consider working within a theoretical paradigm that changes so often and has such inconclusive answers. An answer to this query is possible by looking ahead to three future developments in this area. First, we may find, as in the case of the pro-drop parameter, that future developments in linguistic theory will give a better account of L2-learner data. Second, with more accurate predictions and analyses, a shift away from parameter setting to developmental stages of acquisition may reveal stages that are not only sanctioned by UG but predictable by UG. Finally, with a prediction of the stages of acquisition and the causes of those stages, additional approaches to instruction can be explored.

Notes

1. While children do receive negative feedback about their utterances, this negative feedback has been examined from a number of different perspectives – e.g. the semantic versus syntactic focus of the input; the usefulness and necessity of the input; and the type, quality, and amount of the input (Brown and Hanlon 1970; Hirsh-Pasek et al. 1986; Newport et al. 1977; Pinker 1989). Research in L1 learnability focuses on how grammars are acquired based on positive input alone.
2. In a work of this length it is necessary to present the theory in a concise and comprehensible manner. Such a presentation requires the elimination of many crucial aspects of the theory – e.g. a detailed account of the Empty Category Principle (ECP). While this treatment is not meant to be comprehensive by any means, it is hoped that the novice reader will gain sufficient understanding of the theory in order to gain an appreciation of the L2-acquisition research conducted within this paradigm.
3. The indexed t_i represents a trace of an element that has been left behind after the movement rule, Move α, has been applied. The trace serves to 'hold the place' of the fronted element in order to preserve the structural relationships generated in the D-structure. In this case, the relationship between the verb, *invite*, and the direct object, *whom*, is preserved.
4. In the Minimalist Program, D-Structure and S-structure have been eliminated and the relevant constraints are checked at PF or at LF.
5. *That-trace* effects are often designated as *that-t* with the *t*, representing the trace that has been left behind. The extracted wh-word leaves behind a co-indexed marker – t_i – to indicate its original position before being fronted.
6. In the principles and parameters version of this theory, language variation is determined by different parameter settings. In the most recent Minimalist version, the morphological properties of functional categories such as Tense (T) and Agreement (Agr) influence language variation (Chomsky 1992).
7. Kayne (1994) proposes that word order is universally specifier–head–complement, as exemplified in SVO word orders. Other word orders are seen to be the result of movement from this initial SVO

order. A result of Kayne's proposal is that X-bar theory is not itself a part of UG, although the predictions of X-bar theory are seen as essentially accurate.

8. This formulation simplifies the actual governing category for English as outlined in Wexler and Manzini (1987).

9. The principles of Binding Theory state the following:
   (a) Principle A: an anaphor must be bound in its local domain.
   (b) Principle B: a pronoun must be free in its local domain.
   (c) Principle C: an r-expression must be free.
   An r-expression (a referring expression) is a noun or a name.

10. Several surface phenomena have been proposed as relevant to binding: morphological structure of reflexives and reciprocals (i.e. mono-morphemic reflexives, e.g. *ziji* for 'self' in Chinese, versus compound reflexives, e.g. *him + self* in English) (Battistella 1989; Katada 1991; Pica 1991), reflexives morphologically marked for person, number, and gender (Katada 1991), modification of reflexives (Hermon 1992), verbal morphological marking for tense (Hyams and Sigurjónsdóttir 1990), and stressed/emphatic pronouns (Grimshaw and Rosen 1990; McDaniel and Maxfield 1992).

11. The account given here is somewhat simplified. These examples from White (1988), follow Chomsky (1981) and Sportiche (1981), which assume that both S and S' are the relevant boundaries, or bounding nodes, in English. The S and S' designations have been replaced by the current IP and CP designations respectively. Also related to movement is the Empty Category Principle (ECP) which constrains the positions out of which an element may be extracted (e.g. subject, verbal complement, or prepositional complement). In English, elements may be extracted more freely out of object positions than they can out of subject positions (e.g. the grammatical *What$_i$ did Mary say that John bought t$_i$?* versus the ungrammatical **Who$_i$ did Mary say that t$_i$ bought a car?* with the extraction sites marked with coindexed traces: t$_i$).

12. While *whom* may be considered the only correct form in questions pertaining to objects, as in 'Whom does John want to see?', *who* is quite common in the spoken form of several varieties of English.

13. This is known as the 'poverty of stimulus' argument or 'Plato's problem' (Baker 1979; Bley-Vroman 1989; Chomsky 1986b, 1988; White 1989).

14. While Hyams (1986, 1992, 1994) argued for +pro-drop as the default, or unmarked setting, there has been disagreement as well as differing accounts in the L1-acquisition literature (Valian 1994) and the L2 literature (White 1985b).

15. For a review of these different approaches, see Thomas (1993) or Hermon (1994).

16. The subscripts used in the examples from Thomas (1993) have been reversed to maintain consistency between all of the examples used here.

17. Because of differences between languages – e.g. in verb raising – the evidence for functional categories will differ somewhat from language to language. In addition, researchers accept diverse evidence to some extent, depending on their analyses. Additional evidence for the IP includes: subject clitic pronouns, case marking of subjects, placement quantifiers after raised verbs in French, null subjects in German, the auxiliary *be* and the copula *be* in English and embedded clauses for the CP.

4

Typological universals

4.1 Introduction

Research on linguistic universals can focus on different aspects of universality, and, in fact, in the previous chapters we have seen different perspectives on the notion of universals: universal constraints on the form of human languages – both native languages and interlanguages – and universal processes in the acquisition of both L1 and L2 languages. There are also diverse approaches to examining and defining linguistic universals. While researchers of linguistic universals may ultimately strive to answer the same question – 'What is a possible human language?' (Croft 1990) – the investigative approaches, or how one goes about arriving at an answer to the question, may differ.

Researchers of typological universals attempt to answer this question by examining a selection of structures from a wide range of diverse languages from the different language families in order to form a broad base of cross-linguistic data. From this data-based or inductive approach, statements of linguistic universals are then developed. In one of the seminal works on universals of language, Greenberg (1966b) offers 45 universals of grammar based on typological analyses. This approach contrasts with work in Universal Grammar (UG), which originally focused on an in-depth analysis of a single language in order to form a theory of human language. Thus, research in L2 acquisition of typological universals represents another view of universals in L2 grammatical development.

The interest in the role of typological universals in L2 acquisition grew out of two bodies of research: (1) theoretical work on typological universals, and (2) the examination of transfer and developmental errors in L2 acquisition. As we have seen in Chapter 2, the early L2-acquisition work on transfer and developmental errors generated many of the questions addressed in the subsequent L2-acquisition research in the UG approach. These factors are similarly examined from a typological approach.

The first section of this chapter outlines the theoretical work on typological universals in order to lay the foundation for the subsequent discussion of the L2 research. A general treatment of the different kinds of universals and the related notion of markedness will be given. A detailed description will be supplied only of those universals which are directly relevant to L2 research – that is, the Noun Phrase Accessibility Hierarchy and question formation universals.

4.2 A typological approach to language universals

Typological universals get their name from the classification of different languages into types. Thus, languages that exhibit verb–subject–object word order are classified as one type – VSO languages – in comparison to languages that have a basic subject–object–verb word order – SOV languages. Within each language type, different structural dependencies exist. For example, VSO languages also have prepositions, whereas SOV languages tend to have postpositions. A broad-based cross-linguistic approach to language analysis and classification is utilized to ensure that the dependencies found between two particular structures, VSO and prepositions, for example, are not in fact accidental. Another reason for a broad sampling of languages is to rule out language similarities due to geographical contact or to genetic relations between two languages, such as the similar structures for marking location and movement found in the genetically related languages Czech and Russian (Croft 1990). As Comrie (1984: 11) states, 'The question of the data base can be put succinctly as follows: in order to be reasonably sure that we are on the right track in investigating language universals, we must test our hypotheses against a representative sample of human language.'

In order to determine the existence of structural dependencies, researchers first select a structure for analysis, then examine the morphological and syntactic characteristics of the structure, and finally look for any structural dependencies that are evidenced in the morphological and syntactic characteristics of that structure. Consider the following example in which the syntactic category of 'subject' is examined (adapted from Croft 1990: 8, with emphasis added):

(4.1)
   (a) *He* congratulated *him/*he.*
   (b) Teresa *likes/*like* horses.
   (c) Jack wants Ø to leave. (Jack = Ø)
   (d) Ø Take out the garbage. (you = Ø)
   (e) John found a ring and Ø took it home with him. (John = Ø)
   (f) *John found a ring and Ø was gold. (the ring = Ø)

A typological analysis of 'subject' would first determine that there is a 'correlation among several grammatical categories and constructions' related to the notion of 'subject' in English: word order (4.1a), case marking (4.1a), subject–verb agreement (4.1b), subject control with the verb *want* (4.1c), imperatives (4.1d), and one type of coordination (4.1e and 4.1f). The next step would be to determine which of these correlations also holds cross-linguistically and, alternatively, which of them is specific to English. With additional cross-linguistic evidence, universal dependencies can be determined – for example, the relationship between the animacy of the noun (animate *humans* and *dogs* versus inanimate *rings* and *garbage*) and case marking for nominative 'subjects' and accusative 'objects' (Croft 1990: 151–2).

Typological universals, then, are statements of structural dependencies that hold to varying degrees across a wide range of languages. Typologists distinguish different kinds of universal statements: absolute universals, universal tendencies, implicational universals, and non-implicational universals (Comrie 1981). Absolute universals have no exceptions; they are universal statements that hold for all of the languages in the sample of languages. Universal tendencies are just that: universal tendencies that have some exceptions evidenced in the languages sampled. Implicational universals state the relationship between one property of a given language and another property of the same language; that is, the presence of one property depends on the presence of another. This is stated logically as 'if p, then q.' If characteristic p is present in a given language, then q is also present. Finally, non-implicational universals are universals that make no reference to other characteristics of a language. These four types of universals result in a four-way classification of typological universals (Comrie 1981: 19), as in (4.2). The universal tendencies are seen as statistical universals in that, although they do not hold for all languages, certain properties occur in languages 'with significantly greater than chance frequency' (Comrie 1984: 12). Comrie cites the example of the word order of subjects and direct objects: the universal tendency is for subjects to precede direct objects. While there are counter-examples to this tendency (e.g. Malagasy and Hixkaryana), 99 per cent of the sampled languages adhere to the universal. As a result, although this implicational relationship cannot be stated absolutely, it occurs with much greater frequency than a random occurrence.

(4.2) Typological universals

	Implicational	Non-implicational
Absolute	'If a language has VSO as its basic word order, then it has prepositions.'	'All languages have vowels.'
Tendency	'If a language has SOV as its basic word order, then it will probably have postpositions.'	'Nearly all languages have nasal consonants.'

The implicational universals also allow for four logical possibilities, as can be seen in the example of the basic word-order universal which was introduced above: 'If a language has VSO as its basic word order, then it has prepositions.'

(4.3)

'If a language has VSO as its basic word order (If p . . .), then it has prepositions (. . . then q).'

(a) p and q Welsh: VSO and prepositions

(b) p and *not-q*   Not a possibility based on 'If p then q.'

(c) *not-p* and q English: SVO and prepositions

(d) *not-p* and *not-q*   Japanese: not VSO and no prepositions

The only type of language that should not occur is a language that *has* VSO word order and that does not have prepositions, and this combination is not found (Comrie 1981). Note that the reverse is not implied: the existence of q in a given language says nothing about the existence of p. Therefore, the existence of prepositions in a given language gives no indication of the basic word order of that language. This is evident from the fact that both Welsh and English have prepositions, but, of the two, only Welsh has VSO word order.

Typological universals have often been contrasted with the universals of UG.[1] One difference has already been noted; typological universals are based on data in that they are derived from a careful analysis and comparison of cross-linguistic data. From the data, universals are proposed. Universal Grammar constraints, on the other hand, have originated from the perspective of an established theory. A possible universal constraint is established within the theory and then tested against different data. Another difference between the two approaches is the level of abstraction. Typological universals are typically seen as based on more concrete, surface levels of analysis, while UG universals are seen as abstract constraints that are not necessarily evident in the surface phenomena that they affect (i.e. the poverty of stimulus argument discussed in Chapter 3).

As in the study of UG constraints, the study of typological universals also includes the notion of markedness, but from a slightly different perspective. Several criteria for markedness are taken into account (Croft 1990; Greenberg 1966a; Moravcsik and Wirth 1983[2]); three are considered here: simplicity/complexity, frequency, and distribution. The first criterion for determining marked and unmarked values is simplicity/complexity: unmarked values are less complex than are marked values. For example, in English, singular nouns are unmarked morphologically for number (*apple* = singular), whereas plural nouns are morphologically marked (*apple* + s = plural). In terms of frequency, unmarked values occur more frequently than do marked values. In frequency counts of texts, singular forms are more frequent than are plural forms (Greenberg 1966a). Finally, one view of the distributional characteristic deals with the distribution of a grammatical structure across languages.[3] Unmarked values occur in more languages than do marked values. For example, plurals (number marking for more than one) occur in more languages than do duals (number marking for two). We can also see this example in terms of an implicational universal, Greenberg's Universal 34 (Greenberg 1966b). In the case of 'if p, then q', q is the unmarked value because its existence is implied by the existence of p, so, if a language has marking for duals, it will also have marking for plurals. This type of an implicational universal, then, represents a hierarchy of markedness relationships. We deal with the markedness of implicational hierarchies in more detail presently.

4.3 Typological universals and second-language acquisition

Although typological universals have been examined for a wide range of grammatical structures and categories (e.g. adverbial clauses, animacy, case marking, complementation, grammatical relations, negation, passive voice, relative clauses, transitivity, and word order), only a few typological universals have been addressed in the L2-acquisition research. L2 syntactic research has centred primarily on the Noun Phrase Accessibility Hierarchy (Keenan and Comrie 1977; Comrie and Keenan 1979) with some additional work on question formation universals.[4]

We begin here with the most frequently studied universal, the Noun Phrase Accessibility Hierarchy (NPAH). The NPAH is an implicational universal which delineates the grammatical functions of noun phrases that are accessible to relativization in relative clauses, that is, subject, direct object, indirect object, oblique (object of a preposition), genitive, and comparative. English, for instance, allows nouns in all of the functions of noun phrases on the hierarchy to be relativized. In the following sentence, the subject of the relative clause has been relativized:

(4.4)
   (a) Subject
      The *man* lives next door.

   (b) Direct object
      The dog bit the *man*.

   (c) Relative clause with the subject relativized
      The dog bit the man [*who* lives next door]

The example sentences below illustrate each of the possible grammatical functions of the nouns that can be relativized (examples adapted from Gass 1979).

(4.5)
   (a) Subject (SUB)
      The dog that bit the man . . .

   (b) Direct object (DO)
      The man that the dog bit . . .

   (c) Indirect object (IO)
      The girl that I wrote a letter to . . .

(d) Object of a preposition (OP)
   The house that I talked to you about . . .

(e) Genitive (GEN)
   The family whose house I like . . .

(f) Object of comparative (OCOMP)
   The woman that I am taller than . . .

Cross-linguistically, languages allow different noun functions to be relativized, forming an implicational hierarchy:

(4.6) SUB > DO > IO > OP > GEN > OCOMP

The symbol > here denotes 'is more accessible than'. Subjects represent the most unmarked accessible function. If a language allows relativization on any of the functions lower on the hierarchy – that is, on the more marked end of the hierarchy – the less marked functions will also be accessible in that language. For example, if a language allows relativization of indirect objects ('If p ...), it will also allow relativization of direct objects and subjects (... then q). Thai is such a language (Gass 1980). The reverse, however, is not true. If a language allows relativization of indirect objects, it will not necessarily allow relativization of noun functions on the more marked end of the hierarchy. This again is the case with Thai, which does not allow relativization farther down on the NPAH below the function of Indirect Object. The question relevant to L2 acquisition is whether or not the NPAH holds for IL grammars.

A second aspect of relative clause formation is pronoun retention – that is, retaining or copying the pronoun that the relative marker represents. According to Keenan and Comrie (1977), pronoun retention is unmarked, whereas pronoun deletion, as in English, is marked. The following examples, all ungrammatical in English, demonstrate pronoun retention in the different relativized functions.

(4.7)
   (a) SUB   *The *woman* that *she* spoke to me . . .
   (b) DO   *The *man* that the car hit *him* . . .
   (c) IO   *The *girl* that I gave the book to *her* . . .
   (d) OP   *The *trip* that she wrote to me about *it* . . .
   (e) GEN   *The *artist* whose *her* painting I like . . .
   (f) OCOMP   *The *runner* that Mary is better than *her* . . .

Additionally, pronoun retention is more common in the more marked positions of the NPAH. This can be seen in the following patterns of pronoun retention adapted from Keenan and Comrie (1977). In the table, pronoun retention is represented with a plus (+), optional retention with parentheses ( ), and deletion with a minus (–); structure-specific retention is represented as plus/minus (+/–), and a question mark (?) indicates some uncertainty of the analysis.

(4.8)

Language	SUB	DO	IO	OP	GEN	OCOMP
(a) Arabic	–	+	+	+	+	+
(b) Greek	–	–	+?	+?	+	+
(c) Japanese	–	–	–	–	+/–	
(d) Korean	–	–	–	–	+	
(e) Persian	–	(+)	+	+	+	+

The NPAH also plays another role in predicting the retention or deletion of pronominal copies; as with relativization, if a language allows the deletion (–) of the pronoun at any position on the NPAH, it also allows deletion of the pronoun in the lesser marked positions. This is readily apparent in (4.8).

The second type of typological universal examined in L2 acquisition concerns question formation. Question formation universals involve both yes/no and wh-questions and pertain to the word-order patterns found in these questions. According to Greenberg's (1966b) Universal 11, subject–verb inversion in wh-questions implies sentence-initial question markers, and subject–verb inversion in yes/no questions implies subject–verb inversion in wh-questions. Eckman *et al.* (1989: 175) restate this universal as the following two implicational universals and add the clarification in parentheses:

(4.9)

(a) *Wh-inversion implies wh-fronting*: 'Inversion of statement order (in wh-questions – FE/EM/JW) so that verb precedes subject occurs only in languages where the question word or phrase is normally initial.'

(b) *Yes/no inversion implies wh-inversion*: 'This same inversion (i.e., inversion of statement order so that verb precedes subject – FE/EM/JW) occurs in yes/no questions only if it also occurs in interrogative word questions.'

Languages such as English manifest all of the structures stated in both of these implicational universals – that is, inversion in yes/no questions, inversion in wh-questions, and wh-fronting:

(4.10)

(a)	yes/no S–V inversion	*Can you* hear the music?
	versus S–V order	**You can* hear the music?[5]
(b)	wh S–V inversion	What *can you* hear?
	versus S–V order	*What *you can* hear?
(c)	wh-fronting	*What* can you hear?
	versus non-initial wh	You can hear *what*?

As with other implicational universals, when stated in terms of 'If p, then q', we find languages that fit each of the possible predictions (examples adapted from Eckman *et al.* 1989):

(4.11)

'If a language has S–V inversion in wh-questions (If p . . .), then it has wh-fronting in wh-questions (. . . then q)'

(a) p and q English

(b) p and *not-q*   Not a possibility based on 'If p then q'.

(c) *not-p* and q Finnish

(d) *not-p* and *not-q*   Japanese

(4.12)

'If a language has S–V inversion in yes/no questions (If p . . .), then it has S–V inversion in wh-questions (. . . then q).'

(a) p and q English

(b) p and *not-q*   Not a possibility based on 'If p then q'.

(c) *not-p* and q Lithuanian

(d) *not-p* and *not-q*   Japanese

Question formation universals, as with the NPAH, give researchers the basis upon which to make two kinds of predictions. First, if these universals are indeed universal to all natural languages, one can predict that such universals also exist in IL systems. Second, one can also make predictions concerning the effects of the universals in L2 acquisition such as order of acquisition or ease of production based on implicational hierarchies and the degree of markedness.

In relating typological universals to L2 acquisition, Eckman (1977, 1985a, b) proposed a hypothesis of how typological markedness could be incorporated into a theory of transfer and contrastive analysis in L2-acquisition research. As with the work in UG universals, this work in typological universals represents an attempt to examine the notion of transfer from the perspective of more abstract linguistic influences. Eckman's Markedness Differential Hypothesis (MDH) combined both the theoretical background of typological universals and the notion of transfer in a way that would provide a stronger predictive power. By using a typological analysis of the native language (NL) and of the target language (TL), one could predict the areas of difficulty that a given L2 learner would have based on the markedness of the structures in the native language and the target language. These predictions, like those of UG parameters, are made based on more abstract properties of the two languages in question – the structural dependencies that emerge from cross-linguistic analysis – than were those used to predict language learning difficulties in the contrastive-analysis approach. The MDH states the following (Eckman, 1985a):

(4.13) Markedness Differential Hypothesis

The areas of difficulty that an L2 learner will have can be predicted on the basis of a comparison of the NL and the TL such that:

(a) those areas of the TL that are different from the NL and are relatively more marked than in the NL will be difficult;

(b) the degree of difficulty associated with those aspects of the TL that are different and more marked than in the NL corresponds to the relative degree of markedness associated with those aspects;

(c) those areas of the TL that are different than the NL but are not relatively more marked than in the NL will not be difficult.

Let us consider the predictions of the MDH with regard to relative clauses and the NPAH for L1 speakers of Thai who are learning English as an L2. First, consider relativization patterns in the languages:

(4.14) Accessible positions for relativization:
(a) English   SUB > DO > IO > OP > GEN > OCOMP
(b) Thai   SUB > DO > IO

English allows relativization for all values on the NPAH; Thai allows relativization of the functions SUB, DO, and IO. According to (4.13a), the relativization of the functions OP, GEN, and OCOMP, which are different from Thai and are relatively more marked, will be difficult for the Thai learner of English. According to (4.13b), the function OCOMP will be more difficult than the function OP because it is farther down on the hierarchy and therefore more marked. Finally, the third comparison of the MDH (4.13c) predicts that there will be no difficulty in learning a structure that is different from but not relatively more marked than the structure in the L1.

Eckman (1977) notes that relative-clause formation in different languages includes a number of additional distinct aspects – for example, the choice of relative pronouns (e.g. *that*, *who*, or *whom*) or the position of the relative clause in relation to the head noun (preceding or following the head noun). Eckman suggests that not all of these distinctions are governed by implicational markedness relations. Therefore, these differences can be viewed as neither more nor less marked and should not cause difficulty for L2 learners. The value of the MDH is that it can predict L2 learner difficulty based not only on the differences between the L1 and the L2 as did contrastive analysis, but on a combined analysis of markedness relations and language differences. The L2 predictions in terms of typological universals have also been made related to L2 acquisition of phonology (Eckman 1977, 1985a, b).

Typological universals, then, form the basis for predictions for L2 acquisition with regard to the interactions between the manifestation of the universal in the L1, the possible transfer of that structural manifestation of the universal to the L2, or the overriding influence of the universal in the L2-acquisition process.

4.4 Questions explored in second-language acquisition

- Do typological universal constraints play a role in second-language acquisition?
- How does typological markedness affect the second-language acquisition process?
- What is the effect of instruction on typological universals in second-language acquisition?

The L2 research in this paradigm has developed from the initial interests in transfer, error analysis, and developmental sequences in the late 1970s; the early research on developmental sequences led to the subsequent examination of the causes of particular developmental sequences. Research within the typological approach first asked whether the process of L2 grammatical development was a result of universal linguistic constraints or of L1 transfer as predicted by contrastive analysis. In other words, the underlying question is 'Do the structures of the L1 transfer to the L2, or do the typological universals affect the form of the IL grammar regardless of the form of the L1 grammar?'

4.4.1 DO TYPOLOGICAL UNIVERSAL CONSTRAINTS PLAY A ROLE IN SECOND-LANGUAGE ACQUISITION?

In order to answer this first question, it is necessary to determine the kinds of roles that typological universals might play in L2 acquisition. Typological universals may determine the order in which certain structures are acquired in terms of markedness, with the less marked structures being acquired first – for example, early acquisition of the less marked positions on the NPAH or of the less marked question forms, wh-questions with fronted wh-pronouns.

A second role may be to influence the strategies that learners utilize. For instance, learners' use of a pronoun–retention strategy in relative-clause formation might be based on markedness. In this case, the effects of markedness may manifest themselves in two ways. Since pronoun retention is cross-linguistically unmarked, L2 learners may apply this strategy in their L2 acquisition regardless of the existence of pronoun copies in the L1. For example, a Japanese learner, whose L1 does not allow pronoun copies in SUB, DO, IO, or OP positions, may utilize pronoun copies in these positions in L2 English, which also prohibits them, because this strategy is unmarked typologically. In other words, it is a common and frequently occurring strategy in languages. A second possible effect would be that pronoun retention may also conform to the NPAH; that is, pronouns would be retained in the more marked positions on the NPAH to make the meaning more transparent than in the less marked positions. If typological universals do influence L2 acquisition, these influences should be in evidence regardless of the differences between the structures of the L1 and the L2. In fact, to show that universal constraints are responsible for the processes and structures evidenced in L2 acquisition, it must be shown that these processes and structures cannot be accounted for by the transfer of the L1 structure to the L2 (Eckman 1988).

While research findings are somewhat conflicting, the simple answer to this first question is 'Yes', typological universals do play a role in L2 acquisition. Support for the role of typological universals in L2 acquisition comes from several studies of relative-clause acquisition and question formation. Gass (1979, 1980) was one of the first to examine the role of typological universals in L2 acquisition, and she specifically addressed the role of linguistic universals in L1 transfer. She examined the acquisition of English relative clauses by speakers of Arabic, Chinese, French, Italian, Japanese, Korean, Persian, Portuguese, and Thai from the perspective of six differences that are manifested in relative clause formation cross-linguistically. The relevant characteristics of English relative clauses are illustrated in (4.15).

(4.15)
    (a) the adjacency of the relative clause to the head noun –
        the relative clause is adjacent to the head noun:
        The *bread* [that Terry baked] was good.
        *The *bread* was good [that Terry baked].

    (b) the retention or omission of the relative-clause marker –
        the relative clause marker is optional:
        I like the car *that* she bought.
        I like the car Ø she bought.

    (c) the ordering of the relative clause with respect to the head noun –
        the relative clause follows the head noun:
        The *woman* [*who* bought my car] works in my office.
        *The [*who* bought my car] *woman* works in my office.

    (d) the positions on the NPAH which can be relativized –
        all positions on the NPAH can be relativized.

    (e) the case markings on the relative marker –
        case marking is variable:
        The *woman* [*whom* you met] is the supervisor.
        The *woman* [*that* you met] is the supervisor.

    (f) pronoun retention or omission –
        pronoun retention does not occur:
        *The woman [whom you spoke to *her*] just left.

With specific regard to the NPAH, Gass examined two hypotheses: whether or not the unmarked, more accessible positions are produced more frequently than the marked positions, and whether or not the unmarked positions are produced more accurately than the marked positions. Gass reported evidence in support of both of these hypotheses. She further noted that in general her results did not show evidence of the L1 language-specific properties noted in (4.15), but do reflect differences based on the predictions of the NPAH. One exception, pronoun retention, will be discussed at length below. Hyltenstam (1984) reports that all learners, regardless of the structure of the L1, use the strategy of pronoun retention, a strategy that is unmarked cross-linguistically, in their relative-clause formation. Therefore, influence of typological universals is evident, regardless of the structure of the L1.

Additional support for the ease of acquisition of the unmarked positions on the NPAH comes from a number of studies (Doughty 1991; Eckman *et al*. 1988; Pavesi 1986). Eckman *et al*. (1988) find that learners' production of relative clauses prior to instruction shows fewer errors on the less marked positions (SUB and DO) than on the more marked position (OP). Pavesi (1986) finds that the NPAH predicts the order of acquisition for L2 learners both in a formal instructional setting and in an informal natural setting. Doughty (1991) reports that learner knowledge of relative clauses prior to instruction reflects the order of the NPAH in general, with the GEN position the most notable exception – an issue that we revisit below.

Support also comes from a study of the reliability of grammaticality judgements, in which Gass (1994) examines learners' judgements of relative clauses in addition to learners' assessments of the degree of confidence they had in their own judgements, ranging from definitely incorrect to unsure to definitely correct. The purpose of the study was to see how reliable grammaticality judgements could be, given the incomplete, or indeterminate, nature of the learners' IL grammatical systems. The learners showed greater consistency and determinacy on the unmarked positions of the NPAH, and greater inconsistency and indeterminacy on the more marked positions of the NPAH.

With regard to question formation, Eckman *et al*. (1988) showed that the implicational universals are upheld without exceptions for wh-questions, and with a single learner exception for yes/no questions. That is, all L2 learners who produced wh-questions with subject–verb inversion also fronted the wh-pronoun, whereas all except one L2 learner who produced subject–verb inversion in yes/no questions also produced inversion in wh-questions. The researchers postulate that the implicational universal for yes/no questions may have been overridden by the processing/production of yes/no questions, which they suggest is easier than the processing/production of wh-questions.

From the perspective of the cited research, typological universals do seem to play a role in L2 acquisition – for example, that markedness can predict order and ease of acquisition. This is not a necessary conclusion, however. L2-acquisition research has examined whether the constraints that govern native languages also pertain to interlanguages (Adjemian 1976). To the extent that typological universals that constrain native languages also apply to interlanguages, interlanguages 'behave' like native languages. A second possibility is that these results can be accounted for by other means; while these studies show support for the effects of the NPAH in L2 acquisition – the simple 'yes' answer – the studies also demonstrate exceptions to the predicted order, which we examine in more detail in the next section.

4.4.2 HOW DOES TYPOLOGICAL MARKEDNESS AFFECT THE SECOND-LANGUAGE ACQUISITION PROCESS?

As noted above, the influence of typological universals in L2 acquisition, while evident, is not so clear-cut in all respects. Here we address typological influences specifically in terms of the strategy of pronoun retention, avoidance of difficult structures in relative clauses, and the ease/frequency of acquisition, and examine the inconsistencies found in the effects of typological universals on L2 learners.

Again we return to the earlier studies by Gass (1979, 1980). Recall that Gass examined the six cross-linguistic differences in relative-clause formation shown in (4.14). Of these six differences, only one – pronoun retention – showed evidence of L1 influence. However, the transfer of pronoun retention did not occur in all of the possible positions on the NPAH in which the pronoun is retained in the L1s – DO, IO, OP, GEN, and OCOMP – but retention occurred only in the three most marked positions on the NPAH – that is, OP, GEN, and OCOMP. This is in accordance with the distribution of pronominal copies cross-linguistically. Hence, there seems to be an interaction between L1 transfer of pronoun retention and universal constraints on relativization.

Earlier findings of Ioup and Kruse (1977) also demonstrate pronoun retention in relative clauses to be significantly more likely to occur in the marked positions OP and GEN, but not in the least marked positions SUB and DO. In this study, however, pronoun retention occurred for all subjects (speakers of Arabic, Chinese, Japanese, Persian, and Spanish) regardless of the existence of pronoun retention in the L1, therefore lacking any evidence of L1 transfer.

In a study of L2 acquisition of Swedish, Hyltenstam (1984) hypothesizes that, since pronoun retention is the unmarked strategy, it will be utilized both by speakers of languages that do not allow for pronoun retention (Spanish and Finnish) and by speakers of languages that do (Persian and Greek). This hypothesis is borne out; native speakers of Persian, Greek, Spanish, and Finnish all produce pronominal copies in their relative clauses in Swedish, but to different degrees depending on whether the L1 allows for pronominal copies. That is, transfer from the L1 is not a matter of *whether* or not pronominal copies are utilized in the L2, but transfer is manifested in the *extent* to which pronominal copies are used. The results also show that pronoun retention occurs to increasing degrees based on the position on the NPAH – that is, pronouns are retained most often in the more marked positions. Again there is an interaction between the markedness of the position of the NPAH and the frequency of occurrence in the L2 production data. The results from these three studies give a mixed picture of the interaction between L1 transfer and markedness as related to pronoun retention and the NPAH: the structure of the

L1 affects the extent to which pronouns are retained, while the NPAH influences the positions in which those pronouns are retained.

The issue of avoidance in which learners are said to avoid structures that differ from the L1 or that cause them difficulty was originally raised by Schachter (1974). Gass (1980) examines the issue of avoidance in two separate tasks. In a sentence-combining task, Gass found that L2 learners avoided structures on the marked of the NPAH.[6] A written composition task similarly showed that learners produced more relative clauses on the unmarked end of the hierarchy (76 per cent for the SUB and 15 per cent for the DO positions). These results again point to the effect of the typological universal in avoidance of more marked forms instead of the effect of transfer from the L1.

As discussed earlier, typological universals play a role in the frequency and ease of acquisition of relative clauses as predicted by the markedness relationships on the NPAH (Doughty 1991; Eckman et al. 1988; Gass 1978, 1980; Hyltenstam 1984; Pavesi 1986). None of these studies, however, follows the predicted order of the NPAH without some deviations. The GEN position is consistently treated differently from predictions, and the IO and OP positions are either switched or treated equally. Several studies (Doughty 1991; Gass 1979, 1980) show that GEN is less problematic for L2 learners than is predicted by the NPAH. For example, in a sentence-combining task Gass (1979) finds that learners respond more correctly to relativization of the GEN position than they do for the DO or IO positions. In addition, Doughty's (1991) pre-instructional results indicate that the GEN position is acquired earlier than would be predicted: some learners who have acquired only the SUB and DO positions also have the GEN. On the other hand, other L2 research (Hyltenstam 1984; Pavesi 1986) reveals that L2 learners treat the GEN position as more difficult than the more marked OCOMP position. Hyltenstam (1984), for instance, finds more pronominal copies in the GEN position than in the more marked OCOMP position.

One reason for the distinction of the GEN position has been suggested: the language-specific peculiarities of the L2 being acquired – specifically, English and Swedish. In English, the GEN has a relative marker that is obligatorily marked for case, *whose*, in contrast to the other relative markers in English: *who*, *which*, *that*, and *whom*. Although *whom* is also marked for case, it is not obligatory in spoken English:

(4.16)
    (a) The woman *that* I spoke to . . .
    (b) The woman *who* I spoke to . . .
    (c) The woman *whom* I spoke to . . .
    (d) The woman to *whom* I spoke . . .

Similarly, in Swedish the GEN relative marker, *vars*, differs from the relative marker utilized in the other positions, *som*. Because of these language-specific characteristics, Gass concludes (1980: 140) that universal constraints such as the NPAH 'determine the general outline of learning' while language-specific L1 factors 'can come into play only where universal factors underdetermine the result'. That is, according to these findings, while universal constraints are the primary influence on the course of L2 acquisition of relative clauses, these constraints interact with language-specific factors.

An additional deviation from the predicted order is that of the IO and OP positions (Doughty 1991; Gass 1979; Hyltenstam 1984; Pavesi 1986). Hyltenstam (1984), for example, finds that, for the Spanish speakers, the accuracy of results is the reverse of the predicted order, with OP more easily produced than IO, whereas Gass (1979) finds no difference between these two positions and, in fact, combines the learners' responses for the two positions. While this research supports the influence of the NPAH on L2 acquisition, the findings are not unproblematic.

In fact, not all L2 researchers agree with the findings in support of the NPAH in L2 acquisition. Other studies (Hamilton 1995; Hawkins 1989; Tarallo and Myhill 1983; and Wolfe-Quintero 1992) point to linguistic factors other than grammatical functions as more relevant. Whereas grammatical functions show the relationships between elements in a sentence such as subjects, verbs, and direct objects, configurational analyses show the groupings of elements into phrases which are arranged in specific linear orders. Configurational analyses form the basis for several alternative views of L2 relative-clause formation.

Hamilton (1995), for instance, notes that the exceptions found in the relative-clause studies by Gass and by Hyltenstam – that is, the ease of production and acquisition of GEN and the lack of distinct differences between the IO and OP positions – can be accounted for from the perspective of a configurational account based on phrase structure (O'Grady 1987). This configurational account explains stages and difficulty of acquisition as due to the amount of embedding of the particular structure that is being extracted for relativization. For example, relative-clause formation includes the extraction of structures from different levels of embedding, from the Inflection Phrase (IP) at the clause level, from verb phrases (VP), and from prepositional phrases (PP):

(4.17)
  (a) SUB   extraction from IP
      The dog [that [$_{IP}$ $\emptyset$[$_{VP}$ bit [$_{NP}$ the man . . .

  (b) DO   extraction from VP within IP
      The man [that [$_{IP}$ the dog [$_{VP}$ bit [$_{NP}$ $\emptyset$ . . .

  (c) IO   extraction from PP within VP within IP
      The girl [that [$_{IP}$ I [$_{VP}$ wrote [$_{NP}$ a letter] [$_{PP}$ to $\emptyset$ . . .

  (d) OP   extraction from PP within VP within IP
      The house [that [$_{IP}$ I [$_{VP}$ talked [$_{PP}$ to you] [$_{PP}$ about $\emptyset$ . . .

  (e) GEN   extraction of an NP in various positions:
      (e′)   extraction of a SUB NP from IP
      The dog [whose tail [$_{IP}$ $\emptyset$ [$_{VP}$ is caught . . .

(e'')   extraction of a DO NP from VP within IP
The family [whose house [$_{IP}$ I [$_{VP}$ like [$_{NP}$ Ø . . .

As seen in (4.17c and d), IO and OP differences do not exist from a configurational account because the amount of embedding of the extraction site is identical: both are extracted from PPs within a VP within an IP. Hamilton also argues that the ease of production of the GEN structures in the studies by Gass (1979) and Doughty (1991) may be accounted for by the fact that the NPs which contain the GEN are extracted from either the SUB or the DO positions.

Other results can also be explained from a configurational perspective. For example, Tarallo and Myhill (1983) find differences in the acceptance of pronoun retention based on the proximity of the relativized position to the head of the relative clause. For example, English-speaking learners of various languages were found to be more accurate in judging relativized subjects in right-branching languages – that is, VO languages in which complements follow verbs, such as German and Portuguese, and more accurate in their judgements of relativized direct objects in left-branching languages, languages with OV word order such as Chinese and Japanese. Tarallo and Myhill suggest that this difference is due to the fact that in right-branching languages the gap (Ø) that is left in the SUB position is closer to the head (emphasized in the English examples in (4.18)) than is the gap for a relativized DO:

(4.18)
   (a) SUB
      The dog [that [Ø [bit [the man . . .

   (b) DO
      The man [that [the dog [bit [Ø . . .

When English speakers were judging relative clauses in left branching languages, they found relativized DOs easier because the gap in the relativized DO position is closer to the head than is the SUB position. This is illustrated in the following Chinese sentences (adapted from Tarallo and Myhill 1983):

(4.19)
   (a) SUB

(Ta)	cong	Zhongguo	lai	de	ren	hen	you	qian
Ø	from	China	come		*man*	very	have	money

      'The man who comes from China is very rich.'

   (b) DO

Wo	da	(ta)	de	ren	shi	Zhongguoren
I	hit	Ø		*man*	is	a Chinese

      'The man who I hit is Chinese.'

The accuracy in grammaticality judgements is argued to have more to do with the proximity of the head and the relativized position than with the function of that position.

As seen above, the analysis of relative-clause acquisition from a configurational perspective offers a contrast to the typological approach and offers alternative analyses for findings that are problematic from a typological markedness perspective. At the present time it is not yet clear to what extent these two approaches account for all or parts of the same set of data.

4.4.3 WHAT IS THE EFFECT OF INSTRUCTION ON TYPOLOGICAL UNIVERSALS IN SECOND-LANGUAGE ACQUISITION?

Several studies have investigated the interaction between instruction and typological universals in the acquisition of relative clauses. In general, the questions asked have focused on whether or not the teaching of a more marked structure – for example, the IO position on the NPAH – generalizes to the less marked structures which have not been taught, a phenomenon which Hamilton (1994) refers to as the Implicational Generalizability effect. In other words, can we get two or more for the price of one? Can we teach the marked structures, and leave the students to learn the unmarked structures automatically?

Research findings have both supported and refuted the notion of generalizability to unmarked structures from marked structures (Croteau 1995; Doughty 1991; Eckman *et al.* 1988; Gass 1979, 1982; Hyltenstam 1984; Pavesi 1986). Gass (1982) examined learners' ability to generalize from a marked position on the NPAH, the OP position, to the less marked positions after three days of explicit instruction on only the OP position. The mixed-instruction group received instruction on restrictive relative clauses in general, including several positions on the NPAH: SUB, DO, IO, OP, and GEN. The results showed that, in the experimental OP group, learners were able to generalize from the more marked OP position to all of the less marked positions on the hierarchy and also to the OCOMP position, which is more marked. Gass hypothesized that the generalization to the OCOMP position was due to the learners' analysis of the comparative *than* as a preposition. The one position that did not generalize was GEN. The mixed-instruction group showed improvement only for the positions of SUB and OP, although they were explicitly instructed on three other positions.

In an attempt to replicate Gass's findings of rule generalization, Eckman *et al.* (1988) instructed three experimental groups on the relativization of three different positions on the NPAH: SUB position, DO position, and OP position. The control group received instruction on a technique for combining sentences. Two days after the one class hour of instruction, all groups were tested on all three types of relative clauses. The results, similar to those of Gass, supported the learners' ability to generalize from the more marked structures to the less marked structures. The OP instruction group scored the best on all three of the positions tested; the DO instruction group was next, followed last by the SUB group. These results further support the NPAH and the MDH in that 'the relative degree of markedness of the structures in question corresponds directly to the number of errors made' (Eckman *et al*. 1988: 11). The findings thus show that the direction of the effects of instruction is towards the less marked structures.

Doughty's (1991) research also shows generalization to both less and more marked positions on the NPAH after various kinds of instruction on texts comprised of sentences with only OP relativization. Three groups worked through a computerized reading programme: a rule-oriented group receiving explicit rules about relativization and sentence-combination instruction, a meaning-oriented group receiving comprehension-based instruction of rephrasings and sentence clarification, and a control group, receiving only a review of the text sentences. All groups were tested on text comprehension with two questions and a recall summary per lesson in addition to written (grammaticality judgements and sentence combination) and oral (picture description) tests of relativization. All three groups showed improvement in relativization on all positions on the hierarchy, with the two instructed groups showing greater improvement.

These instructional studies point to the 'two or more for the price of one' result. By teaching a more marked position of the NPAH, learners will learn relativization of the less marked positions also. This has been found with both explicit grammar instruction (rule instruction and grammatical practice) and implicit comprehension-based instruction (text comprehension and semantic paraphrasing). Nevertheless, some questions do remain about the instructional studies. First, it is not clear why the instruction should lead to generalization to the more marked structures also. While misanalysis of the comparative *than* may be a factor, it has not been proven to be the cause of these results. Hamilton (1995) tests the unidirectional nature of rule generalization from marked to unmarked against a bidirectional generalization from marked to both unmarked and more marked positions on a different type of relative-clause hierarchy, the SO Hierarchy which is based on a combination of the NPAH and types of embedded clauses.[7] The results showed a unidirectional generalization to the unmarked structures. As with the NPAH research, the results are somewhat ambiguous because there is also some generalization to the more marked structures. In addition, contradictory results have been reported by Croteau (1995), who found that instruction on the OP position generalized only to the DO position and not to the SUB position, the least marked position of all, and that instruction on the GEN position did not generalize at all.

Instruction has other effects in addition to generalization to less marked positions on the NPAH. Pavesi (1986) examined the relative-clause formation of formally instructed learners of English and informal learners who learned English in a natural setting. She found two major differences between the formal and informal groups. Formally instructed learners acquired relative clauses farther down the more marked end of the NPAH (the OCOMP position for formal learners versus the OP position for informal learners). Moreover, when these learners used a pronoun-retention strategy, the formal learners used pronoun copies (e.g. the boy who the dog is biting *him*), while the informal learners used noun copies (e.g. the boy who the dog is biting *the boy*).

Clearly, instruction has a beneficial effect on L2 relative-clause acquisition. The instructional studies give some indication of the implications of teaching marked and unmarked structures. The question that these studies cannot answer is why the instruction on the marked structures sometimes generalizes to all of the lesser marked structures and sometimes not. Additionally, if the NPAH is a universal that holds for ILs, how does one account for the exceptions to the predictions of the universal? In order to clarify the status of the NPAH in L2 acquisition, one would have to address these issues from both a typological and a configurational approach.

4.5 Conclusion

Although the typological approach to L2 acquisition has produced far less research than has the Universal Grammar approach, it is important because it offers us a different view of language universals and because it is possibly related to processing constraints as well as mental representations (Hawkins 1989; Tarallo and Myhill 1983). The implicational hierarchy exemplified in the NPAH would seem to be a partial explanation for learners' acquisition of restrictive relative clauses, since L2 learners follow the unmarked-to-marked ordering, as evidenced in L2 research examining the NPAH in both tutored and untutored environments. Given the findings of configurational effects in L2 acquisition, the role of typological universals in L2 acquisition needs to be reassessed.

In support of typological universals in L2 acquisition, Gass and Ard (1984; Gass 1995) discussed the origins of different types of language universals and the evidence for those universals in language acquisition. They noted that universals can originate from different sources – for example, physical sources, perceptual/cognitive sources, a language-acquisition device, or an interactional basis. They hypothesized that those universals of perceptual/cognitive origins, such as the typological hierarchies, would have the greatest influence on L2 acquisition. Gass (1995a) expands on this model and notes that phenomena that are accessible in the surface structure will be more noticeable for learners and consequently more teachable than those structures that are connected by abstract linguistic universals. From this perspective, typological universals may offer a more practical view of how learners utilize and interact with the L2 input with which they are presented.

Notes

1. Typological universals are often referred to as Greenbergian universals after Joseph Greenberg (1966a, b; Greenberg, *et al.* 1978), and the generative

universals are referred to as Chomskyan universals after Noam Chomsky, as discussed at length in Chapter 3.

2. Greenberg (1966a) discusses eight characteristics of unmarked/marked oppositions.

3. Croft (1990) distinguishes between two forms of the distributional characteristic of markedness: the intra-lingual and the cross-linguistic. The intra-lingual criterion of distribution addresses the number of grammatical environments in which a given linguistic item occurs. In a comparison of the active and passive voices in English, if 'the element which occurs in a larger number of constructions is the less marked one', then the active voice is unmarked and the passive voice is marked in English.

4. Typological universals have also been examined in L2 phonology – e.g. the work of Eckman (1985b). Limited work has also been done on L2 word order (M. Schmidt 1980).

5. This word order is ungrammatical in English if it has the falling intonation pattern of a declarative statement as opposed to the rising intonation pattern of a yes/no question.

6. Evidence for avoidance was found in substituting different lexical items, changing the order of the two sentences to be combined, changing the identical noun phrase to be relativized, and changing the structure of the second sentence.

7. The SO Hierarchy delineates four types of relativization based on the position of the head noun and the position of the relativized noun. For example, an OS relative clause is one in which the head noun is a direct object and the relative pronoun is a subject: OS: They saw the *boy who* entered the room (Hamilton 1995). For early work, see Sheldon (1974).

5

Processing approaches

5.1 Introduction to processing theories

In discussing L2 acquisition of syntax, we have primarily been concerned up to this point with the examination of linguistic representations of IL grammars and the linguistic factors that contribute to the forms of those IL grammars (for example, UG constraints and typological universals). While much research in L2 grammatical development focuses exclusively on what is termed grammatical competence, other approaches examine the role of processing in grammatical development, several of which have been discussed extensively in the L2 literature (Bates and MacWhinney 1981; Bialystok 1978, 1981, 1990a; Bialystok and Sharwood Smith 1985; Clahsen 1980; McLaughlin 1987, 1990; Pienemann 1984; 1997; Sharwood Smith 1986).

The traditional distinction between grammatical competence models and processing models is 'to consider competence models as descriptions of knowledge of rules for linguistic structure and processing models as descriptions of methods of storage and means of accessing those rules' (Bialystok 1990a: 637).[1] One's perspective on the relevance of processing models to the L2 acquisition of syntax is related to one's answer to the following question: what is acquired in the L2-acquisition process? Possible answers include the following: an abstract system of grammatical rules, language-specific processing procedures, or a set of complex cognitive skills. The models discussed here offer different answers to this question and, as a result, are relevant to different aspects of the acquisition process.

In a departure from the formats of the previous chapters, this chapter includes three different theoretical approaches to L2 processing: (1) the Input Processing Model and Processing Instruction, (2) the Competition Model, and (3) the Multidimensional Model and Processability Theory. Each of these processing approaches will be discussed individually, followed immediately by an examination of the questions explored within each theoretical paradigm. Since we are concerned with the possible relationships between the processing models of L2 acquisition and L2 grammar-building, the essential question becomes 'What can processing models tell us about how L2 learners learn the L2 grammar?' The chapter concludes with an exploration of this question.

In addition to these three approaches, we also briefly discuss two information-processing models. Information processing has been applied to a broad range of L2 issues, including the learning of artificial languages. Although the information-processing approach has not been applied with specific experiments to natural L2 acquisition, it is included in this introduction because it lays the foundation for other L2 research related to the acquisition of syntax.

5.1.2 INFORMATION PROCESSING

Information-processing models (Hulstijn 1990; McLaughlin 1987, 1990; McLaughlin, Rossman, and McLeod 1983) generally account for how linguistic information undergoes controlled processing until that information becomes available through more automatic processing strategies and is integrated into one's existing linguistic knowledge structure. L2 learning, then, can be seen as the learning of a complex cognitive skill.

Initial learning requires controlled processes, which require attention and time. With practice, the linguistic skill requires less attention and time to execute and becomes routinized, thus freeing up the controlled processes for application to new linguistic skills. From the perspective of L2 learning as a complex cognitive skill, language acquisition is viewed as the process by which linguistic skills become automatic.

McLaughlin (1990: 114) offers a non-linguistic example of the procedure for learning a skill: learning to drive a car with a clutch. At the beginning of the learning process, the task requires a great deal of attention – controlled processing. With continued practice the different components of the skill of using a clutch become automatic – that is, determining when to shift gears, putting in the clutch, shifting gears, and releasing the clutch at the same time as applying the accelerator in order to avoid stalling the car. The experienced driver can drive with a clutch without paying attention to these necessary procedures – for example, carrying on a conversation and driving at the same time. Controlled processing may be called into play again in situations where attention is once again needed – for example, driving on an icy road or driving with a faulty clutch.

What happens once a skill becomes automatic? Hulstijn (1990: 32) points out that learning is not simply a matter of speeding up the necessary procedures and sub-procedures, but rather learning involves 'the establishment of new procedures which *reorganize* a body of facts and rules previously acquired'. This reorganization, or restructuring, is seen in the qualitative differences between one stage of acquisition and another.[2] Numerous examples of restructuring are available from both L1 and L2 acquisition.

In the L1 acquisition of English, children commonly exhibit the following developmental sequence. They first learn the correct past tense forms of irregular verbs such as *went*. Once they have learned the *-ed* past tense forms for regular verbs such as *walked*, children restructure their grammars to include a past tense rule which marks all past tense verbs with the regular *-ed* form resulting in verb forms such as *goed*. Children then restructure their grammars once again so that the past tense *-ed* rule applies only to regular verbs. Such 'U-shaped' behaviour (that is, behaviour that changes from being on the right track to adopting incorrect rules and then returning to an appropriate hypothesis) demonstrates the learner's restructuring of the existing linguistic knowledge system. Examples of syntactic restructuring from L2 acquisition are readily evident in the stages of acquisition seen in Chapter 2.

From this perspective, L2 acquisition is the process by which attention-demanding controlled processes become more automatic through practice and can result in a restructuring of the existing mental representation. McLaughlin (1990) perceives this processing account as a 'partial account' of L2 acquisition to be complemented by a linguistic theory which deals with the linguistic constraints on the developing grammatical system.

A different framework of information processing proposed by Bialystok (Bialystok and Ryan 1985; Bialystok 1978, 1981, 1988, 1990a, 1994; Bialystok and Sharwood Smith 1985) explores the relationship between the form and content of knowledge and the mechanisms that operate to access that knowledge. Bialystok proposes that language develops along two dimensions: an analysed dimension of a learner's control over the form and content of knowledge and an automatic dimension of access to that knowledge.[3]

The notions of knowledge, control, and access are illustrated nicely by a library analogy (Bialystok and Sharwood Smith 1985: 105). The language user is seen as a mental library. That library contains various books that are organized in a particular system. The library user needs to know what the books are, which books are relevant to the user's immediate goals, how the books are arranged, and how one goes about retrieving the desired books. The mental library represents the content of the learner's linguistic knowledge. That knowledge can be structured to different degrees representing different degrees of control over the knowledge. Different degrees of structure in the library analogy might be the amount of detail in the organizational system – for example, a system similar to the North American Dewey Decimal System versus a simple system of two categories: books that I have and have not read. The retrieval of the books represents the learner's access to the linguistic knowledge; the learner may be more or less adept at retrieving the desired knowledge.

On the analysed dimension, one may picture a continuum on which a learner's knowledge representation may be more or less analysed. 'At any point along the dimension, the information itself may be the same, but as control over that information moves towards the Analysed, then the learner becomes increasingly aware as well of the structure of that information' (Bialystok 1988: 33). Once that knowledge is analysed, it is qualitatively different from the unanalysed form; the analysed form *cow + s* is qualitatively different from the unanalysed *cows*. Differences in a learner's control over the structure of knowledge allows the learner to apply that knowledge differentially in various situations and not always in a target-like manner: *cowses*. A learner who has had a formal classroom experience with the L2 would most likely have a highly analysed representation of the L2. On the automatic dimension, a learner may range from having automatic to non-automatic access to information. As in the previous model, the learner gains automatic access to information through practice and experience.

The two dimensions, however, are seen as independent. For example, automatic access does not necessarily imply either unanalysed or analysed knowledge; a learner may have automatic access to both analysed and unanalysed knowledge. L2-acquisition research shows evidence of learners using unanalysed chunks of language – for example, phrases such as *I don't know* and the initial correct usage of *went* with automatic access. In addition, highly proficient speakers can access analysed knowledge automatically, while other learners with analysed knowledge may access that knowledge less automatically owing to lack of experience. As a result, the independence of the two dimensions allows for a four-way distinction:

(5.1)
   (a) −analysed knowledge/−automatic access
   (b) −analysed knowledge/+automatic access
   (c) +analysed knowledge/−automatic access
   (d) +analysed knowledge/+automatic access

Bialystok's model, therefore, includes the analysis of the representation of the linguistic knowledge as well as the learner's access to that knowledge.

It is important to note that neither of these information-processing models makes the claim that the learner can state what he or she 'knows'. Increased analysis or restructuring of knowledge does not imply the learner's conscious awareness of the structure; in other words, learners cannot necessarily *state* the rule for analysed knowledge. Although L2 learners can and do have both implicit L2 knowledge (abstract grammatical constraints unavailable to consciousness) and explicit L2 knowledge (in the form of grammatical rules that can be stated), analysed knowledge is not necessarily explicit. This distinction is important because some researchers of L2 acquisition argue that grammar building involves only implicit knowledge (e.g. Krashen 1982; Schwartz 1993; Zobl 1995).[4]

Aspects of the information-processing models have formed the basis of research in diverse areas of L2 acquisition: L2 reading (Harrington 1992; Harrington and Sawyer 1992; McLeod and McLaughlin 1986), L2 ultimate attainment (Bialystok 1997), L2 learning of miniature artificial languages (DeKeyser 1995, 1997; Hulstijn 1989; Nation and McLaughlin 1986; Nayak *et al.* 1990), L2 aptitude (McLaughlin 1995), and L2 learning and knowledge representation (Bialystok 1994; Hulstijn 1989; Robinson 1996, 1997). While L2 research has utilized some aspects of information processing, the direct application of these models to the L2 acquisition of syntax is less obvious, however.

Nevertheless, the information-processing models make several contributions to an understanding of L2 acquisition and of the issues addressed within other processing approaches. First, they highlight the fact that L2 acquisition involves both knowledge representation and knowledge retrieval and that the structure of that representation (analysed or unanalysed) affects the learner's ability to use that L2 knowledge. In addition, the notion of restructuring as applied to L2 acquisition of syntax has been seen in several examples of stages of acquisition and U-shaped behaviour. It is clear that L2 grammars are restructured; however, one might argue, as Long (1990) does, that it is not enough to describe the changes that take place from one grammatical representation to another or from one stage of acquisition to another. One must be able to state what the mechanism is that accounts for that change. McLaughlin (1990: 120) concedes that 'not enough is currently known about the mechanisms involved in restructuring'. Finally, these models emphasize the fact that learners have limitations on the amount of information that can be processed in short-term or working memory. This limited-capacity processing forms the basis for aspects of Input Processing, the Competition Model, and the Multidimensional Model and Processability Theory, to which we now turn.

5.2 Input processing: the Input Processing Model and Processing Instruction

Input has been seen as one of the determining factors in L2 acquisition, and much research since the late 1970s has focused on the role of input in the acquisition process: the types of input necessary for acquisition, learner interaction and input, and learner processing of input.[5] Krashen's Input Hypothesis (1982, 1985) makes the claim that humans acquire language by understanding messages and that these messages come in the form of comprehensible input – that is, input that contains both structures that have already been acquired – structures at the learner's current level of competence – and also structures that are slightly beyond the learner's current level of competence.[6] Krashen's focus on the importance of meaningful input is also highlighted in a corollary to the Input Hypothesis: 'if input is understood, and there is enough of it, the necessary grammar is automatically provided' (Krashen 1985: 2).

VanPatten's theory of input processing (1996: 6) is also built on the notion of meaning-bearing input, which he defines as 'language that the learner hears or sees that is used to communicate a message'. But, as any L2 researcher, teacher, or learner knows, everything that goes in does not necessarily contribute to the learner's grammar building. In other words, not all input becomes intake, as noted by Corder (1967). VanPatten distinguishes between three different sets of processes: the processes that transform input into intake (I), the processes that utilize intake in building the developing grammatical system (II), and the processes needed to access the developing system for language production (III) (adapted from VanPatten 1996: 154):

(5.2)   I   II   III
        input →   intake → developing system   → output
    I = input processing
    II = accommodation (of intake), restructuring (of the developing system)
    III = access

VanPatten's focus is on the processing of input that allows that input to become intake, processing set I. He proposes that learners filter input so that only a small subset of the input becomes intake.

An important constraint on input processing is the learner's cognitive capacity for processing information. VanPatten argues that attention is required for learning (VanPatten 1990; also Schmidt 1990, 1994, 1995; Schmidt and Frota, 1986).[7] Learners must first *attend* to form before they can *detect* a particular linguistic form. Detection is the process that makes that piece of information available for further processing. One problem is that learners cannot attend to both the content and the grammatical form of a message (VanPatten 1990). When a learner attends to the form of the message, this attention to form competes for the processing capacity available to attend to the content. If L2 learners are seen as limited-capacity processors, they can attend to only so much linguistic information at one time, therefore limiting the subset of information that can be detected (VanPatten 1996: 14).

VanPatten proposes that learners follow particular principles in order to process the incoming input. His Input Processing Model is comprised of two types of processing principles. The first type deals with the cognitive aspects of input processing, or how learners attend to the input (VanPatten 1996: 14–15):

(5.3) Input processing principles: cognitive aspects
    P1   Learners process input for meaning before they process it for form.
    P1(a)   Learners process content words in the input before anything else.
    P1(b)   Learners prefer processing lexical items to grammatical items (e.g. morphological markings) for semantic information.
    P1(c)   Learners prefer processing 'more meaningful' morphology before 'less or non-meaningful morphology'.
    P2   For learners to process form that is not meaningful, they must be able to process informational or communicative content at no (or little) cost to attention.

'Meaningful' as used in P1(c) refers to communicative value. An example of 'meaningful' morphology is the English morpheme *-ing*. As the marking of progressive aspect, the morpheme has inherent semantic value, and the progressive is not usually marked redundantly by other lexical context (e.g. *at this moment*). Less meaningful morphology has little communicative value; for instance, the third person singular -*s* in English is somewhat redundant, because subjects are obligatorily present in most cases. These processing principles highlight the fact, that in terms of learner processing, meaning is primary; form is secondary. In order for learners to be able to attend to non-meaningful form, the processing of meaningful input must be fairly effortless or automatic.

The second type of principle concerns sentence-level aspects of input processing. These strategies focus on learner interpretation of sentence meaning – that is, how learners assign grammatical roles (subject and object) and semantic roles (agent and patient) to nouns (VanPatten 1996: 32):

(5.4) Input processing principles: sentence-level aspects

P3   Learners possess a default strategy that assigns the role of agent to the first noun (phrase) they encounter in a sentence. We call this the 'first noun strategy'.

P3(a) The first noun strategy can be overridden by lexical semantics and event probabilities.

P3(b) Learners will adopt other processing strategies for grammatical role assignment only after their developing system has incorporated other cues (e.g. case marking, acoustic stress).

Principle P3 and its corollaries have as an underlying assumption that learners use word order as the primary strategy for sentence interpretation. These combined principles (P1–P3) produce a semantic and grammatical interpretation of the input, which is then available as intake.

To summarize, attention to and detection of grammatical form require processing capacity. VanPatten argues that the principles developed in the Input Processing Model suggest conditions under which learners can attend to both meaning and form in order to facilitate form-meaning mappings. While recognizing that certain kinds of grammatical form (i.e. less meaningful forms) present detection difficulties for learners, VanPatten advocates grammatical instruction that directs learners' attention to form within meaning-bearing input.

Briefly, the 'processing instruction' that is advocated 'seeks to alter the way in which learners perceive and process linguistic data in the input' (VanPatten and Sanz 1995: 169). It consists of two different types of input: explicit explanation and 'structured input'. The explicit explanation focuses on both the instructed grammatical item, for example, direct object pronouns, and the processing strategies, for example, the 'first noun strategy', as in (5.4) P3(a). Structured input is input that is manipulated, but meaning-bearing. In the structured input phase of instruction, learners are asked to focus on the selected grammatical structure in order to interpret the meaning of the input sentences. These instructional activities are termed 'referentially oriented' activities because they focus on meaning. A follow-up activity requires that learners understand the input sentences in order to comment on their attitudes towards the content of the input sentences; for example, learners state whether they agree or disagree with the sentence. Thus, processing instruction emphasizes the comprehension of the instructed form–meaning mappings and not the production of the structures, which is emphasized in traditional grammar instruction.

How do these input-processing strategies contribute to learner intake and grammar building? VanPatten (1996: 134) argues that, according to the Input Processing Model,

> learners' processing of input results in a reduced and sometimes altered subset of the input data. These data, called intake data, are subject to further processing (accommodation) that, when it occurs, can lead to restructuring of the developing system. In this view, the developing system uses intake data and not input data for growth.

The input-processing strategies are, therefore, seen as a filter that produces intake data which are 'accommodated or not by the developing system with subsequent restructuring of the system depending on the nature of the intake data' (VanPatten 1996: 134). Therefore, VanPatten sees the Input Processing Model as complementary to a model of grammar-building mechanisms such as Universal Grammar.

A specific example can be seen in the application of processing principle P1(a) in (5.3). If it is true as P1(a) states that 'learners process content words in the input before anything else', then the intake data to the developing grammatical system consist of lexical items without grammatical functors. The prediction for L2 acquisition would be that learners at this stage should then begin by producing only content words. VanPatten cites unpublished evidence by Zobl that shows that lexical categories are acquired before functional categories in support of this claim.

The relationship then between input processing and grammar building is that input processing determines the body of data to which the grammar-building mechanisms have access. Processing instruction is seen as a way to make the form–meaning mappings more accessible to the learner's grammar-building mechanisms – that is, to give learners a more grammatically rich intake (VanPatten 1995).

5.3 Questions explored: the Input Processing Model and Processing Instruction

5.3.1 HOW CAN INSTRUCTION AFFECT INPUT PROCESSING AND SECOND-LANGUAGE ACQUISITION?

VanPatten and his colleagues (VanPatten and Cadierno 1993a, b; VanPatten and Oikkenon 1996; VanPatten and Sanz 1995) have investigated the effect of input-processing instruction on learners' comprehension and production of L2 Spanish. A few comments on Spanish direct objects are in order here. Direct object pronouns in Spanish are marked for person, number, and, in some cases, gender and formality.

(5.5)

(a) me	me	1st person, singular
(b) te	you	2nd person, singular, informal
(c) lo	you	2nd person, singular, formal, masculine
	him/it	3rd person, singular, masculine
(d) la	you	2nd person, singular, formal, feminine
	her/it	3rd person, singular, feminine
(e) nos	us	1st person, plural
(f) os	you	2nd person, plural, informal
(g) los	you	2nd person, plural, formal, masculine
	them	3rd person, plural, masculine
(h) las	you	2nd person, plural, formal, feminine
	them	3rd person, plural, feminine

Direct object pronouns occur before the verb that they complement. In addition, Spanish word order is flexible, so that subject noun phrases can occur after the verb; subjects are also optional in Spanish. If the direct object is manifested as a noun phrase, it is case-marked with the 'personal *a*'. These syntactic rules result in the following possible manifestations of the sentence *His parents call him*. The direct object pronoun in this case is *lo* (him); the subject pronoun is *ellos* (them), and the direct object noun phrase is *a Tomás* (to Tomás).

(5.6)

(a)	Sus padres	lo	llaman.
	His parents	him	call-3rd person plural-present tense
	Subj	Obj	
(b)	Ellos	lo	llaman.
	They	him	call-3rd person plural-present tense
	Subj	Obj	

    (c) Lo llaman sus padres.
    (d) Lo llaman ellos.
    (e) A Tomás lo llaman sus padres.
    (f) A Tomás lo llaman ellos.
    (g) A Tomás lo llaman.
    (h) Lo llaman.

In a series of studies on the L2 acquisition of direct object pronouns and word order in Spanish, the effect of input-processing instruction on sentence interpretation and production is compared with the effect of traditional production-based grammar instruction. The input-processing instruction consists of explicit grammatical and processing explanations plus structured input with meaning-focused practice. The traditional instruction includes explicit grammatical explanation and output practice (mechanical, meaningful, and communicative practice).

VanPatten and Cadierno (1993a, b) find that the processing instruction increases learners' ability both to interpret and to produce direct-object structures correctly, while traditional instruction only aids production. VanPatten and Sanz (1995) expand on this previous work to test whether processing instruction also affects learners' communicative production in discourse-oriented language use – in a question-and-answer interview and a video narration task. Their findings further support the hypothesis that processing instruction significantly affects learners' interpretation and production in both written (sentence-completion, interview, and narration) and oral (sentence-completion) tasks.

Finally, VanPatten and Oikkenon (1996) examine the separate effects of the explicit explanation and the structured input on the learners' interpretation and production of Spanish object pronouns and word order in sentence-level tasks. This study was undertaken to clarify further the effects of structured input. Three instructional groups were included: processing instruction (explanation plus structured input), structured input only, and explicit explanation only. Only the combined processing instruction and the structured input had significant effects on both the interpretation and production tasks, whereas explicit explanation alone had no or limited effects. These results suggest that the structured-input aspect of processing instruction is the most significant aspect of processing instruction.

However, these results in favour of input-processing instruction may not be as clear-cut as suggested. In addition to VanPatten and Oikkenon (1996), DeKeyser and Sokalski (1996) question the results of the studies by VanPatten and Cadierno (1993a, b). In a replication study, they note that the input-processing comprehension group and the traditional output group differ in a number of ways: the quality of the instruction, the quantity of the instruction, and the amount of focus on attention to form and to meaning. For example, the input group received an explanation contrasting the subject and object forms as well as examples of each possible combination. In contrast, the output practice group was presented with a simple identification of the subject and object forms and a chart of the object pronoun forms only.

An additional factor possibly contributing to the results is the choice of object pronouns as the focus of the studies. DeKeyser and Sokalski point out that different kinds of practice (input or output) may be more appropriate for different kinds of structures (pronominal versus verbal morphology) in different kinds of tasks (comprehension versus production). They suggest that Spanish object pronouns are difficult to detect in the input but relatively easy to produce, whereas conditional verb forms (e.g. *hablaría, hablarías,* etc.) are easy to detect but comparatively difficult to produce correctly owing to multiple verb endings and word-order differences. The results of the VanPatten and

Cadierno studies can be explained by the fact that the input group received practice on the difficult task – comprehension of object pronouns – while the output group received practice on a task that was relatively easy – production of object pronouns – without practice on the difficult task.

In a comparison of L2 comprehension and production of Spanish object pronouns and conditional verbs, DeKeyser and Sokalski (1996) find that input practice aids comprehension and output practice aids production of object pronouns. In the comprehension and production of conditional verb forms, output practice was better for both. They note, however, that the effects of input practice seem to be longer lasting than the effects of output practice.[8]

The results of the processing-instruction research offer preliminary evidence that structured input, which requires learners to focus on meaningful grammatical form, may alter the quality of the input that is accessible as intake for the developing grammatical system. Research findings also indicate that the levels of difficulty of the particular structures and of the task types need to be considered. This research paradigm highlights the issue of learner attention to grammatical form as a prerequisite for grammatical development – an issue which is under examination in L2 instructional research.

The influence of correct meaning–form mappings on subsequent grammar development is underscored when one considers the possible effects of misinterpretations of sentences with direct object pronouns (VanPatten and Cadierno 1993a; VanPatten 1996):

(5.7)
   (a) absence of object pronouns;
   (b) misuse of object pronouns for subjects;
   (c) incorrect placement of object pronouns;
   (d) a general over-reliance on subject pronouns;
   (e) a complete lack of use of the direct object case marker *a*;
   (f) an over-reliance on subject–verb–object word order and problems in the acquisition of object pronouns;
   (g) a delay in the acquisition of person-number endings;
   (h) difficulty in the acquisition of verbs that require post-verbal subjects (e.g. *gustar*).

In other words, learners' interpretation of the grammatical form in the first set of input processes determines how the intake facilitates accommodation into and restructuring of the developing IL. Another approach to the processing and interpretation of input is seen in the Competition Model, to which we now turn.

5.4 Input processing: the Competition Model

The Competition Model (Bates and MacWhinney 1981, 1982, 1987; Bates *et al.* 1983) is a model of linguistic performance which incorporates the mapping between form and function in language performance and acquisition. While a modular approach to language such as the Government and Binding Theory separates the notions of linguistic competence (the grammar) and performance (the use), the Competition Model takes a functional approach which links the grammatical form to its communicative function. From this perspective, the Competition Model differs from the other processing approaches discussed (e.g. Processability Theory, and the other approaches to information processing (discussed in Section 5.1.2)), which also present speech and input processing as separate from the linguistic component. Nevertheless, the Competition Model does incorporate concepts that we have already seen – for instance, limited processing capacity. This performance model has been developed to account for data from L1 acquisition and from cross-linguistic speech processing by highly proficient bilinguals and less proficient L2 learners, as well as by native speakers.

In accordance with a functional perspective, the Competition Model is based on the assumption that 'the surface conventions of natural languages are created, governed, constrained, acquired, and used in the service of communicative functions' (Bates and MacWhinney 1981: 192). This assumption leads to the creation of a two-levelled mapping: the communicative function is one level and the formal grammatical manifestation of that function is the other level. Languages encode the communicative functions – for example, 'topic' and 'agent' – onto surface grammatical conventions in various ways – such as word order, morphological case marking, or subject–verb agreement. Because of the limits on processing, these functional categories compete for control of the surface grammatical conventions.

Speakers of a language use a variety of cues – word order, morphology, lexical meaning – to facilitate their interpretation of these form–function mappings. For example, speakers of English may use word order, subject–verb agreement, and the meaning of the lexical items *dog* and *flower* to determine that *dog* is the semantic agent and syntactic subject of the sentence: *The dog eats flowers*. The frequent connection between word order and subjecthood/agenthood in English increases the strength of word order as a cue for interpreting *the dog* as the subject/agent of *eats*. Word order, however, is not as strong a cue for speakers of Italian, because word order is more flexible in Italian than it is in English:

(5.8)

(a)	Il cane	mangia	i fiori	SVO
	The dog	eats	the flowers	
(b)	I fiori	mangia	il cane	OVS
(c)	Il cane	i fiori	mangia	SOV
(d)	Mangia	i fiori	il cane	VOS

As a result, some cues have more value for speakers of a given language than do others, and cue validity can be predicted based on 'cue availability (i.e. how often is this piece of information offered during a decision-making process?) and cue reliability (i.e. how often does the cue lead to a correct conclusion when it is used?)' (MacWhinney 1987: 321). Word order, in this case pre-verbal position, is both an available and a reliable cue for subjecthood/agenthood in English, whereas this is not the case for Italian, in which subjects are often omitted or appear both pre- and post-verbally.

MacWhinney (1987: 321) argues that cue availability and cue reliability allow speakers to 'control 95% of the grammar in actual sentence production and comprehension'. The last 5 per cent require attention to the interaction between cues within the particular language system. Cues can either converge on a single interpretation or conflict to allow for conflicting interpretations. Consider the following examples in English:

(5.9)
   (a) The boy is eating the apple.
   (b) The apple is eating the boy.
   (c) The apples is eating the boy.

Three cues are at work here: animacy, subject–verb agreement, and word order. In (5.9a) all three cues converge to indicate that *the boy* is the subject/agent of the sentence. In (5.9b) there is a conflict between the animacy cue and the word-order cue, and the listener must select only one noun as the subject/agent. In (5.9c) there is a conflict between the animacy, the subject–verb agreement, and the word-order cues. In conflict sentences such as (5.9b) and (5.9c), cue strengths compete to determine the interpretation (McDonald 1986). The usefulness of a cue in resolving such interpretation conflicts is referred to as conflict validity. McDonald proposes that conflict validity accounts for adult processing whereas overall cue validity (the product of availability and reliability) is predictive in child language acquisition.

Another factor relevant to the acquisition of processing strategies is cue cost – that is, the relative effort of processing a particular cue (Bates and MacWhinney 1987). Cue cost can be affected by two factors: perceivability and assignability. Some cues are difficult to perceive – for example, the third person singular/plural distinction in certain French verbs: *décrit/décrivent* – 'describe(s)', *suit/suivent* – 'follow(s)', or *choisis/choississent* – 'choose(s)' (McDonald and Heilenman 1991).[9] The perceivability of this cue will interact with its validity; if the cue is difficult to detect in the input, it is less probable that speakers will rely on this information for sentence interpretation.

' "Assignability" refers to the ease with which a given cue can be assigned to a role' (Bates and MacWhinney 1987: 180). Cues can be assigned locally or globally; a local cue, such as nominative case marking on the subject noun phrase, can be used as soon as it is perceived and is high in assignability. Global cues are those which must be held onto before they can be assigned, such as subject–verb agreement marking. Global cues are seen as more costly because they require auditory storage, which may be limited.

In terms of cross-linguistic processing, the question is to determine which cues L2 learners use in L2-sentence interpretation. One solution of L2 learners is to transfer the L1 processing strategies to the L2 (forward transfer) so that the English-speaking learner of Italian will transfer a reliance on a word-order cue to the production and comprehension of the Italian L2. Other patterns of how L2 speakers deal with cue weight are also possible: abandonment of L1 strategies for L2 strategies (backward transfer), merger of L1 and L2 strategies (amalgamation), and partial attainment of separate L1 and L2 systems (differentiation) (Liu *et al.* 1992; Kilborn and Ito 1989; MacWhinney 1987).

In sum, the issues discussed above – two-level mapping, cue strength and competition, cue validity, systematic interactions between cues, and processing limitations – comprise the core concepts of the Competition Model (MacWhinney 1987: 317). The learner's ability to interpret form–function mappings will affect the learner's subsequent L2 acquisition. MacWhinney offers the transfer of Japanese topicalization as a clear example of this. Japanese learners of English produce structures which transfer the Japanese function of topic into a sentence-initial position, resulting in structures such as '*As for the doll, it was a gift from my aunt.*' In Japanese, and as seen in this English example, the discourse function of 'topic' is marked separately from that of the grammatical form of 'subject'. The more common structure in English results from the coalition of the topic and the subject into one grammatical form: '*The doll was a gift from my aunt.*' While the 'as for ...' structure is not ungrammatical in English, it is relatively uncommon.

The Competition Model is seen as one approach to L2 acquisition that can shed light on how and why learners construct the form–function interpretations that they do. It is also seen as a way to study how 'learners handle conflicting and competing language data and the generalizations that result' (Gass 1989b: 525).

5.5 Questions explored: the Competition Model

● What types of strategies are used in sentence interpretation?
● How do second-language learners use cue strategies in sentence interpretation?

Research based on the Competition Model has examined both native-speaker and learner use of different kinds of cue strategies (syntactic, morphological, semantic, and pragmatic) to interpret language input in a variety of languages (e.g. L2 research in Chinese, Dutch, English, French, German, Italian, Japanese, and Spanish). Languages utilize different combinations of the possible cues. A subset of the cues which have been examined in this research is seen in (5.10):

(5.10) Sentence interpretation cue strategies
   (a) Syntax   word order

    (b) Morphology   subject–verb agreement, nominal case marking, subject and object clitic pronouns
    (c) Semantics   animacy
    (d) Pragmatics   contrastive stress, topicalization

The format of the studies is relatively uniform. The subjects are presented with sentence strings consisting of at least one verb and two nouns and are asked to identify which noun in the string is the subject of the sentence (syntactic strategy) or the doer of the action (semantic cue). These instructions aim to present subjects with an unbiased approach to interpreting the sentences. Research subjects select the subject/agent in either a timed (on-line) or a non-timed (off-line) condition. The sentence strings are formulated so that different cues combine in all of the possible variations. The possible word-order combinations are NVN, NNV, and VNN. When subjects interpret the grammatical functions of these word orders, the following subject and object combinations are possible:

(5.11)

    (a) NVN   SVO   OVS
    (b) NNV   SOV   OSV
    (c) VNN   VSO   VOS

The nouns can be either animate (A) or inanimate (I). The possible combinations of the animacy of the first and/or second noun(s) in the different word orders are as follows:

(5.12)

    (a) both nouns animate (AA)   AVA   AAV   VAA
    (b) first noun animate (AI)   AVI   AIV   VAI
    (c) second noun animate (IA)   IVA   IAV   VIA

While animacy and word order are the two common cue strategies studied, the L2 learner research has explored learner use of several additional cues in the following languages:[10]

(5.13)

    (a) Chinese   animacy, word order
    (c) Dutch   animacy, case inflection, subject–verb agreement, word order
    (c) English   animacy, subject–verb agreement, topic, word order
    (d) French   animacy, clitic pronoun agreement, subject–verb agreement, topic, word order
    (e) German   animacy, subject–verb agreement, word order
    (f) Italian   animacy, subject–verb agreement, topic, word order
    (g) Japanese   animacy, case inflection, contrastive stress, word order
    (h) Spanish   animacy, subject–verb agreement, word order

5.5.1 WHAT TYPES OF STRATEGIES ARE USED IN SENTENCE INTERPRETATION?

Returning now to the questions explored in this paradigm, we see that monolingual native speakers of various languages utilize cues that match to some extent the language input that they get in the native language. Cue strength in a given language is relative to the validity of the cue in that language. Recall that cue validity includes the notions of cue availability and reliability. While there is no absolute agreement among studies as to one rank order of various native speaker interpretation strategies, there is some agreement on the strongest cue strategy for native speakers of different language groups.

Speakers of morphologically rich languages such as Dutch, Italian, and Spanish rely most on morphological cues, either case inflection or subject–verb agreement cues (Bates and MacWhinney 1981; Hernandez *et al.* 1994; Kilborn 1989; Kilborn and Cooreman 1987; McDonald 1986, 1987a, b), while speakers of a morphologically impoverished language such as English rely on strict word order as the most reliable cue to the subject/agent of a sentence (Bates and MacWhinney 1981; Harrington 1987; Heilenman and McDonald 1993; Kilborn 1989; Kilborn and Cooreman 1987; McDonald, 1986, 1987a, b; MacWhinney *et al.* 1984). However, speakers of Chinese, a language with little morphology and fairly strict word order, utilize animacy as the most reliable cue (Miao 1981; Li *et al.* 1992). For native speakers of the following languages, the cue strategies listed below are proposed to be the strongest. In some cases, two cues are proposed, based on the different configurations of cues examined in the research:[11]

(5.14)

(a)	Chinese	animacy
(b)	Dutch	case inflection/subject–verb agreement
(c)	English	word order
(d)	French	clitic pronoun agreement
(e)	German	subject–verb agreement/animacy
(f)	Italian	subject–verb agreement
(g)	Japanese	animacy
(h)	Spanish	subject-verb agreement

Two points must be noted. First, speakers of a language do not use cue strategies in isolation. For example, while Italian native speakers use subject–verb agreement as the strongest cue, when this agreement is ambiguous, there is a strong reliance on animacy. In a sentence such as *La gomma il maialino bacia* (The eraser the pig kisses), the animate *pig* is chosen as the subject/agent (MacWhinney *et al.* 1984). It has also been shown that native speakers may use all cues to some degree and that those cue interactions result in the strengthening and weakening of cues based on the presence or absence of competing cues (Li *et al.* 1993).

Second, in some studies, morphological marking is omitted from the test sentences. For instance, case marking in German and Japanese was omitted (Harrington 1987; MacWhinney *et al.* 1984) to facilitate the comparison of processing strategies with languages that do not mark nouns for case such as English. It is probable that case marking is the strongest cue. In fact, in studies where case marking was included (McDonald 1986, 1987a, b), nominal case inflection was the strongest cue for Dutch native speakers.

What types of strategies are used by L2 learners in sentence interpretation? The simple answer is that L2 learners use a wide variety of cue strategies: word order, subject–verb agreement, and case-marking. The more complicated answer involves patterns of strategy use. Recall the four possible L2 conditions explained above: (1) L1 forward transfer, (2) L2 backward transfer, (3) amalgamation, and (4) differentiation. While the research of L2 processing demonstrates some evidence for each of the four possibilities, forward transfer of L1 processing strategies to the interpretation of sentences in the L2 is the most common finding (Bates and MacWhinney 1981; Gass 1987; Harrington 1987; Heilenman and McDonald 1993; Kilborn 1989; Kilborn and Cooreman 1987; Kilborn and Ito 1989; Sasaki 1991, 1994). For instance, Kilborn (1989) finds that German L2 learners of English utilize the L1 agreement and animacy strategies in both German and English. Japanese L2 learners of English transfer their L1 animacy strategy to English (Harrington 1987; Sasaki 1991), as do Italian learners of English when subject–verb agreement is not available as a cue (Gass 1987).

Transfer, however, may be affected by the actual types of cues – semantic versus syntactic – that are most valid in the L1 and the L2. In addition to the L1 transfer of animacy strategies into the L2, several studies have suggested that it is easier to adopt L2 semantic strategies such as animacy than it is to adopt L2 syntactic strategies (e.g. Gass 1987; Liu *et al.* 1992; McDonald and Heilenman 1991; Miao 1981; Sasaki 1994; cf. Kilborn and Ito 1989). For instance, Gass (1987) finds that English learners of Italian in an Italian-speaking environment readily adopt animacy strategies. Sasaki (1991) also finds that English learners of Japanese are similar to native Japanese speakers in their use of animacy strategies. One caveat to this proposal is that morphological marking for case in Japanese and for subject–verb agreement in Italian, which may be a competing cue in these languages, were absent from these studies. However, the primacy of animacy is also indicated in a study of English L2 learners of Japanese in which morphological case is indicated (Sasaki 1994), and in a subset of English native speakers who adopt an animacy cue over word order in the processing of their L1 English (Harrington 1987). MacWhinney (1987) suggests that animacy might be seen as a last resort cue when no other cue offers reliable information.

L2 research also shows some evidence of differentiation; some learners are able to adopt L2 processing strategies as separate from their L1 strategies. This differentiation is found in highly proficient L2 speakers (Bates and

MacWhinney 1981; McDonald and Heilenman 1991) and in some bilinguals who had early exposure to the L2 (Liu *et al.* 1992). For instance, Sasaki (1994) finds that English-speaking L2 learners of Japanese increase their use of the L2 morphological case marking cues with increased proficiency.

But L2 proficiency and/or bilingualism is not a reliable predictor of differentiation since there is also evidence of highly proficient L2 speakers who transfer L1 strategies to the L2 (Bates and MacWhinney 1981) and of bilingual speakers who combine the L1 and L2 strategies into one amalgamation of language-processing strategies (Hernandez *et al.* 1994; Wulfeck *et al.* 1986). In one study, Wulfeck *et al.* (1986) find two groups of Spanish–English bilinguals who have adopted two distinct sets of processing strategies that are applied to both English and Spanish sentences (one set of ordered cues was word order > subject–verb agreement > animacy and the other ordered set was subject–verb agreement > animacy > word order). In another study (Hernandez *et al.* 1994), Spanish–English bilinguals also have an amalgamation of strategies but show some evidence of differentiated strategies in timed on-line tasks. Hernandez *et al.* (1994), who pose the question, 'What does it mean to be "in-between"?', note that there is a wide array of in-between patterns including 'partially differentiated patterns of amalgamation (e.g. Spanish–English bilinguals who rely primarily on agreement in both of their languages, but make greater use of word order in English)' (p. 421). These researchers suggest that bilinguals use cues that optimally fit the bilingual processing conditions but which may not work as well for monolinguals.

The final possibility of backward transfer is reported in a study of Chinese–English bilinguals which includes age of arrival in the English environment as a factor (Liu *et al.* 1992). Two groups were shown to exhibit English word-order strategies in Chinese: Chinese–English bilinguals who were exposed to both Chinese and English before the age of 4 and those who were exposed to English between the ages of 12 and 16. The former group is best categorized as English-dominant bilinguals, in which case English cannot necessarily be considered the L2. It seems that backward transfer then applies only to the latter group.

Perhaps there is a need for a fifth category to distinguish better between the distinct processing patterns of developing L2 learners from those of bilinguals. 'Developing differentiation' captures the situation in which L2 learners demonstrate a growing sensitivity to the L2 processing strategies but do not yet process the L2 using the same cues in the same ways as do native speakers. That is, they are moving beyond L1 forward transfer, but they are somewhere on an IL processing continuum.

As Gass (1989a) points out, not only do L2 learners need to learn the appropriate L2 cues; they also need to learn the relative strengths of those cues – that is, which L2 cues 'win' in a competition condition. The most valid cue in a language, the one that is both the most applicable *and* the most reliable, is the first one chosen for a particular function (Bates *et al.* 1984; McDonald 1986).

McDonald (1986) proposes that L2 learners do not change cue weights for cues that result in correct interpretations but do alter cue weights that result in incorrect interpretations over time. 'With increasing exposure to the language, the strengths of the relevant cues will increase more rapidly than those of the irrelevant ones' (McDonald 1986: 321). This may account for the ease with which English learners of languages with flexible word order readily abandon a strict word-order strategy in favour of more relevant animacy or morphological cues (Gass 1987; McDonald and Heilenman 1991, 1992; Sasaki 1991).

The L2 research shows that L2 learners use all of the same types of cue strategies – semantic, syntactic, and morphological – as do native speakers. How L2 learners differ is that they do not necessarily rely on the same cues in the same ways that native speakers do – a question that we now turn to.

5.5.2 HOW DO SECOND-LANGUAGE LEARNERS USE CUE STRATEGIES IN SENTENCE INTERPRETATION?

Examination of L2 learners' developing differentiation of cue strategies reveals a complex picture. Kilborn and Cooreman (1987) note that Dutch learners of English utilize the L1 Dutch agreement strategy in their L2 English, but do show some movement towards a sensitivity to the English word-order strategy. Their processing strategies are complex, however. The consistent word-order strategy of native speakers of English is to select the first noun as the subject/agent in canonical NVN sequences (SVO: '*The cat* is kissing the girl') and the second noun as the subject/agent in the non-canonical VNN and NNV sequences (VOS: 'Is kissing the girl the *cat*' and OSV: 'The girl *the cat* is kissing' respectively). The L1 Dutch speakers' sensitivity to word order in L2 English is selective: they transfer 'exportable' L1 cues (the selection of the first noun in a VSO sequence which resembles Dutch question formation: 'Is kissing *the girl* the cat'), but they also abandon L1 cues in favour of L2 word-order cues (second noun selection in OSV) as the only likely solution in the absence of other cues.

Kilborn and Ito (1989) also cite English learners of L2 Japanese who interpret Japanese NNV strings as SOV – the canonical word order in Japanese – rather than directly transferring the L1 English OSV interpretation. Similar to the Dutch learners of English, these English learners of L2 Japanese have not adopted the L2 strategy (no preference for one noun over the other in NNV sequences), nor have they directly transferred the L1 English strategy.

Based on this type of evidence, Kilborn and Ito point out that L2 learners do not always directly transfer L1 strategies or develop L2 strategies in ways that are predicted by the Competition Model. What these English learners of L2 Japanese have done is developed a meta-strategy – the strategy of paying attention to word order as a cue to sentence meaning – rather than transferring the English-specific word-order strategy noted above (see also Sasaki 1994). Utilizing *a* word-order cue in the L2 is not the same as using the L1 word-order cue.

Second, cue cost has been found to be a factor in L2 acquisition of processing strategies (McDonald and Heilenman 1991) as well as in L1 acquisition (Kail 1989). Perceivability, one of the elements of cue cost, affects L2 learners' reliance on a given type of cue. Advanced L2 French learners who are able to use L2 subject–verb agreement cues are less likely to use this same cue when it is less phonologically salient with a subset of verbs, although they do use it as a cue when it is easily detectable (McDonald and Heilenman 1991).[12] The other aspect of cue cost, assignability, is a factor in L1 child and adult processing (Bates et al. 1984; Kail 1989), but has not yet been conclusively linked to the processing of L2 cues. For example, in L1 acquisition, Bates et al. (1984) find that L1 learners of Italian and English learn the local cues related to contrastive stress and word order before they develop a more global discourse interpretation of these cues beginning at age 7.

A third factor in L2 learners' cue use appears to be increased proficiency or increased access to the L2. While some studies have indicated that highly advanced L2 learners may not use the L2 cues (Bates and MacWhinney 1981), other studies do demonstrate that increased access to the L2 facilitates increased utilization of L2 cue strategies. For instance, Gass (1987) finds that English L2 learners of Italian as opposed to their foreign-language learner counterparts begin to adopt L2-appropriate strategies, possibly owing to the increased exposure that they get in the second-language environment. In addition, studies which include L2 learners at different levels of proficiency do find evidence of a gradual shift from L1 strategy use by beginning learners to L2-like strategies by more advanced learners (Heilenman and McDonald 1993; McDonald and Heilenman 1992; Sasaki 1994).

L2 cue use seems to be affected by three factors: type of transfer (direct versus indirect), cue cost (perceivability), and access to the L2. The difficulty is in predicting L2 learner use of cues. Although findings have been inconclusive, several predictive influences have been suggested: word-order frequencies in the input, cue cost including both perceivability and assignability, and cue universality (Gass 1987; McDonald and Heilenman 1992).

Finally, the Competition Model as applied to L2 acquisition also raises some interesting issues concerning the quality of the input and individual differences. One might argue that the experimental input that is presented to these learners is at best awkward, as in the case of non-canonical word orders, and at worst completely ungrammatical, as in the instances of the omission of case markers. Sasaki (1991) cites this issue as a factor in the interpretation of Japanese word sequences by native Japanese speakers, and notes that the strings are seen as simply that: strings of words rather than possible utterances. The interpretations result from the fact that the sequences lack 'utteranceness' and are therefore not processed in the same way as are real language sequences. However, MacWhinney et al. (1985) report that Hungarian native speakers use the same strategies to process both grammatical and ungrammatical word sequences (that is, lacking obligatory accusative case marking). The issue of input is most probably language specific, and in a given language there are differing degrees of grammaticality (Gibson 1992).[13] As Sasaki (1991) notes, the Hungarian sequences are much more acceptable than are the Japanese sequences. A related input issue is the effect of presenting both canonical and non-canonical word orders. Sasaki (1997) finds that canonical word orders in Japanese and English are processed differently when they are presented alone from when they are presented together with non-canonical sequences. Clearly, the quality of the input and the type of presentation condition has an effect on L2 processing.

Many studies indicate interesting individual differences – for example, native speakers with diverse processing strategies (Harrington 1987; Wulfeck *et al.* 1986) and differences between foreign-language learners and L2 learners (Gass 1987; Sasaki 1991). Many other approaches to L2 acquisition also cite individual differences as an influential factor (e.g. the Multidimensional Model). The processing differences evidenced in these studies occur both with native and non-native speakers and do not appear to be language specific. In their review of the L2 studies, Kilborn and Ito (1989) discuss several possibilities for these differences: different treatments of canonical and non-canonical orders, a universal bias towards animacy, the effect of timed tasks on conflict resolution, and the immediately preceding context of the test sentences. While some of these factors are directly relevant to natural language use (e.g. the universality of animacy), others are more a matter of the experimental design (e.g. the presentation of non-canonical orders).

A Competition Model perspective on L2 acquisition generally deals with two issues: how L2 learners interpret the L2 input they get and whether L2 learners are able to learn to adopt the L2 processing strategies. These issues are related to the question of what learners attend to and how the learners' form–function mappings affect grammatical development.

5.6 Speech processing: the Multidimensional Model and Processability Theory

In addition to the information and input processing models, the Multidimensional Model (Meisel *et al.* 1981) introduced in Chapter 2 includes a processing dimension based on the notion of speech processing complexity. The Multidimensional Model grew out of the work of the ZISA (Zweitspracherwerb Italienischer und Spanischer Arbeiter) Project on L2 acquisition of German by foreign workers in Germany. Clahsen (1984) proposed a set of processing strategies as a component of the Multidimensional Model, which has been developed into Processability Theory (Pienemann 1997). We first examine the processing strategies proposed by Clahsen and then discuss the development of the Processability Theory formulated by Pienemann.

The processing component of the Multidimensional Model was explained by Clahsen (1984: 221), who proposed that linguistic structures which required a 'high degree of processing capacity will be acquired late'. His proposals were based on a linguistic analysis requiring movement rules (transformations) and a processing analysis applying different processing strategies to produce different grammatical structures. Crucially, the linguistic analysis relates one structure to another by means of movement. For example, a declarative sentence in English is related to a yes/no question by means of movement of the auxiliary verb from its canonical order after the subject to sentence-initial position: 'Jamie *can* bake good cookies' is transformed into '*Can* Jamie bake good cookies?' The canonical order of Subject–Aux–Verb–Object is seen as the basic underlying form which is transformed into a related, more complex form.

Language processing can be seen as the mapping of linguistic structure onto meaning, or, put differently, how the meaning of an utterance is encoded into a grammatical form. The underlying meaning of an utterance may be represented in different grammatical forms:

(5.15)
- (a) Tom gave the book to Mary yesterday.
- (b) Tom gave Mary the book yesterday.
- (c) Yesterday Tom gave the book to Mary.
- (d) The book was given to Mary yesterday by Tom.
- (e) Yesterday Mary was given the book by Tom.

Given that Clahsen's linguistic analysis is based on movement, the underlying linguistic elements may be restructured in several ways to produce the grammatical form of the utterance. Clahsen's processing analysis reflects the types of restructuring that the underlying meaning structure undergoes, and the processing complexity of an utterance for a learner is based on these different restructurings. Clahsen (1984: 221) argues that, 'As far as syntax is concerned, processing complexity results from reorderings and restructurings of various levels of underlying linguistic units' and proposes that a learner's degree of processing capacity is related to three processing constraints: the Canonical Order Strategy (COS), the Initialization/Finalization Strategy (IFS), and the Subordinate Clause Strategy (SCS). Clahsen (1980, 1984, 1988a, b; Clahsen and Muysken 1986) further claims that it is the combination of these three processing constraints that can account for the sequence of developmental stages of L2 acquisition of German word order and negation, as explicated below.

Clahsen (1988b: 58) defines the three processing constraints as follows:

(5.16) The Canonical Order Strategy (COS) allows only direct mappings of underlying structure to surface form due to the ease of processing.

(5.17) The Initialization/Finalization Strategy (IFS) allows sentence-initial and sentence-final permutations of underlying form.

(5.18) Subordinate Clause Strategy (SCS) prohibits any sort of permutation in embeddings.

The COS, as stated in (5.16), prohibits learners from moving a syntactic element out of its canonical order; in other words, nothing can be moved in or out of a sequence. For instance, given the canonical order W X Y Z, the only possible production is W X Y Z, which maintains the given canonical order.[14] This represents the easiest level of processing, because it is a direct mapping of underlying meaning structure (W X Y Z) to the grammatical form (W X Y Z).

The second strategy, the IFS as seen in (5.17), allows movement from sentence-final to sentence-initial position or from sentence-initial to sentence-final position. The canonical order, W X Y Z, can thus become respectively Z W X Y __ or __ X Y Z W. Sentence-initial and sentence-final positions are seen as salient positions; if movement is to be allowed, an element can only be moved into one of these easier sentence positions, and no permutations of elements into sentence-internal positions are allowed. The canonical order can, therefore, be altered but only in a prescribed way.

The third strategy, the SCS, prohibits any movement from canonical order in embedded clauses. At a level of processing complexity in which the L2 learner allows for movement in the main clause, movement is still prohibited in embedded clauses.

Each processing strategy above represents a different level of processing complexity. The COS, which prohibits any movement whatsoever, represents the most restrictive strategy. The IFS allows for permutations, which increase processing complexity, but restricts the types of permutations that are allowed. With the elimination of both the COS and the IFS, any permutations may be applied to non-embedded clauses. However, the SCS still restricts permutations in embedded clauses, which, because of their embedded structure, are more complex than non-embedded structures.[15] The learner's easing of each of these processing constraints has the following effects and accounts for the demonstrated developmental orders of acquisition of German word order (stages are designated by roman numerals) (adapted from Clahsen 1984; Pienemann 1984; and Pienemann and Johnston 1986):

(5.19)

	Processing complexity	Processing constraints
(I) W X Y Z	Do not interrupt the basic linguistic units by moving an element.	+COS, +IFS, +SCS
(II) W X Y Z → Z W X Y __	Move an element into an easy, salient position.	−COS, +IFS, +SCS
W X Y Z → __ X Y Z W		

(III) W X Y Z   →   Move an element   −COS, −IFS, +SCS
       W X Z Y __   into a less salient
                        position.

       W X Y Z   →
       W __ Y X Z
(IV)   W X Y Z   Move an element in   −COS, −IFS, −SCS
       [A B C]   →   embedded clauses.
       W X Y Z
       [B A __ C]

The processing constraints serve to determine the different stages of L2 development. The model is seen as multidimensional because it accounts for both developmental grammatical features that determine different stages of acquisition and grammatical features that vary within a given developmental stage. These two dimensions, the developmental and the variational, are seen as two different components comprising the Multidimensional Model, which thus offers a 'dynamic description of a developing grammatical system' (Pienemann *et al.* 1993).

The developmental features are the rules, such as those designated for German word order (e.g. particle shift or inversion), whose emergence is determined by the processing constraints. As discussed in Chapter 2, these rules emerge in an implicational order (ADV preposing > particle shift > inversion > verb to end), such that the rule of inversion in stage III cannot be acquired before the prerequisite rule of particle shift in stage II. A learner is said to have moved from one stage to the next based on the evidence of the first systematic use of a designated developmental grammatical feature in his or her speech production. Thus, it is the emergence of a designated grammatical feature rather than the learner's accuracy in producing the feature that determines the learner's stage of development. The acquisition of other grammatical features is not determined by processing constraints; these features have been designated as variational grammatical features. For example, the acquisition of the copula is not determined by processing constraints, and its emergence is therefore unrelated to the implicationally ordered rules.

Once a learner's developmental stage is determined by the emergence of the critical structures, not all learners are alike in their speech production at a given stage (Meisel *et al.* 1981). For instance, although two learners may be at stage III because they both produce inversion in required contexts such as questions, these two learners may differ in how often and how accurately they produce inversion. These differences are attributed to the learners' orientations. One learner may see language in terms of its integrative function and therefore values standard-like usage of the L2 in order to be seen as a member of the L2 community. Another learner may see language in terms of its instrumental function and therefore values the communication of information rather than membership in the L2 speech community. The result of such different orientations is that the first learner will strive towards accurate production of inversion, whereas the second learner will focus on communication and may produce the required inversion infrequently and inaccurately.

To sum up, the Multidimensional Model proposes that processing constraints determine the emergence of particular structural rules which are the indicators of successive developmental stages of L2 acquisition. Other structural rules, representing variational features, are not determined by the processing constraints. At each stage of development, L2 learners exhibit greater or lesser degrees of accuracy, and these learner differences can be attributed to differences in learners' orientations to language learning and communicating.

Various aspects of the Multidimensional Model have come under scrutiny – for example, the linguistic analysis (du Plessis *et al.* 1987; Mellow 1996; Pienemann and Johnston 1996; Tomaselli and Schwartz 1990), the distinction between developmental and variational features (Larsen-Freeman and Long 1991), the data collection techniques, the statistical analyses, and the applicability of the model (Hudson 1993; Pienemann *et al.* 1993; White 1991b). Perhaps for our purposes the most important issue involves the applicability of the model. If L2 acquisition is seen primarily as a process of grammar building, what can speech-processing constraints contribute to the acquisition process? In addition, much of the empirical research in support of the Multidimensional Model involves the acquisition of word order in German, a fairly limited application of a theory of L2 acquisition.

Pienemann (1997; Pienemann and Håkansson 1996) has extended this earlier work on processing into the Processability Theory and has addressed the issues of the applicability of the theory as well as the relation between language processing and language acquisition. Simply put, the Processability Theory states that 'the learner cannot access [structural] hypotheses which he/she cannot process' (Pienemann 1997: 3). In other words, given that processing mechanisms are distinct from linguistic knowledge, there may be linguistic structural options, or hypotheses, that the learner cannot access because the learner does not have the necessary processing resources available. From a processability perspective, L2 acquisition can be seen as the 'gradual acquisition of those very computational mechanisms.' Pienemann (1997: 3) argues that 'if one can determine how language processing develops in the learner, then one can predict which structural hypotheses the learner can entertain at what point in development'. The availability of these processing procedures then serves to determine L2 developmental stages. It is important to note that Pienemann is dealing not with the origin of the linguistic knowledge, but rather with the learners' ability to process that information in speech production. One's notion of linguistic knowledge and its origins is dependent upon the theory of language that is adopted – for example, Government and Binding Theory or Lexical Functional Grammar Theory.

The Processability Theory derives from three basic areas: a processing model of language production – the Incremental Procedural Grammar (Kempen and Hoenkamp 1987; Levelt 1989), a model of grammar – Lexical Functional Grammar (Kaplan and Bresnan 1982; Pinker 1984), and language acquisition data. Let us first look at a brief sketch of speech processing.

The process of speech production involves both grammatical information (e.g. morphological marking for number, tense, and gender) and propositional information (*the girl* and *her younger brother* as participants in the event of *watching* in 'The girl watches her younger brother'). The production of an utterance proceeds in step-by-step hierarchical fashion. For example, once the intended message has been conceptualized, the word, *girl*, is selected from the lexicon and is identified as a member of the noun category.[16] As a noun, the word *girl* may select from a number of options: it may take a definite or indefinite article based on its accessibility in the discourse; it may be marked for number as plural or singular, and it is designated as third person.

At the category level, these noun options are selected, and separate grammatical functorization rules begin to activate the necessary morphological markings: *the girl* selects the features of accessible, singular, and third person, and the grammatical rules activate the morpheme *the*. At the next level, the phrasal level, *the girl* is marked for grammatical function – in this case, the subject of the sentence. As the subject of the sentence, the noun phrase contains grammatical information (third person singular) that must be transferred to the verb. This grammatical information is held temporarily in a grammatical storage until the verb phrase is activated. As the procedure progresses, the sentence level, or syntactic procedures, relate the subject of the sentence to the verb and its complements, and word-order rules determine the order of these phrases in the sentence.

The grammatical information required is language specific, so that L2 learners must acquire the specifications for the particular lexical items in the L2 lexicon – for example, accessibility, number, and person for nouns in English but accessibility, number, person, gender, and case for nouns in German. Therefore, L1 English learners of L2 German must acquire the additional gender and case features for nouns. L2 learners must also acquire the specialized procedures for processing the specific L2 grammatical information; hence, L2 learners must learn the language-specific processing procedures for lexical categories, morphological marking, syntactic procedures, and word order rules.

According to Pienemann, this grammatical information derives from various sources which jointly produce grammatical morphemes during speech processing. He has designated *lexical* morphemes as those morphemes that are produced with the activation of the word from the lexicon; for example, the grammatical morpheme for past tense *-ed* is selected from the lexicon with the verb *talked*, and no syntactic procedure is required. *Phrasal* morphemes require the exchange of grammatical information based on the grammatical relationships within a given phrase. *Girls* is the head of the noun phrase *girls in* *my class*, and as a plural noun *girls* requires the agreement of other elements in the phrase: in this case the selection of the English marker for plural, *-s*, and the Ø marker to denote indefiniteness (rather than the indefinite article *a*). Finally, *inter-phrasal* morphemes involve the exchange of grammatical information across phrase boundaries, as in the singular, third person subject–verb agreement in *the girl watches*.

Two additional factors need to be considered. The first is that language processing is incremental; that is, the structure of the sentence is generated ' "from left to right" as successive fragments of the message become available' (Levelt 1989: 235). As a result, the subject noun phrase may be proceeding through the later sentence-level procedure while the agreeing verb phrase has yet to be activated at the lexical level. In such a case, any inter-phrasal morpheme must be held in the grammatical storage until the appropriate level of production is reached for the related phrases. Additionally, the grammatical information processed at a lower level is seen as a prerequisite for the processing procedures at the next higher level; lexical level information, such as the category designation of noun or verb, is a prerequisite for the subsequent category procedures, and so on. A visual display of this procedure might look like (5.20):

(5.20) Step-by-step left-to-right incremental processing

levels:

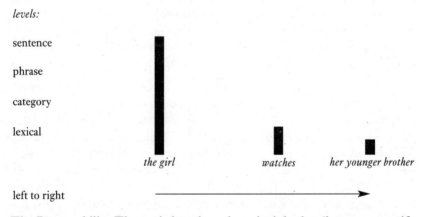

left to right

The Processability Theory is based on the principle that 'language-specific processing resources have to be acquired to make the processing of the L2 possible' (Pienemann and Håkansson 1996: 19). Given the incremental and ordered nature of the procedures, the processing procedures form a hierarchy – the Processability Hierarchy. Pienemann hypothesizes that the processing procedures will be acquired in their implicational sequence (from 1 to 6), as seen in (5.21) (adapted from Pienemann 1997: 10):

(5.21) Processability Hierarchy
   6 clause boundary
   5 sentence-procedure/word order rules
   4 grammatical function

3 phrasal procedure
2 category procedure
1 word procedure

This Processability Hierarchy represents Pienemann's hypothesis of 'how language processing develops in the learner'. The prediction of 'which structural hypotheses the learner can entertain at what point in development' is based partially on Pienemann's classification of grammatical morphemes into lexical, phrasal, and inter-phrasal morphemes and on the different processing mechanisms to be acquired. Also incorporated into these predictions is Clahsen's notion of perceptual saliency as stated in the IFS – that is, initial and final positions are seen as more prominent. These salient word order positions are proposed to be processable before non-salient positions. The Processability Hierarchy makes the following predictions for the acquisition of L2 grammatical structures (adapted from Pienemann 1997: 11):

(5.22) Predictions of the Processability Hierarchy

6 clause boundary	6 main and subordinate clauses
5 sentence procedure/word order rules B	5 inter-phrasal information exchange/ –saliency
4 sentence procedure/word order rules A	4 inter-phrasal information exchange/ +saliency
3 phrasal procedure	3 phrasal informational exchange
2 category procedure	2 lexical morphemes
1 word	1 words

The L2 learner entertains hypotheses about the structure of the L2 based on the Processability Hierarchy. This 'hypothesis space' is determined by applying the processability hierarchy to the grammar of the L2. Each developmental stage represents a hypothesis space in which certain structural hypotheses are possible because they are processable. As a result, the hypothesis space defines which IL grammars are options but does not determine which ones will be chosen. Pienemann has thus incorporated the developmental focus of the Multidimensional Model and has extended the application of the earlier model to grammatical information exchange beyond word order phenomena. He has formulated the Processability Theory as a component in L2 acquisition that is complementary to a linguistic theory (such as Lexical Functional Grammar), which would in turn address the issues of the nature and the origins of the learner's IL grammatical rules.

5.7 Questions explored: the Multidimensional Model and Processability Theory

● What is the role of cognitive processing in determining developmental stages?

- What is the role of cognitive processing in natural versus instructed second-language acquisition?
- How do processing constraints affect non-native speakers differently from the way they do native speakers?

5.7.1 WHAT IS THE ROLE OF COGNITIVE PROCESSING IN DETERMINING DEVELOPMENTAL STAGES?

The Multidimensional Model and the Processability Theory both propose speech-processing accounts for L2 developmental stages. Let us first reconsider the acquisition of German word order rules in the light of the application of Clahsen's proposed processing strategies. Clahsen proposes that L2 learners of German regardless of their L1 begin with a basic SVO word order[17] and arrive at the native-like word order by relaxing the processing constraints. This process results in the following stages of development (designated below with roman numerals) (adapted from Clahsen 1984: 224–5):[18]

(5.23)

    (I) SVO   +COS +IFS (+SCS)

    None of the German word order rules is applied. The constituents appear in the fixed linear order:

    NP   ({ AUX/MOD })   V   (NP)   (PP)

    Sie hat gekauft das Buch in der Buchhandlung.

    She has bought the book in the bookstore.

    (II) ADV-preposing   +COS +IFS (+SCS)

    Adverbials (=adverbs and prepositional phrases) are moved into sentence-initial position.

    Gestern   sie hat gekauft das Buch.

    Yesterday she has bought the book.

    (III) Particle shift   –COS +IFS (+SCS)

    Nonfinite parts of discontinuous verbal elements are moved into sentence-final position. This rule applies to the following structural contexts:

    (a) separable prefixes

    (b) participles in AUX + V structures

    (c) infinitives in MOD + V structures

    (a) Sie schlägt das Buch *auf*.

       She opens the book up.

    (b) Sie hat   das Buch *gekauft*.

       She has   the book bought.

    (c) Sie muss   das Buch *lesen*.

       She must   the book read.

(IV) (Subject–Verb) inversion   –COS   –IFS   (+SCS)
Following preposed complements and in interrogatives, the subject
appears immediately after the finite verb.
Wo   hat *sie* das Buch gekauft.
Where has she the book bought.

(V) ADV–VP   –COS   –IFS   (+SCS)
Adverbials can be placed optionally between the finite verb and the
object.
Sie hat *gestern*   das Buch gekauft.
She has yesterday the book bought.

(VI) V to end   –COS   –IFS   –SCS
In embedded sentences the finite verb appears in clause-final
position.
Ich weiß dass sie gestern   das Buch gekauft *hat*.
I   know that she yesterday the book bought has.

As Clahsen accounts for the evidenced developmental stages by the easing of
the COS, IFS, and SCS, he has suggested that certain stages could be collapsed.
For example, stage I and stage II above both conform to the same processing
strategies (+COS, +IFS, +SCS) since the movement of adverbials to sentence-
initial position does not involve the disruption of the canonical order of
subjects, verbs, and objects. Similarly, stage IV and stage V can be collapsed into
one stage (–COS, –IFS, +SCS). Since the SCS is only relevant to embedded
clauses, it is not seen as applicable to the structures produced in stages I
through IV. The revised stages of development are represented in (5.24).

(5.24)
  (I) SVO   ADV-Preposing
 (II) Topicalization[19]   Particle Shift
(III) Inversion   ADV-VP
(IV) V to End (only in embedded clauses)

These stages of acquisition in accordance with the three proposed processing
strategies have been confirmed in a number of different studies for German word
order (Clahsen 1984; Clahsen and Muysken 1986; Meisel *et al.* 1981; Pienemann
1980), German negation (Clahsen 1984, 1988a), and German verbal morphology
(Pienemann 1987). Work has also been completed on the application of the
model to L2 acquisition of English (Pienemann and Johnston 1986, 1987).
    Pienemann (1997; Pienemann and Håkansson 1996) reconsiders these
findings from the perspective of the predictions of Processability Theory and
extends the analysis to L2 acquisition of Swedish. Pienemann has chosen to
interpret the Processability Hierarchy through a Lexical Functional Grammar
analysis, because of its compatibility with the Incremental Procedural
Grammar model of speech processing. Unlike the movement-driven linguistic
analysis employed by Clahsen, this linguistic analysis (Kaplan and Bresnan

1982; Pinker 1984) lists a number of equations which interact to create the correct word orders; a grammatical sentence must conform to all of the relevant constraining equations.

By applying a Lexical Functional Grammar-based analysis to the L2 German structures under investigation, Pienemann makes the following predictions for L2 developmental stages (Pienemann 1997):

(5.25) Predictions of the Processability Hierarchy for German word order rules

6 main and subordinate clauses	6 V to End
5 inter-phrasal information exchange/−saliency	5 Inversion
4 inter-phrasal information exchange/+saliency	4 Particle Shift
3 phrasal informational exchange	3 ADV Preposing
2 lexical morphemes	2 SVO
1 words	1 words

The predictions of the Processability Hierarchy are borne out in the studies of L2 German word order. Similarly, Pienemann and Håkansson (1996) re-evaluate the findings of 14 empirical studies of L2 acquisition of Swedish in light of the predictions of the Processability Hierarchy. The reanalysis confirms that the predictions of the Processability Hierarchy are consistent with the orders of acquisition demonstrated in the body of research on L2 Swedish.

The original German word-order studies and the reanalysis of the Swedish studies demonstrate that the processability of grammatical structures may be a determining factor in the L2 developmental stages evidenced in these studies. While these accounts do not address the origins of the linguistic knowledge in the L2 learner's grammar, Pienemann (1997) argues that a processability approach can define the hypothesis space in which a learner may produce a given linguistic structure.

5.7.2 WHAT IS THE ROLE OF COGNITIVE PROCESSING IN NATURAL VERSUS INSTRUCTED SECOND-LANGUAGE ACQUISITION?

While the original research which led to the proposal of the Multidimensional Model was based on natural L2 acquisition, one extension of the model is the examination of the interaction between instruction and the developmental stages demonstrated in natural L2 acquisition. Do the developmental stages that are manifested in natural L2 acquisition also occur in an instructed language acquisition setting or does language instruction influence the course of L2 development? The answer to both of these questions is 'yes'. Pienemann (1984, 1989) found that learners followed the same sequence of development in an instructed L2 setting as did learners in a natural setting; in other words, the demonstrated stages of development were determined by the processing constraints regardless of instruction.

In one study (Pienemann 1984), child L2 learners of German who had not yet learned the rule for inversion were given explicit instruction on inversion and were taped in both formal interview and informal play settings. Recall the implicational hierarchy of the rules determining the developmental stages: ADV preposing > particle shift > inversion > verb to end. Learners who had not yet acquired the prerequisite rule particle shift were unable to use inversion productively, although they were able to produce memorized phrases containing inversion and to repeat phrases with inversion. Only those learners who had already reached the prerequisite stage of particle shift were able to learn and use the inversion rule productively.

This is not to say that instruction did not have any influence. While only those learners who were 'ready' actually acquired the structure, instruction did have an effect. The learners who learned the inversion rule did differ from natural learners in three ways: they learned the rule more quickly; they provided more frequent applications of the inversion rule, and they applied the rule in a larger range of obligatory contexts (with preposed adverbs, preposed object noun phrases, wh-questions, and yes/no questions).

Pienemann (1989) also examined classroom input to the learners in relation to the learners' acquisition of the different word order rules. No matter how early a given structure was introduced either explicitly or implicitly, the adult L2 learners of German followed the same natural developmental sequence. These instructed L2-acquisition results led Pienemann to propose the Teachability Hypothesis, in which he suggests that the influence of formal instruction is subject to some of the same constraints which determine the course of natural acquisition.

One final finding from these instructional studies helps to support the distinction between developmental features and variational features. While instruction did not change the order of acquisition of the developmental features, it did have an effect on the variational features; in this case, the frequency with which the learners produced the copula increased considerably following the instruction. Pienemann concluded from this finding that 'variational features appear to be free of the kinds of constraints which affect the teachability of developmental features: once a variational feature can be produced at all, it can be said to be teachable' (1989: 61).

In short, the instructional studies show that, in terms of developmental features, learners cannot skip developmental stages, but they can be helped through the appropriate stages with instruction. Variational features, however, are not constrained by processing mechanisms, as are the developmental features.

5.7.3 HOW DO PROCESSING CONSTRAINTS AFFECT NON-NATIVE SPEAKERS DIFFERENTLY FROM THE WAY THEY DO NATIVE SPEAKERS?

Much of L2-acquisition research examines the differences between L1 acquisition and L2 acquisition, as in the UG accessibility research. From a processing perspective, one might ask whether or not language processing is a determining factor in L1- and L2-acquisition differences.

Pienemann (1997) poses this question in terms of the Processability Theory. In a comparison of developmental stages for monolingual L1, L2, bilingual L1 (2L1), and specific language impairment (SLI) learners, he shows that each of the demonstrated developmental sequences, while not identical in comparison to each other, produces stages which fall within the hypothesis space predicted by the Processability Hierarchy, as exemplified in (5.25). Because of this adherence to the Processability Hierarchy, he concludes that processability does not account for the differences between L1, L2, 2L1, and SLI acquisition.[20]

Instead, he suggests that the differences in developmental sequences result from a process of 'generative entrenchment'. Generative entrenchment essentially constrains the process of development by preserving and refining all structures throughout the course of development. As a result, initial structural decisions cannot be discarded and must, therefore, be incorporated into later stages. While the Processability Hierarchy defines the possible grammars within the hypothesis space, generative entrenchment determines that one path of development must be followed as opposed to another because of the previous hypotheses that the learner has made.

Pienemann exemplifies this effect of generative entrenchment by comparing the stages of German word order development for monolingual L1 and L2 learners. German word order follows a verb–second rule which requires that the finite verb always occurs in the second position in a main clause; the first position may be filled by a subject NP, a wh-pronoun, a preposed adverbial, or a preposed object NP, as shown in (5.26):

(5.26)

Position	1	2	3	4	5
(a) subject	Sie	*hat*	das Buch	gekauft.	
	She	has	the book	bought.	
(b) wh-pronoun	Was	*hat*	sie	gekauft?	
	What	has	she	bought?	
(c) adverb	Gestern	*hat*	sie	das Buch	gekauft.
	Yesterday	has	she	the book	bought.
(d) object	Das Buch	*hat*	sie	gekauft.	
	the book	has	she	bought.	

The basic difference between the L2 and L1 sequences, as indicated in (5.27) (adapted from Pienemann 1997), is that L2 learners begin with an SVO canonical word order, whereas L1 learners begin with an SOV order. This initial L2 choice of SVO necessitates that the L2 learners develop the particle shift and inversion rules to get the finite and nonfinite verbs in the correct positions; these rules are not necessary to arrive at the correct word order with the initial SOV hypothesis found in the L1 sequences.

(5.27) Processability Hierarchy Hypothesis Space and developmental stages
for German monolingual L1 and L2 word order

Stage resources	German L2	German L1
6 +/- ROOT clauses	6 V to End	6 V to End (no errors)
5 S-procedures/ Word Order rules	5 Inversion (+/- verbal agreement)	5 V 2nd (+ verbal agreement)
4 S-procedures/ Word Order rules	4 Particle Shift	4 ——
3 phrasal procedures	3 ADV Preposing	3 ——
2 lexical categories	2 SVO	2 SOV
1 words	1 words	1 words

From this analysis of language-acquisition data, the Processability Hierarchy
defines the ordered stages through which a learner may pass, but the actual
paths taken depend upon the previous structural decisions that have been
made. In accordance with his separation of the linguistic and processing
components of L2 acquisition, Pienemann relegates the question of why L1
and L2 learners make different developmental choices in the first place to the
research which explores the linguistic component.

One contribution of this speech-processing approach is that it correctly
predicts the developmental stages that occur in L2 acquisition. As a result, it
also identifies the 'hypothesis space' within which a learner at a given stage will
operate. One problem with this approach may be the over-reliance on
performance data, an issue that we return to below.

5.8 Conclusion

Let us now return to our original concern: 'What can processing models tell us
about how L2 learners acquire an L2 grammar?' In part, the answer to this
question depends on one's definition of 'acquire an L2'. In Chapter 1 we
discussed different perspectives on definitions of syntax and definitions of
acquisition. One's view of the relevance of processing models depends on one's
perspective on the scope of the acquisition of syntax. As we shall see, this
question is also not so easily answered in view of the complexity of the issues
involved: processing of input versus processing of output or speech
production, the relationship between the IL grammar and the IL production,
the relationship between input and intake, and the role of comprehension and
production in language acquisition. In addition, several input and processing
factors are proposed to be influential in L2 acquisition. An examination of these

factors will help to organize the information that is available from the processing research.

One can argue, as White (1991b) does, that we must be careful to distinguish between the processing of input – reception – and the processing of output – production of sentences. The processing of input involves the assignment of grammatical structure onto the incoming linguistic data. Input-processing mechanisms are seen as separate from the grammar, although the processing mechanisms do have access to that grammar in order to assign structure to the input. White also notes that the mechanisms involved in input processing are unlikely to be the same as those involved in speech production, and, while speech–production mechanisms also have access to the grammar, there is no direct connection between the two distinct types of processing mechanisms. White concludes that processing mechanisms involved with the parsing of incoming input may have an influence on grammar building, but speech-production processes do not.

Another issue related to the reception/production question is the relationship between IL grammatical competence and IL production. Learners can often comprehend more than they can produce. If a learner can comprehend a given input, the learner must have an IL grammar that can assign an interpretation to that input. What can account for the learner's ability to comprehend but not produce a given structure? White (1991b) suggests that, while a rule may be a part of the IL grammar, its absence in the production may be related to speech-production factors rather than competence factors. In the same manner, Sharwood Smith (1986) proposes that the distinction between competence and control makes the difference. The learner may have acquired a given grammatical structure but may not have the requisite control to produce that structure. In other words, developmental sequences may in fact reflect two different orders: a competence order and a control order. Sharwood Smith further suggests that the relationship between competence and performance is not as transparent as we would like to believe. White (1991b) points out that this is a problem with production data because the relationship between the acquisition of an IL grammar and the IL production is not clear.

Given a distinction between reception and production processes and grammatical competence and performance, we can begin to examine the input and output processing factors that have an effect on L2 acquisition. Krashen (1982, 1985) and VanPatten (1990, 1996) have argued that comprehensible, meaning-bearing input facilitates L2 acquisition. White (1987a) has proposed that 'incomprehensible input', or input that cannot be parsed by the IL grammar, is necessary for grammar building. That is, the learner must be pushed by the incomprehensible input to restructure the IL grammar to account for that input. Faerch and Kasper (1986: 257) also point to the lack of comprehension as the determining factor. They suggest that there is a distinction between 'input functioning as intake for comprehension and input functioning as intake for learning' and that theories of acquisition need to be able to predict when input for comprehension will become intake for learning and when it will not. They state that:

> if input is to function as intake to the learning of high-level L2 material, learners need to experience comprehension problems; such problems have to be perceived as deficits in their knowledge structure, not in the input; finally, these gaps need to be considered the responsibility of the learner herself and not of the interlocutor. (Faerch and Kasper 1986: 270)

While the comprehension of input, and the lack thereof, can be seen as factors contributing to the restructuring of IL grammar, the relationship between comprehension and grammatical competence is also all but clear. For example, Bley-Vroman (1991) points out that learners can comprehend L2 input that does not match the rules of the IL grammar by 'suspending' the IL rules to allow for a partial interpretation of the L2 input.

In addition to comprehensible and incomprehensible input, Schmidt (1990, 1993, 1994, 1995; Schmidt and Frota 1986) suggests that learners must 'notice' a grammatical form as a necessary condition for acquisition – i.e. that intake is the part of the input that the learner attends to and notices. Similarly, Gass (1988a) has proposed that there are different levels of input as it is processed by the learner. 'Apperceived input', the first level, is characterized as input that is noticed by the learner. Gass claims (1988a: 203) that attention is 'what allows a learner to notice a mismatch between what he or she produces/knows and what is produced by speakers of the second language'. The next level of input is 'comprehended input', input that is accepted by the learner as intake. Tomlin and Villa (1994: 190–3), however, argue that the notion of attention as applied to L2 acquisition actually conflates three separate notions: alertness (the learner's state of readiness with regards to incoming data), orientation (the direction of attentional resources to the data), and detection (the 'cognitive registration' of the data). From this perspective, Tomlin and Villa (1994: 199) redefine Schmidt's notion of 'noticing' as 'detection within selective attention'.[21] As the notions of comprehensible, incomprehensible, apperceived and comprehended input, and attention demonstrate, any discussion of input in relation to acquisition must include both the input conditions necessary to provide learners with the appropriate kind of input and learner conditions that facilitate the processing of that input into intake.

What do the processing approaches reveal about how input becomes intake? The research on structured input shows that in some learning contexts – with difficult-to-detect structures – structured, meaning-bearing input can focus the learners' attention on the grammatical form and can result in improved comprehension and production, thus providing comprehensible, apperceived, and comprehended input. The Competition Model research demonstrates what L2 learners attend to in their interpretations of L2 sequences – for example, word order, animacy, verbal morphology, or pronominal morphology.

The fact that L2 learners can and do change their processing strategies suggests that using incorrect strategies results in incomprehensible input – an incorrect form–function mapping. These incorrect results force the learner eventually to adopt the correct processing strategy leading to a form–function mapping that is consistent with the L2 input. Hence, L2 research examining the processing of input from the perspective of the Input Processing Model and the Competition Model offers insights into how learners attend to and interpret input, making that input available as possible intake.

What about L2 production? Pienemann (1997) has specifically stated that Processability Theory is not directed at how linguistic knowledge is created – that is, the theory is not about grammar building. This perspective is consistent with White's (1991b) view that speech processing relates more to language use than the building of grammatical competence and with Sharwood Smith's (1986) proposal of different competence and control orders. This is also supported by the fact that the German L2 data come from speech-production tasks.

The results of these studies are intriguing, however. For example, in addition to the German L2 data, the Processability Hierarchy also accounts for the Swedish L2 data, some of which does not come from speech production tasks but from a written cloze test in which learners fill in the blanks (Hyltenstam 1977). Clearly, written production is a type of production, but it is also clear that speech production in an interview setting is not the same task as filling in a cloze passage.

Several other questions also come to mind. Does the Processability Hierarchy also constrain the L2 learner's ability to make grammaticality judgements about L2 structures? Is the Processability Hierarchy also related to the processing of input? This question is pertinent, since the increasing domains of the hypothesis space of the Processability Hierarchy from lexical to phrasal to inter-phrasal are similar to the local and global cue strategies hypothesized in the Competition Model.

For instance, does the Processability Hierarchy also constrain a learner's focus of attention in comprehension? Recall that one of the instructional studies (Pienemann 1989) shows that L2 learners of German are unable to produce a grammatical structure until the prerequisite stage has been reached no matter how much earlier the structure had been available in the input either explicitly or implicitly. Similarly, Schmidt and Frota (1986: 280) report that, until a particular structure – the long question form in Portuguese, *o que é que* – was noticed (in journal entry, week 21), Schmidt was unable to produce it and unaware of it in the input, even though it was commonly available in the input and had been instructed 'way back in the beginning'. Further research in this area with a greater variety of elicitation techniques and tasks may be able to address some of these issues.

Finally, Swain (1985) has suggested that learner production may be required for language development. Swain posits 'comprehensible output' as necessary for advanced L2 acquisition because her research into L2 acquisition by immersion students shows that 'comprehensible input' is not a sufficient condition for L2 acquisition. In her view, learners reach a stage where they can understand and be understood based on the IL grammar they have developed, but language development fossilizes before native-like performance is achieved. In this early work, Swain (1985: 248–9) suggests that the L2 output serves various purposes: (1) as 'contextualized' language in which one learns to speak by speaking, (2) as 'pushed' language use in which the learner is forced to restate the message due to negative feedback, (3) as a hypothesis-testing function, and (4) as a means to move from semantic to syntactic processing.[22] More recently, Swain (1995) has proposed that output can promote grammatical accuracy in three ways: by serving a noticing function, a hypothesis-testing function, and a reflective function. In other words, output can force a learner to notice the 'gap between what they *want* to say and what they *can* say' (Swain 1995: 126). Output also offers the learner a context in which to test hypotheses and get feedback. Finally, output allows learners to reflect on their own language. Swain is careful to note that not all output serves this function, but rather output in which learners 'negotiate about form'.

If the learner is indeed forced to analyse the L2 syntactically in the production process (as opposed to predominantly semantic analyses in the comprehension process), the push to produce 'comprehensible output' may serve as the mechanism that forces the learner to attend to a particular grammatical form. While Swain has proposed 'comprehensible output' as necessary for advanced L2 acquisition, is it also required for all levels of L2 acquisition? From the perspective of the Processability Theory, the learner would be unable to consider a structural hypothesis until the prerequisite processing mechanisms had been acquired. In this case, the hypothesis space allowed by the Processability Hierarchy would constrain the possible forms that 'comprehensible output' could take.

This current L2 research that focuses on grammatical form underscores the importance of many of the issues addressed in these different processing approaches. Moreover, the processing approaches highlight the various aspects of L2 acquisition – input, intake, grammar development, and production – that are not often directly addressed in other L2 research paradigms.

Notes

1. Bialystok (1990a) argues, however, that this distinction is not so clear-cut in the case of IL, which represents an incomplete grammatical rule system and is marked by variability.
2. McLaughlin (1990) traces the concept of restructuring to the work of Jean Piaget.
3. Bialystok (1992: 504) refers to these two dimensions as two cognitive processes: analysis of representational structures and control of attentional processing.

4. Robinson (1996: 10–11) notes three different senses of the term 'implicit knowledge' – innate grammatical constraints (such as UG), linguistic knowledge that has become automatized through practice, and knowledge that has been learned without conscious awareness of or intent to learn the rules.

5. While it is impossible to cite all of the research on input here, several issues have been examined quite extensively: the types of input necessary for acquisition (Lightbown 1985, 1992; Schwartz 1993b; Sharwood Smith 1993; White 1987a, 1992b; White *et al.* 1991), learner interaction and input (Braidi 1995; Chaudron 1988; Gass and Varonis 1989; Long 1983a, b, c; Pica 1988, 1994; Pica and Doughty, 1985; Wesche 1994), and learner processing of input (Faerch and Kasper 1986; Gass 1988a; Schmidt and Frota 1986; Sharwood Smith 1991).

6. Krashen (1985: 2) formulated 'comprehensible input' as 'i + 1', where 'i' represents the learner's current level of competence, and 'i + 1' represents the next level of acquisition along a proposed natural order of acquisition.

7. The issues of learner attention, consciousness, and awareness are currently under debate. One issue in the debate concerns whether or not conscious attention is required for learning (e.g. Hulstijn and de Graff 1994; Robinson 1996, Schmidt 1990, 1994, 1995; Tomlin and Villa 1994; VanPatten 1994).

8. In a study of the effects of written input enhancement with the grammatical items (Spanish relative pronouns and present perfect verb forms) printed in emboldened, upper-case letters, Shook (1994) finds that calling the learners' attention to the grammatical form results in better overall production of the forms as opposed to recognition of the forms.

9. In each case, the difference in pronunciation is minimal.

10. Additional cues have been studied in native-speaker sentence processing. For example, research in Chinese has included the object marker *ba* and the passive marker *bei* (Li *et al.* 1992) and research in English and Dutch has included relative clauses and dative constructions (McDonald 1987b).

11. In a study in which case marking in German was not included, MacWhinney *et al.* (1984) state that, since subject–verb agreement may be ambiguous, native German speakers also use animacy cues as a reliable cue. Li *et al.* (1993) find both word-order and morphological cues used in Chinese in addition to the dominant animacy cue.

12. While perceivability should also be a factor in L2 learners' processing of unstressed clitic pronouns in French, Heilenman and McDonald (1993) find that low-level L2 learners of French are able to perceive object clitic pronouns in the experimental sentences, all of which are clearly pronounced with definite word boundaries. In these cases, the learners interpret the object clitic pronouns based on the transfer of English word order strategies: they translate the sentences word by word and assign the subject role to the object pronouns.

13. Gibson (1992) reviews the soundness of the Competition Model as a model of language acquisition and language processing and cites several difficulties with the model, including the definitions of cue and cue validity, the identification of cues, the measuring of cue validities, and the experimental paradigm.
14. This schema is based on Pienemann and Johnston (1986).
15. Clahsen (1984: 221–2) formalized the Canonical Order Strategy and the Initialization/Finalization Strategy as follows:
    Canonical Order Strategy (COS): in underlying sequences
    $[X_1 + X_2 + \ldots + X_n]_{CX}[\ ]_{CX+1} \ldots [\ ]_{CX+m'}$ in which each subconstituent X_1, X_2, $\ldots X_n$ contributes information to the internal structure of the constituent C_X, no subconstituent is moved out of C_X, and no material from the subsequent constituents C_{X+1}, C_{X+2}, $\ldots C_{X+m}$ is moved into C_X.
    Initialization/Finalization Strategy (IFS): in underlying sequences $[X\ Y\ Z]_S$ permutations are blocked which move X between Y and Z and/or Z between X and Y.
16. Each lexical entry in the mental lexicon contains four types of features: meaning, syntactic, morphological, and phonological features. The term *word* is used here in place of the technical term *lemma*, which designates the meaning and syntactic features of a word's lexical entry as separate from the word's morphological and phonological features (Levelt 1989: 187).
17. This preliminary analysis has been challenged (e.g. du Plessis *et al.* 1987; Tomaselli and Schwartz 1990).
18. The specification of the applicability of the processing constraints (±COS, ±IFS and ±SCS) and the example sentences have been added.
19. Topicalization refers to movement of the object NP out of the VP and into initial position, as seen in
    Das Buch sie hat gekauft gestern.
    the book   she has bought yesterday.
20. Interestingly, he reports two similar sequences: one sequence for child L2, adult L2, SLI, and L1 acquisition of the weaker language in bilingual children and another sequence for monolingual L1 and L1 acquisition of the stronger language in bilingual children.
21. For reviews of the issue of attention in L2 acquisition, see Schmidt (1990, 1994, 1995) and Robinson (1996).
22. Braidi (1991a) points out that 'comprehensible output' is a misnomer; Swain implies that the output must not only be comprehensible, but must also be grammatically accurate. As Swain herself notes (1985: 249), learners do not appear to be under pressure to be more comprehensible than they already are. Thus, Swain implies that it is *accurate* comprehensible output that is a 'necessary mechanism' for L2 acquisition.

6

Functional approaches

6.1 Introduction

6.1.1 FUNCTIONAL GRAMMAR

Functional approaches to grammar, as indicated in Chapter 1, are much broader in scope than purely syntactic approaches. The first section of the present chapter introduces the notions of functional grammar (Givón 1984a, b, 1990, 1993; Halliday 1994) and grammaticalization (Dittmar 1992) and presents a number of the specific functions and structures that are explored in the L2 research. The remainder of the chapter, as in previous chapters, examines the questions addressed in the L2 literature.

The assumption underlying functional approaches to grammar is that the grammatical structures in a language are closely related to the semantic – (meaning) – and pragmatic – (use) – functions that they perform. Givón (1993: 21) suggests that human language has two major tasks: mental representation of experience and its communication to others.[1] From this perspective, grammar is seen as a 'set of strategies that one employs in order to produce *coherent communication*' (Givón 1993: 1, emphasis in the original). A functional view of grammar thus unites the notions of grammar and use of grammar within a context, unlike an autonomous view of grammar, which separates grammatical competence from performance. Such a pragmatic view also takes into account the use of language in social interaction and the effects of that interaction on the form of the language used.

While we may already have a sense of what a grammatical structure or grammatical rule is, it is important at this point to specify what is included in the semantic and pragmatic functions of language. Semantic functions include the thematic roles of the participants in the activity that is denoted by the verb. For example, a participant may be the agent of an action, as is *Charlie* in (6.1a), or a participant may be seen as a recipient or beneficiary, as is *Jill* in (6.1c). In addition, several distinct thematic roles are possible:

(6.1)
  (a) *Charlie* read the book.   agent

(b) Sally took *Tracy* to the airport.   patient
(c) Marie gave the book to *Jill*.   beneficiary
(d) The bird came from *Brazil*.   source
(e) We are going to the *store*.   goal
(f) Chase cut the pie with a *knife*.   instrument
(g) The *children* saw the rainbow.   experiencer
(h) I felt the *breeze* on my face.   stimulus

All systems which characterize the various thematic roles (e.g. Fillmore 1968; Frawley 1992; Jackendoff 1987; Van Valin 1996) differentiate between the grammatical function of an entity – for example, the subject of the sentence – and the thematic role of an entity. If we compare (6.1a) and (6.1g) above, both *Charlie* and the *children* are the grammatical subjects of their respective sentences, but their thematic roles differ. *Charlie* is seen as an active agent in the activity, whereas the *children* do not purposefully seek to *see* the rainbow in the same way that *Charlie* goes about *reading* the book. To understand this difference, the more passive meaning of *see* can be contrasted with the more purposeful meaning of *look for*, which, like *read*, would require the thematic role of agent.

In addition to thematic roles, semantic functions also include the semantic properties of an entity. For example, is the entity animate; is the entity human? Clearly, in (6.1), *Charlie* is both animate and human; the *bird* is animate only, and the *breeze* is neither. Not only do thematic roles and semantic properties of entities and verbs contribute to the meaning of a sentence, but so too do the semantic concepts of time, space, and modality. All of these semantic concepts are included in the semantic functions of grammatical structures.

The pragmatic function relates to the use of grammatical structures. Let us take the notion of topic as an example. We can examine this notion from both a syntactic and a discourse perspective. Within a sentence we can simply consider the topic of the sentence as the 'entity (person, thing, etc.) about which something is said' (Crystal 1991: 354). The sentence will also contain a comment about the sentence topic.

(6.2)
(a) John bought a book.
(b) As for that book, John bought it.
(c) That book, I don't like (it).

In (6.2a), *John* is seen as the topic of the sentence and *bought a book* is the comment that is being made about *John*. In English, the sentence topic is most closely identified with the noun that functions as the grammatical subject of the sentence, and the comment is identified with the predicate. However, English does have structures which serve to topicalize elements other than the subject of the sentence, such as the *as for* construction in (6.2b) and the leftward movement – the left dislocation – of the direct object *that book* in (6.2c). Other languages, such as Japanese, use grammatical particles explicitly to mark the topic of the sentence as opposed to the subject, as seen in (6.3) (adapted from Levinson 1983: 88):

(6.3)
   (a) ano-hon-wa   John-ga   kat-ta
   (b) That book-topic John-subject bought
   (c) 'As for that book, John bought it.'

The particle *wa* marks the topic, and the particle *ga* marks the subject.

From a typological perspective, according to Li and Thompson (1976), languages differ as to their basic underlying sentential structures; some languages are classified as subject-prominent languages with a subject-predicate sentence structure as in English, while other languages are classified as topic-prominent with an underlying topic-comment sentence structure as in Chinese.[2] Li and Thompson outline a number of identifying characteristics of both topic-prominent and subject-prominent languages. For example, topic-prominent languages have the following characteristics (adapted from Li and Thompson: 466–70):

(6.4) Characteristics of topic-prominent languages
   (a) Topics will be overtly marked as topics; subjects need not be marked as subjects.
      Mandarin (the topic is always in initial position):
      Nèike shù yèzi   dà
      that   tree leaves big
      'That tree (topic), the leaves are big.'
      Japanese (the topic is overtly marked):
      Sakana wa   tai   ga   oisii
      fish   topic, red snapper subject delicious
      'Fish (topic), red snapper is delicious.'

   (b) Passive constructions either do not occur or occur rarely as marginal constructions with specialized meanings.

   (c) 'Dummy' subjects, such as English *it* and *there*, German *es*, and French *il* and *ce*, do not occur.
      Mandarin:
      Zhèr   hěn   rè
      here   very   hot
      'It is hot in here.'

   (d) 'Double-subject' constructions, with two consecutive noun phrases, are pervasive.
      Japanese:
      Sakana wa   tai   ga oisii
      fish   topic, red snapper subj delicious
      'Fish (topic), red snapper is delicious.'

(e) The topic, not the subject, controls coreferential constituent deletion.
Mandarin:
Nèike shù yèzi   dà, suǒyi wǒ bu xǐhuan Ø
that tree   leaves big so I not like   Ø
'That tree (topic), the leaves are big, so I don't like *it*.'
Nèi kuài tián dàozi zhǎnge hěn dà, suǒyi Ø hěn zhìgián.
that piece land rice grow very big so   Ø very valuable.
'That piece of land (topic), rice grows very big, so *it* (the land) is very valuable.'

(f) Verbs tend to occur in clause-final position.

(g) There are no constraints on what may be the topic.

(h) Topic-comment sentence structure is considered a basic sentence structure.

While topic-prominent and subject-prominent sentence structures are a syntactic notion, as we will see below, these structures figure prominently in predictions about the pragmatic nature of early L2 acquisition.

The notion of topic is also related to how a discourse is structured. Written and spoken discourses relate both new and known – or given – information.[3] In this case, the topic is the given information. However, in a specific discourse, how do we identify whether the information being communicated is considered new information or given information identifying the topic? While, in an idealized situation, the structures contain both given and new information, as in the examples noted in (6.3), in some instances only new information is presented, because, as Halliday (1994: 296) notes, the 'discourse has to start somewhere'. Therefore, how is the topic of the discourse first established, and how is that topic maintained throughout the discourse? In order to exemplify these issues, consider the following discourse in English, the beginning of a fable entitled 'The Boy who Called Wolf':

(6.5)
(a) Once upon a time, *there* was *a* young shepherd.
(b) *The* shepherd was responsible for guarding *a* small flock of sheep.
(c) However, instead of watching the sheep, *he* preferred to watch the clouds in the sky and Ø daydream.

In this discourse, the existence of the shepherd is presented as new information in (6.5a) with the grammatical structure '*there was*'. We also know that the shepherd is not known because of the use of the indefinite article *a*. In (6.5b) the use of the definite article *the* indicates that the shepherd is now a familiar, known entity at this point in the discourse, but '*a* small flock of sheep' is not. In addition, once the topic of the discourse, the shepherd, is introduced, this topic is maintained through the use of anaphora – that is, the use of grammatical devices which get their meaning from a previously mentioned element. In this case, the anaphoric pronoun *he* and the zero anaphor Ø both refer back to *the shepherd* in (6.5c).

The distinction between given and new information may not be refined enough for the distinctions that speakers and writers actually make. In creating a discourse, speakers and writers make assumptions about the addressee's different levels of knowledge about and levels of attention to the participants in the discourse (Gundel *et al.* 1993; Prince 1981). For instance, Gundel, Hedberg, and Zacharski (1993) propose a Givenness Hierarchy that consists of six categories: in focus > activated > familiar > uniquely identifiable > referential > type identifiable.[4] These narrower distinctions give a clearer indication of how speakers and writers continually make assumptions about the addressee's awareness of the participants in the discourse. Based on these assumptions, speakers and writers choose the grammatical devices to match the addressees' appropriate assumed levels of knowledge and awareness. For instance, Gundel *et al.* (1993: 275) propose the following grammatical structures to correspond to different levels of givenness:

(6.6)

(a)	in focus	it
(b)	activated	that, this
(c)	familiar	that
(d)	uniquely identifiable	the N
(e)	referential indefinite	indefinite this N
(f)	type identifiable	a N

In spoken question-and-answer discourse, we also see the structure of the discourse influenced by the type of information being provided. Lyons (1977: 503) suggests that the asking of a simple question includes information that is presupposed and information that is in focus. For example, the question 'Who is X?' presupposes that X is an existing person, and the focus of the question is the identity of X. Similarly, the question 'What happened?' presupposes the existence of an event, and the focus of the question is the identification of that event.

Perdue and Klein (1992a: 51), in their discussion of pragmatic factors in L2 acquisition, note that 'very often, a statement is used to answer a specific question, this question raising an alternative, and the answer specifying one of the "candidates" of that alternative'. In such a situation, the topic represents the given information and the focus in the answer represents 'that part of a statement which specifies the appropriate candidate of an alternative raised by the question' (pp. 51–2)[5], or the new information.[6]

These various examples of topic structures and given/new information structures demonstrate that grammatical structure is related to the status of the information being presented and to the structure of the discourse in which that information is presented. It is also clear that different authors use distinct terminology – presupposition/given/known and focus/new/asserted – to characterize the status of information in discourse.

A final look at the notion of discourse topic is based on the work of Givón because much of the L2 research under discussion applies his analyses to L2-learner data. We here detail his approach to the issue of grammatical encoding of discourse topic. According to Givón (1984b), the particular structural device that is used to introduce and/or maintain a topic in a discourse is determined by the predictability of the topic. He has proposed a continuum of most continuous/predictable topics to least continuous/predictable topics, as seen in (6.7) (Givón 1984b: 112):

(6.7) *Most continuous/predictable topics*
  (a) Zero anaphora
  (b) Clitic/unstressed/agreement pronouns
  (c) Independent/stressed pronouns
  (d) Right-dislocated definite NPs or comment-topic word order
  (e) Simple definite NPs in the neutral/fixed word order (if any)
  (f) Left-dislocated definite NPs or topic-comment word order
      Least continuous/predictable topics

To encode the first mention of a participant as a topic in the discourse, the device that is used is seen to be highly structurally marked – or heavy; for example, a full NP (6.7e) or a left-dislocated NP (6.7f) as exemplified in the reference to *that book* in (6.2c) and (6.3c): (6.2c) *That book, I don't like (it)*, and 6.3c. *As for that book, John bought it*. These newly mentioned topics are seen as the least predictable or continuous topics owing to their 'new' status. Once the topic has been introduced into the discourse, less structurally marked – or lighter – devices are used to refer to the participant – for example, zero anaphors (6.7a) or stressed pronouns (6.7c) rather than full nouns, because these are seen as more predictable topics. These lighter devices are exemplified in the reference to *the shepherd* in (6.5c): *However, instead of watching the sheep, he preferred to watch the clouds in the sky and Ø daydream.*

Givón arrived at this continuum by conducting a cross-linguistic study which utilized three quantitative measurements for determining topic continuity and ease of topic identification in a discourse (1984b: 111, emphasis in the original):

(6.8) Topic continuity measurements
  (a) *Referential distance to the left:* 'The distance from the present mention of a topic NP and the last clause where the same referent was a semantic argument within the clause, in terms of *number of clauses*.'

  (b) *Potential ambiguity:* 'The number of other referents within the immediately preceding environment (3 clauses to the left) which could qualify in terms of their semantic/syntactic selectional restrictions to compete for referential identification with the topic/argument under study.'

(c) *Topical persistence:* 'The number of clauses to the right, from the locus under study, in which the same topic/referent persists in the discourse register as argument of some clause.'

These three measurements essentially assess how easy it is to identify the topic in terms of the distance between one mention of the topic and the next, the uniqueness of the topic, and the importance/persistence of the topic in the discourse. In other words, 'topic continuity without interfering *gaps* or *other topics* thus yields easier topic identification', as does the importance of the topic in the discourse (Givón 1984b: 112).

The devices chosen from the topic continuity continuum (6.7) will be affected by the constraints of referential distance, potential ambiguity, and topical persistence. For instance, if the topic has been absent from the discourse for a number of clauses, thus creating a gap in the topic continuity, a heavier device – a full NP rather than a pronoun – will once again be chosen in order to reinstate the participant as a topic. Similarly, the existence of competing, potentially ambiguous topics will also result in the use of a heavier device. Consider the following additions to 'The Boy who Called Wolf':

(6.9)
    (d) One day, *the shepherd's father* caught *him* sleeping.
    (e) *The man* scolded *his son* and Ø warned *him* to be more vigilant.

The addition of a competing participant requires the selection of full NPs, *the man* and *his son*, to identify the participants more easily. The question explored by L2 researchers is whether or not Givón's measures of topic continuity and topic predictability also constrain L2-learner discourse.

From these examples, we see then that the functional approach to grammar assumes an integral relationship between syntax, semantics, and pragmatics. In general, all functional approaches to grammar consist of three basic elements: syntactic forms, the semantic and pragmatic functions that they encode, and rules that specify how the semantic and pragmatic functions are mapped into syntactic forms (Tomlin 1990).

6.1.2 RELATIONAL FUNCTIONALISM, ECOLOGICAL FUNCTIONALISM, AND GRAMMATICALIZATION

Functionalism can be approached from two different perspectives, which Tomlin (1990) designates as relational functionalism and ecological functionalism. Relational functionalism represents a descriptive orientation which deals with the relation between form and function: either how particular semantic and pragmatic functions are encoded in grammatical form in a particular language or what semantic or pragmatic function a particular grammatical form encodes. An examination of Japanese from a relational functional perspective could examine the grammatical particle *wa* to determine the semantic or pragmatic functions that this particular form encodes – that is, the pragmatic function *topic* that we have seen in (6.3) (Tomlin 1990: 159).

Ecological functionalism, on the other hand, addresses the issues of the origins of grammatical forms and how these forms are related historically or developmentally to their functions. Givón (1993) compares a grammar to a biological organism, whose anatomical structures adapt with evolution to the particular functions that they perform. Similarly, he argues that grammar rules are the way they are because of the functions that they perform in the coding and communication of information.

Why should it be the case that grammatical forms are so closely linked to their functions in discourse? From an ecological functional view, it is argued that these forms develop historically – or diachronically – from their functions. Moreover, Givón (1979) proposes that several types of linguistic processes represent a shift from pragmatic discourse structures to grammatical structures. He argues that these processes – historical language change, the development of pidgin languages into creoles, L1 acquisition, and the relationship between informal and formal registers – all represent a single process of grammaticalization through which loose ' "pragmatic" discourse structures develop – over time – into tight, "grammaticalized" syntactic structures' (p. 208). This process of grammaticalization[7] is exemplified as follows (Givón 1979: 214):

(6.10)

(a) I want	I-go subject- finite verb	→ I want	to-go subordinate- infinitive verb	
(b) I tell	you object	you-go subject- finite verb	→ I tell	you object	to-go subordinate- infinitive verb

In the example, the simple linking of elements through juxtaposition (that is, in paratactic constructions) – *I want I – go –* is developed into a more complex subordinate structure with the development of a grammatical marker – the infinitive verb *to-go*.

Thus, the process of grammaticalization is seen as a diachronic process in which semantic and pragmatic factors interact to influence the emergence of grammatical structures. Dittmar (1992) extends the notion of grammaticalization to L2 acquisition by suggesting that L2 grammatical development be considered but one type of linguistic change that is affected by the process of grammaticalization.

In addition, Givón (1979, 1993) links this move from a pre-syntactic pragmatic mode to a syntactic mode to different levels of information processing. The pre-syntactic mode is analytic and slow whereas the syntactic mode is seen as more automatic. The characteristics of pre-syntactic language and syntactic language are summarized as follows (Givón 1984: 110):

(6.11) *Pre-syntactic mode*   *Syntactic mode*

   (a) Topic-comment structure   Subject-predicate structure

   (b) Loose conjunction   Tight subordination

   (c) Slow rate of delivery   Fast rate of delivery

   (d) Pragmatic government of   Semantic government of word order
       word order

   (e) Low noun/verb ratio   Higher noun/verb ratio within
       within clauses   clauses

   (f) Scant use of grammatical   Extensive use of grammatical
       morphology   morphology

The unification of semantic, syntactic, and pragmatic/discourse constraints in the functional view of grammar provides a broader basis on which to explore L2 grammatical development. One prediction, for instance, is that L2 acquisition also precedes from a pragmatic mode to a syntactic mode. One of the primary approaches to investigating this prediction is the analysis of topic-comment structures in IL grammars.

6.2 Functional approaches to second-language acquisition of grammar

L2 researchers began to argue for a more functional/discourse-based approach to L2 acquisition in reaction to earlier approaches to L2 acquisition. Contrastive analysis, error analysis, and creative construction focused primarily on the grammatical forms produced by the learner without paying attention to the function of those grammatical forms. Long and Sato (1984: 265) have categorized this type of analysis as a 'form-only' analysis which focuses on the measurement of 'increasing target-like production of particular forms'. With the move away from examining language products, L2 researchers began to focus more on the process of acquisition. Within this movement from product to process, several argued for an increased focus on the relations between language forms and their functions within the L2-acquisition process. For instance, even though the creative construction approach highlighted the L2 learner's construction process, the resulting morpheme acquisition studies (Bailey *et al.* 1974; Dulay and Burt, 1973, 1974a, b; Larsen-Freeman 1975, 1976) charted the acquisitional orders of several grammatical morphemes but did not offer an explanation of whether or not the corresponding functions were also acquired.

Support for a functional/discourse approach derives from the fact that L2 learners do not necessarily acquire a grammatical form and its corresponding function simultaneously. In a study of child L2 acquisition, Wagner-Gough

(1978) noted that L2 learners may acquire the grammatical form before they acquire the target-language function of that form. Wagner-Gough's subject produced different variations of the *be V+ing* progressive form to denote the semantic temporal functions of present, past, and future, as in (6.12a–b). This L2 learner also produced different grammatical forms – *I'm find* and *found* – to represent the same meaning, i.e. that the event occurred in the past, as in (6.12d) (adapted from Wagner-Gough 1978: 159):

(6.12)
  (a) It's a sleeping in there a room.
      'It's sleeping in the room in there (right now).'

  (b) I'm playing with that Mark.
      'Mark was playing with that.'

  (c) I'm going /in/ give it to Mark.
      'I'm going to give it to Mark (sometime).'

  (d) I'm find it. Bobbie found one to me.
      'I found it. Bobbie found it for me.'

Long and Sato (1984: 266) have argued that, in addition to omitting the functional variation of a form, a 'form-only' approach also ignores 'all occasions where other forms in learners' ILs may have covered roughly the same functional/semantic scope as the forms actually analyzed'. These types of form–function variations are obscured in an analysis that examines the suppliance of a given form, in this case *be V+ing*, only in an obligatory context.

Long and Sato (1984) present two different functional alternatives to the 'form-only' approach: a form-to-function analysis which includes a 'comprehensive analysis of the functional distribution of a particular form in a learner's IL' and a function-to-form analysis which 'begins with a functional domain, such as the expression of temporality, and documents the evolution of grammatical encoding of that functional domain' (pp. 265–6). A form-to-function analysis allows us to examine the systematicity of the developing form–function mappings. In other words, by looking at the acquisition both of the form and of its function, we see that learner grammars begin to look less chaotic (Long and Sato 1984: 267).

A function-to-form analysis allows for the examination of the different grammatical forms which may be utilized to mark a single function – for instance, adverbials such as *yesterday* or *last week* – to mark past tense in the absence of morphological tense markers. Long and Sato ultimately propose a combination of these two approaches – that is, a function-to-form analysis complemented by a form-to-function analysis. In their view, either functional approach alone can present only an incomplete picture of L2 form–function development, whereas a combined approach allows for careful analysis of the learner's form–function mappings from both the formal and the functional perspectives.

Research which has taken functional approaches to L2 acquisition has focused on several different grammatical phenomena: tense/aspect marking (Bailey 1989; Bardovi-Harlig 1992a, b; Dietrich *et al.* 1995; Kumpf 1984; Sato 1990; Schumann 1987; Tomlin 1984), clause structure (Perdue 1990; Sato 1988), word order (Perdue and Klein 1989, 1992b; Trévise *et al.* 1991), and noun phrase reference (Chaudron and Parker 1990; Kumpf 1992; Polio 1995; Williams 1988, 1989). We focus here on one area of the L2 research: the development of noun phrases. This particular aspect has been chosen because of the wide variety of nominal forms, the interactions between these forms and discourse topic, and the variety of approaches taken to the study of noun phrases.

6.3 Questions explored

● What are the form–function relationships exhibited in interlanguage?
● What types of principles constrain the mapping of grammatical forms onto function in second-language grammatical development?
● How do first-language grammaticalizations influence the development of the second language?

6.3.1 WHAT ARE THE FORM–FUNCTION RELATIONSHIPS EXHIBITED IN INTERLANGUAGE?

With a focus on the acquisition of functions as well as of forms, L2 researchers began to look at L2 acquisition of syntax from a more detailed perspective. One of the first studies to examine form–function mappings in L2 acquisition was that of Huebner (1983), who examined an adult Hmong speaker's form–function acquisition of three different types of forms in English: the copula *is(a)*, the definite article *da*, or *the*, and the subject and object pronouns. Over the course of a twelve-month period, Huebner looked at his informant Ge's suppliance of these forms in obligatory, optional, and ungrammatical contexts. In his analysis, Huebner found similarities in Ge's acquisition process of the *is(a)* and *da* forms. For example, Ge would initially utilize a given form in both obligatory and ungrammatical contexts, would then decrease the suppliance of the form in all contexts, and would eventually increase the suppliance of the form in obligatory contexts and decrease the suppliance of the form in ungrammatical contexts.

However, the most informative aspect of Huebner's study is the development of the form–function mappings of these grammatical structures and the underlying discourse basis of this development. While Huebner identifies the origin of the *is(a)* form as 'it's' and 'it's a', the form does not originally function as a copula verb. Although Ge initially utilized *is(a)* in 80 per cent of the obligatory copula environments (for example, following an NP and preceding an equative NP, an attribute or quantifier, or a time or place locative), he also used the form over half of the time in non-copula environments. Ge used *is(a)* both in sentence-initial position and in sentence-medial position, and *is(a)* appeared to mark the boundary between given and new/asserted information, as seen in the examples in (6.13) (adapted from Huebner 1983: 107–13). The new/asserted information is in italic.

(6.13)
    (a) T: How many people slept in each house?
        G: ow. in wan haws -n- piipow sliip, isa tuw handred.
           'Oh. *Two hundred* people slet [*sic*] in each house.'

    (b) T: What time did you begin working?
        G: ai werk, isa ei' owklok, tu -n- fo owklok.
           'I worked *from eight to four.*'

    (c) T: How long did it take to walk from Laos to Thailand?
        G: ow. isa -n- twentii dei.
           '(It took) *twenty days.*'

Huebner posits the following rules for Ge's early use of *is(a)* (pp. 109–14):

(6.14) Rules for *is(a)*

    (a) Mark all new/asserted constituents with *is(a)*.

    (b) Mark new/asserted major constituents (i.e. noun phrases, verbs, and adjectives) with *is(a)*.

    (c) Mark those constituents which are least likely to be assertions with *is(a)*.

Ge's IL at this point (tapes one and two with an interval of two and a half weeks between tapes) consisted of agent–verb–object sequences which for the most part followed a given–new word order. Within this system, object NPs are the most likely candidates to be new/asserted constituents, and therefore, the least likely to be marked with *is(a)*. Those elements that were least consistent with the given–new word order – for example, new/asserted agents – were always marked with *is(a)*. By the time of tape six (roughly three and a half months into the study), Ge's use of *is(a)* had begun to appear more consistently in obligatory copula verb environments – i.e. before equative NPs and before attributes and quantifiers:

(6.15)
    (a) (NP) —— NP$_{equative}$
    (b) (NP) —— Attribute/Quantifier

From this example, we see that the initial function as a topic boundary of the *is(a)* form slowly evolved into the native-like copula function. This example of a form-to-function analysis nicely illustrates the interaction between the grammatical form (*is(a)*), syntactic and semantic factors (word order and thematic role), and information structure (new/asserted information).

Huebner found a similar pattern of development with the article *da*, or *the*. Huebner suggested (1983: 130) that the characteristics that determine the use of the definite article *the* and the indefinite articles *a/an* and Ø in English can be specified by two binary features: [±Information Assumed Known to the Hearer] ([±HK]) and [±Specific Referent] ([±SR]).[8] For example, an entity that is unknown to the hearer but that has a specific referent ([−HK], [+SR]) would require an indefinite article – *a/an* or Ø – whereas an entity that is known to the hearer and that has a specific referent requires the obligatory use of *the*:

(6.16)
    (a) I bought *a* book.   [−HK, +SR]
    (b) I gave *the* book to Marie.   [+HK, +SR]

In (6.16a) the entity is unknown to the hearer, but, once it has been identified to the hearer in (6.16a), it is assumed to be known to the hearer, as in (6.16b). Note that the grammatical use of *the* in English occurs obligatorily in [+HK, +SR] environments, as in (6.16b) and optionally in [+HK, −SR] environments with generics such as in 'The telephone is necessary in modern life' and 'Telephones are necessary in modern life'.

In characterizing Ge's acquisition of the form–function mapping for *da*, Huebner again noted the relevance of the concept of topic in Ge's early IL grammar. Initially, Ge used *da* for noun phrases that are [+SR, +HK] which are not functioning as the topic [−Tp]. The topics are identified by word order and do not need to be redundantly marked by *da* because, as a topic, the noun phrase is already characterized as [+HK]. The rules for Ge's use of *da* throughout the first seven and a half months of the study are shown in (6.17) (adapted from Huebner, 1983: 140–5).

(6.17) Rules for *da*
    (a) Rule for *da*, I
        Mark with *da* those noun phrases which have the features [+SR, +HK], but [−Tp].

    (b) Rule for *da*, II
        Use *da* with all noun phrases.

    (c) Rule for *da*, III
        Use *da* with all noun phrases except those that are [−SR, −HK].

    (d) Rule for *da*, IV
        Use *da* to mark noun phrases which are [+HK].

    (e) Rule for *da*, V
        Use *da* for all [+SR], except those found in existential constructions.

(f) Rule for *da*, VI – a return to Rule IV
Use *da* to mark noun phrases which are [+HK].

Huebner further characterizes these rules into six distinct stages of acquisition (p. 145):

(6.18)
(a) Stage 1 [+SR, +HK, –Tp]
(b) Stage 2 [+NP]
(c) Stage 3 [+NP], except [–SR, –HK]
(d) Stage 4 [+HK]
(e) Stage 5 [–SR, –Exist]
(f) Stage 6 [+HK]

Ge eventually arrived at a native-speaker-like rule when he returned to Rule IV in Stage 6.

As seen in these two examples, *is(a)* and *da*, the L2 learner first acquired the grammatical form and then gradually acquired the appropriate functions of the form. More importantly, it is shown that the learner used a combination of functional information (topic, given/new information) and syntactic information (syntactic category) to arrive at his form–function mappings.

In another example of a form–function analysis, Pfaff (1987) examined the L2 acquisition of German pronouns and articles by Turkish adolescents who had lived in Germany on average from four to seven years. In German, the grammatical forms for definite articles, indefinite articles, and pronouns are all morphologically marked for case (nominative, accusative, dative, genitive), number (singular or plural), and gender (feminine, masculine, or neuter), thus complicating the choice of accurate grammatical forms. In the study the L2 learners produced narratives about two sequences of pictures which differed in degrees of complexity: the thematic subject, the number of participants, animacy, the participants' amount of participation, and the existence of the participants in the pictures.

Pfaff found general trends for most of the learners. In the simpler narrative, 'The Cat and the Milk', all learners marked the same discourse functions, although they chose different grammatical forms. The sentence subjects were introduced with a definite article + noun, and, in the subsequent mentions, a pronoun was used until an additional participant was introduced. The sentence objects were introduced with a definite article + noun, and subsequent mentions were referred to with either the definite article + noun or with a pronoun.

The more complex narrative, 'The Snowman', included many participants – both visible and not visible in the pictures – as well as animate and inanimate participants. Again, the L2 learners consistently distinguished discourse functions in conjunction with semantic and syntactic factors: the interaction between first mention/subsequent mention, unspecified agents/specified agents, and subject/object position. Although a complete account of the form–function mappings of these L2 learners is beyond the scope of our discussion, a few examples should suffice to demonstrate the systematicity of their ILs. For instance, the first mention of animate agents as subject/protagonists was marked with the definite article + noun or a pronoun. Specified non-protagonist agents were marked with either the definite article + noun if they were known, or the indefinite article + noun if they were unknown. The first mention of inanimate agents was as objects, and these agents were marked with a Ø article + noun at an early stage of development which was replaced by a definite article + noun. Again, there was a distinction between known and unknown participants as marked with definite articles versus indefinite articles. Although the gender and case marking was far from native-like for these L2 learners, Pfaff found that the acquisition of case marking preceded the acquisition of gender marking. From this form–function analysis, Pfaff concluded that discourse functions, such as given and new information and first and subsequent mention, develop before grammatical functions, such as case marking.

These two studies demonstrate clearly that the previous form-only analyses obscure the actual L2-acquisition process. In addition, they show that L2-learner production is a result of several different kinds of factors: discourse, syntactic, and semantic factors.

6.3.2 WHAT TYPES OF PRINCIPLES CONSTRAIN THE MAPPING OF GRAMMATICAL FORMS ONTO FUNCTION IN SECOND-LANGUAGE GRAMMATICAL DEVELOPMENT?

Several studies have tried to determine the types of principles which constrain the mapping of grammatical forms onto function in L2 grammatical development (Klein and Perdue 1992b; Perdue and Klein 1992c). As noted above, Tomlin (1990) points out that all functional approaches to grammar consist of three basic elements: syntactic forms, the semantic and pragmatic functions that they encode, and rules that specify how the semantic and pragmatic functions are mapped into syntactic forms. A number of L2 studies completed as part of the longitudinal European Science Foundation Project (Klein and Perdue 1992b) examined the syntactic, semantic, and pragmatic constraints which were evident in the early stages of L2 acquisition of several different L2 target languages (i.e. Dutch, English, French, German, and Swedish) by speakers of several L1 source languages (i.e. Arabic, Finnish, Italian, Punjabi, Spanish, and Turkish).

(6.19) *Target languages*

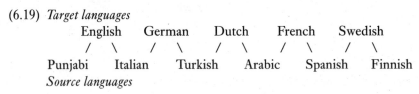

Source languages

The target languages were European languages with large populations of adult immigrant learners. The studies paired speakers of diverse source languages as learners of a single target language. In this way, the studies could distinguish between recurrent common features of L2 acquisition (e.g. the features common to L2 acquisition of any language) and L1-specific features (e.g. the features common to Italian L1 speakers, Turkish L1 speakers, and so on).

Perdue (1993a: 3) outlines the underlying assumptions of the project as follows:

(6.20)
  (a) the internal organization of an interlanguage (or *learner variety*) at a given time is essentially systematic, and

  (b) the transition from one variety to the next over time is essentially systematic.

In order to study this systematic development, the learners were regularly recorded over a two-and-a-half-year period, resulting in 20–25 recordings of approximately two hours' length for 40 learners (Perdue and Klein 1992b: 6). The partial database reported on consisted of the retelling of a film – a montage of extracts from Charlie Chaplin's film, *Modern Times*. The montage was divided into two episodes: (1) the researcher and the learner watched the first episode together; (2) the researcher left the room during the second episode and then returned and asked the learner to tell him/her the rest of the story. The 'Chaplin retelling' represented a complex verbal task for the learner with several characters and events and offered a controlled body of information for the researcher: a comparison between the film and the retold narrative.

In terms of systematic learner varieties, the researchers identified three types: Nominal Utterance Organization (NUO), Infinite Utterance Organization (IUO), and Finite Utterance Organization (FUO) (Perdue and Klein 1992: 302). The initial NUO is characterized by the presence of sequences of nouns, adverbs, and particles, with the occasional addition of adjectives and participles and the absence of verbs. Example utterances from the NUO varieties (Perdue and Klein 1992: 313–14) are given below:

(6.21) Nominal Utterance Organization (NUO)
  (a) NP_1 —   PP
      one man   for the window

  (b) NP   —   Particle
      de boot   weg
      'the boat   off/away'

  (c) NP_1 — NP_2
      daughter's dad   no job

(d) NP$_1$ —   Adj
    les deux   content
    'the two of them   happy'

(e) Adv   —   NP
    daar   ook de man
    'there   also the man'

The subsequent IUO variety includes verbs and their noun arguments. With the inclusion of the verb comes the influence of different kinds of arguments (e.g. animate agents, inanimate patients, or animate patients), which affects the organization of the utterances. The rules for the phrasal patterns of the IUO are given in (6.22) (Perdue and Klein 1992a: 312).

(6.22) Infinite Utterance Organization (IUO)
   (a) NP$_1$–V–(NP$_2$)

   (b) NP$_1$ (Cop)   {NP$_2$}
                        {Adj}
                        {PP}

   (c) V–NP$_2$

The final learner variety – FUO – which was not reached by the learners in this project, distinguishes between finite verbs marked for tense, person, and number and the non-finite, unmarked verbs found in the IUO variety.

What then are the constraints that determine the form of learner varieties? Based on the results of the different language group projects, Perdue and Klein (1992a) identify pragmatic, semantic, and syntactic constraints in the data, which determine the form of what they call the 'basic variety', or the IUO. Two types of pragmatic constraints were found: one determines the position in the utterance of the focus element (6.23a); the other determines the type of NP which is used to introduce and maintain the information in the discourse (6.23b and c). The semantic constraints relate to the thematic roles of the participants and to the amount of control that an NP-referent with a given thematic role may have over another NP-referent (6.23d and e) (adapted from Perdue and Klein 1992a: 302–3):

(6.23)
   (a) Focus last.

   (b) Lexical nouns (alternatively names or deictic pronouns) are used if the referent is introduced.

   (c) Zero anaphors are used if the referent is maintained from the immediately preceding clause and neither its topic-focus status nor its thematic role ('controller') is changed.

   (d) Controller first (i.e. 'The NP-referent with [the] highest degree of control comes first').

(e) Controller of source state outweighs controller of target state.

Consider first topic introduction and maintenance (6.23b and c). In the examples in (6.24) (adapted from Perdue and Klein 1992: 316), the referent is introduced with a lexical noun, namely Chaplin in (6.24a). The topic is then maintained from the immediately preceding clause through the use of zero anaphors – that is, the null subjects in (6.24b–d) that refer back to the previously identified topic, Chaplin.

(6.24)
   (a) Chaplin think the return in the prison.
   (b) Ø go to the restaurant.
   (c) Ø eat too much.
   (d) Ø tell the police 'when you pay'.

As noted above, Perdue and Klein define focus as the one possibility that is selected from a set of several alternative possible answers to a question – i.e. the topic of the utterance. Therefore, in (6.25), the phrase *stole a loaf of bread* is the focus, and the topic is the set of alternative actions that *the girl* may have performed (Perdue and Klein 1992a: 307–8).

(6.25) Then, this girl stole a loaf of bread.

In this instance, the utterance follows both the pragmatic principle of placing the focus last in the utterance and the semantic principle of placing the controller, the NP-referent with the most potential control over another, first. In terms of control, compare the following examples supplied by Perdue and Klein (1992: 310–11):

(6.26)
   (a) The girl stole the bread.
   (b) The girl saw the bread.
   (c) Charlie was in love with this girl.
   (d) The girl passed the bread to Charlie.

Recall from the discussion of (6.1) that thematic roles are determined by the verb. In (6.26a) the amount of control of the two NP-referents – *the girl* and *the bread* – is clearly asymmetrical with *the girl* having more control over *the bread*. In (6.26b) the control asymmetry is still evident but is weaker than in (6.26a). Finally, Perdue and Klein argue that in (6.26c) there is almost no asymmetry in the amounts of control between the two NP-referents, *Charlie* and *the girl*. In instances with little control asymmetry, the strength of the semantic principle of 'Controller first' (6.23d) is diminished. In the case of (6.26d) both NP-referents have some control over the bread, but, according to the second semantic principle (6.23e), the thematic role of the source state outweighs that of the target state – i.e. *the girl* has higher control over *Charlie*.

While both the focus constraint (6.23a) and the controller constraint (6.23d) are followed in (6.26a), there may be conflicts between these constraints. For example, the controller may him/herself be in focus, as in the answer to the question 'Who stole the loaf?', as seen in (6.27) (Perdue and Klein 1992a: 320):

(6.27) mädchen   nehme   brot   nix mann
       girl   take   bread   not man

In such a conflict, learners must override one of the constraints – either 'Focus last' or 'Controller first' – in order to resolve this conflict. In this case, the learner chose to override the 'Focus-last' constraint. In fact, Perdue and Klein (1992a: 315) argue that such conflicts force learners to move beyond the basic variety by developing new devices to accommodate the conflict, such as intonation or cleft constructions (e.g. *c'est ... que* 'it is ... who'). Thus, the 'basic variety' is further developed because it is no longer structurally adequate for the task at hand.

Perdue and Klein (1992a) report that, although not all learners in the project went beyond the basic variety, further development was evident in the case of third person pronouns, focalization devices, subordination, and verb morphology. They hypothesized that the third person pronouns developed because of limitations in the topic-presentation/topic-maintenance constraints. For example, with two female protagonists, the identification of the NP-referents becomes more complicated. One result is the over-repetition of the lexical nouns used to present topic NP-referents. Similarly, the development of focalization devices was seen as the resolution of conflicts between the focus and controller constraints (adapted from Perdue *et al.* 1992: 278):

(6.28) et   [se] la   fille [le vju]
       and it's the girl see him

Overall, the project researchers find that the interaction of the pragmatic and semantic constraints of the basic variety primarily determine the form of the learners' utterances. It is also suggested that the conflicts between different constraints are the motivating factors that force learners to continue developing towards the target language.

Several L2 studies have also examined the constraints on nominal reference in L2 acquisition from the perspective of Givón's proposed constraints for topic continuity. Recall from (6.8) that Givón based his constraints on topic referential distance, potential ambiguity, and topic persistence – that is, the distance between one mention of the topic and the next, the uniqueness of the topic, and the importance/persistence of the topic in the discourse. Using Givón's framework in conjunction with three additional structural norms, Williams (1988, 1989) examined how native and non-native speakers of English use pronouns and zero anaphors to mark topics in spoken discourse. In addition to Givón's referential distance and potential ambiguity constraints, Williams explored the effects of prescriptive grammatical norms and types of descriptive grammatical norms on nominal reference. The prescriptive grammatical norms for pronouns require that, 'in general, a pronoun can only be used successfully if its referent can be found in the preceding discourse or in the context of the speech situation' (Williams 1989: 153). An example is the use of *he* to refer back to the shepherd in (6.5). The prescriptive grammatical norms for zero anaphora are quite restrictive in English and allow zero anaphora for subjects in only one instance; that is, subject pronouns may be omitted when the second subject is coreferential with the subject of a coordinated verb, as in (6.29):

(6.29) Sally ate breakfast and Ø left for work.

Williams analysed instances of zero anaphora matching this prescriptive rule as meeting the native-speaker prescriptive norm.

However, in spoken discourse, native speakers themselves do not always follow prescriptive grammar rules. Accordingly, Williams also explored constraints that accurately describe native-speaker spoken discourse but that do not conform to the prescriptive grammatical constraints of English (adapted from Williams 1988: 340):

(6.30)
   (a) Subject pronouns may be omitted when two clauses represent a coordinate relationship but without the requisite coordinating conjunction (*and, but,* or *or*) present.
      He just walked into the crossfire. Ø Never knew what hit him.

   (b) Subject pronouns may be omitted when they can be clearly identified by the immediate situational context.
      (while attending a lecture) Ø Sure knows his stuff.

Instances of zero anaphora that follow these constraints are said to meet native-speaker descriptive norms. Non-native speakers of English also use zero anaphors in discourse contexts which are inconsistent with native-speaker use. Williams categorized these instances of zero anaphors as non-target-like, as exemplified in (6.31) (excerpted from Williams 1988: 362):

(6.31) I am having problem with *my children* because Ø don't like speak language anymore. Just English. I teach, but *they* don't like. Ø say 'Mommy, please not Africa. We don't have to speak your language from Africa. We are not from Africa. Maybe you are, but not us.' ...

In an experiment with two groups of non-native speakers of English, Williams (1988, 1989) questioned to what extent these discourse and grammatical constraints account for both native and non-native use of pronouns and zero anaphors in spoken discourse. The first group consisted of speakers of Singaporean English, a non-native lingua franca, tested in Singapore. The second group was made up of L2 learners of English studying in the United States.

In terms of Givón's discourse constraints, there were significant differences between the non-native speakers and the native speakers. As for referential distance, native speakers used zero anaphora to refer back to a referent that occurred in either the preceding clause or less than two clauses back. Both groups of non-native speakers, on the other hand, used zero anaphora to refer back to a referent that was on the average over three clauses back. There were no significant differences between the native-speaker and non-native speaker groups in terms of Givón's potential ambiguity constraint for the use of zero anaphora; all groups used a pronoun or a full NP where there was potential ambiguity instead of using the zero anaphor.

The subjects' adherence to the grammatical constraints resulted again in native-speaker/non-native speaker differences. In order fully to understand these differences, it was also necessary to consider the discourse context – that is, the difference between topic-initiating, topic-reinstating, and topic-continuing contexts. These contexts were defined in terms of referential distance: a topic-initiating context is the initial occurrence of the topic, topic-reinstating contexts include the reintroduction of topics after a distance of more than eight clauses, and topic-continuing contexts include the reappearance of topics within a distance of eight clauses.

The results indicated that the greatest portion of native-speaker zero anaphora was used in accordance with native-speaker prescriptive norms – that is, in the context of coordinate verb constructions in topic-continuing contexts. Non-native speakers followed the prescriptive norm to a much lesser extent. Native-speaker descriptive norms included cases of coordinate verb construction in which the coordinate conjunction had been omitted. In these constructions, native speakers and non-native speakers alike used zero anaphora in non-adjacent clauses. However, as in the results within the prescriptive norms given above, native speakers and non-native speakers differed in the distance between the zero anaphor and the previous mention of the referent.

Non-native speakers also used zero anaphora in accordance with non-target-like structural norms. In these cases, the zero anaphors generally marked a change in grammatical function. As seen in (6.32), the first referent was an object in its clause, and the zero anaphor occurred as a subject in an adjacent clause.

(6.32) You$_i$ see them$_j$ and $\emptyset_j$ ask you$_i$ for money.

Williams pointed out that, in these cases, although they broke the native-speaker prescriptive norm, the reference relationship was clear from the context. Williams concluded that, while there were differences in native and non-native speaker use of zero anaphors, both groups followed principles related to both discourse constraints and grammatical constraints.

Williams (1989) explored these phenomena further with the inclusion of subject pronoun copies and an analysis based on Givón's continuum of devices for marking the most to the least continuous/predictable topics, as seen in (6.7). Pronoun copies, sometimes referred to as left dislocation of the NP, are essentially pronominal copies of an NP which denote the same referent as the noun phrase, as in (6.33):

(6.33) *That man$_i$, he$_i$ is my neighbour.*

Pronoun copies differ from the double-subject constructions found in topic-prominent languages because the pronoun copies refer to the same entity as the subject, whereas in double-subject constructions the first entity is the topic and the second is a subject.

Williams found that native-speaker and non-native speaker choice of referring device – pronoun copy, definite noun, pronominal anaphor, and zero anaphor – was related to Givón's referential distance constraint with pronoun copies occurring with the most intervening clauses, from an average of 12.41 to 15.06 intervening clauses, and zero anaphors occurring with the least intervening clauses, from 1.88 to 3.52 clauses. In terms of potential ambiguity, native speakers and non-native speakers essentially used pronoun copies and definite nouns in ambiguous contexts and pronouns in unambiguous contexts. These findings for subject pronoun copies indicated that pronoun copies were used in topic-initiating contexts, in instances of topic-reinstatement after considerable referential distance, in potentially ambiguous contexts, and with topics that were seen as important. In general, these functions of pronoun copies did not overlap with those discussed above for pronominal and zero anaphors and coincided with Givón's prediction of left-dislocated nouns as markers of the least continuous and least predicable topics.

Givón's topic-continuity measures also figured in a study of L2 learners of French. Fakhri's (1989) study of current and previous L2 learners of French explored the effects of foreign-language loss on the use of nominal referents in L2 French written narratives. Fakhri based his analysis on Givón's continuum of referential marking devices and constraints of referential distance and potential ambiguity. The constraint of referential distance was neutralized because the great majority of instances of nominal reference in the data occurred at the distance of only one clause, and the analysis was therefore limited to only those examples of nominal reference. To account for the constraint of potential ambiguity, Fakhri calculated the actual use of pronouns against the possible use of pronouns in instances in which there was no risk of ambiguity. Based on the notion that lighter marking devices are more grammaticalized and heavier marking devices are less grammaticalized, Fakhri predicted that the current French learners would use the lighter, more grammaticalized forms – pronouns – while the group of previous French learners would use the heavier, less grammaticalized forms – NPs – for these instances of one-clause nominal referents. The results showed that, as predicted, there was a significant difference between the previous and the current learner groups: the previous learner groups used more full NPs after one clause and avoided pronouns in non-ambiguous contexts more than did the current learners.

Polio (1995) also investigated the constraints on the acquisition of zero anaphora, but from the perspective of the L2 acquisition of Mandarin Chinese, a language that requires zero anaphora. Polio's subjects were L1 speakers of languages that have dissimilar constraints on zero anaphora – English with very restricted use of zero anaphora and Japanese with extensive use of zero anaphora. She examined the L2 Chinese spoken narratives of learners at three different levels of proficiency: low, middle, and high. In their retelling of a short non-verbal film,[9] Polio analysed the form (e.g. full NP, lexical pronoun, or zero pronoun) and the syntactic position (e.g. subject, indirect object, direct object) of all NPs functioning as a non-initial mention of a previously mentioned NP.

The results showed that the grammatically correct use of zero pronouns increased with increased proficiency and weakly suggested that there was no difference between the English and Japanese subjects. Polio found that all of the L2 learners seemed to follow first syntactic, then semantic and discourse constraints in their decisions concerning the use of zero versus lexical pronouns. At the syntactic level, learners first distinguished between subject and direct object positions versus other object positions, marking other objects with lexical pronouns. At the semantic level, non-human entities were marked with zero pronouns in subject and direct object positions, while human entities were not. At the next decision-making level, the discourse level, the choice between zero and lexical pronouns was determined by clause distance. If the referent did not occur in the immediately preceding clause, a lexical pronoun would usually be used. Up to the discourse level, the non-native speakers performed similarly to the native speakers. At the discourse level, non-native speakers used fewer zero pronouns than do native speakers. Polio concluded that other factors may be influencing the non-native speakers' production. One possible factor was clarity; that is, L2 learners used lexical pronouns to remedy possibly ambiguous reference, similar to the learners in Fakhri's study.

The nominal forms which encode the notion of topic within a discourse context are also the focus of a study by Chaudron and Parker (1990). In their investigation, they examined the interactions between structural and discourse factors in the L2 acquisition of English nominal reference by L1 Japanese speakers. One aspect of this interaction is the notion of markedness – that is, are some structural forms more frequent, structurally simpler, or more common than others? Do some discourse contexts provide more of the information needed to process and identify the noun referents than do others? Chaudron and Parker proposed two scales of markedness to capture these influences. In structural terms, they examined the use of the following nominal reference forms: definite or indefinite NPs, pronouns, or zero anaphora, and proposed the following markedness scale of nominal forms (adapted from Chaudron and Parker 1990: 48):

(6.34) *Less marked*
zero anaphora
pronoun/bare noun
left-dislocated noun/existential noun
definite noun/indefinite noun
left-dislocated definite noun/existential indefinite noun
More marked

The discourse contexts included the following three types of topics: topics that are new to the hearer, topics that are known to the hearer but not previously the topic, and topics that are already established as the current topic. The discourse markedness scale was represented as follows (adapted from Chaudron and Parker 1990: 48):

(6.35) *Less marked*
refer to current topic
introduce known referent as topic
introduced new referent as topic
More marked

Current topics are known and available and therefore easier to process than are new, unknown topics.

By manipulating the three discourse contexts, the researchers could determine how various factors interacted in the L2 acquisition of nominal reference. In a three-picture sequence, a discourse was established with two noun referents – for example, a woman and a child in a grocery store. One referent was established as the topic – the woman reaching for and reading a box of cookies. The fourth test picture picks out either the current topic referent – the woman – the other known referent – the child – or a newly introduced referent – another shopper – as the topic. The subjects produced oral narratives of each type of sequence with the topic continuity controlled by the pictures.

Chaudron and Parker found interesting interactions between these two scales of structural and discourse markedness: L2 learners increased their use of structurally marked forms with increased proficiency; L2 learners at all levels of proficiency treated the three discourse contexts as distinct, with the use of different nominal reference devices, although native-like usage increased with proficiency; beginning-level L2 learners overgeneralized devices for less marked discourse contexts such as pronouns to other discourse contexts, and, even though learners generally increased their use of more syntacticized forms with proficiency, there was no simultaneous decrease in the use of the less syntacticized forms. These researchers concluded that both the structural and discourse markedness scales adequately describe the acquisition sequences of nominal reference marking.

These studies taken as a whole seem to indicate that L2 learners' production is guided by a multi-levelled set of constraints, including syntactic, semantic, and discourse/pragmatic constraints. In arguing for a discourse-functional approach to L2-acquisition studies, Williams (1989: 159) noted that the absolute occurrence of zero pronominal forms may be explained by factors such as UG or L1 influence, but 'a discourse-functional approach may be more appropriate to account for variation in *pro-drop*'. This proposal suggests that it is possible to combine grammatical constraints of UG with the pragmatic/discourse constraints of a functional approach in order to account for all aspects of L2 acquisition.

6.3.3 HOW DO FIRST-LANGUAGE GRAMMATICALIZATIONS INFLUENCE THE DEVELOPMENT OF THE SECOND LANGUAGE?

Another functional approach to L2 acquisition is to examine the proposal that all L2 learners begin the L2-acquisition process in a pragmatic discourse mode regardless of the structure of the L1 and then gradually grammaticalize into a more syntactic mode. Several studies have examined the L2 development of nominal reference from this perspective and have come up with conflicting results. One approach to this question is to examine the basic sentence structure of the learners' IL for evidence of topic prominence, because this is one of the proposed characteristics of a pragmatic mode.

Fuller and Gundel (1987) examined the use of nominal reference in the English IL narratives of native speakers of Arabic, Chinese, Farsi, Japanese, Korean, and Spanish. They categorized Chinese, Japanese, and Korean as topic-prominent languages and Arabic, Farsi, and Spanish as non-topic-prominent. Included in their analysis of the IL narratives were the following topic-prominent characteristics: topic markers, sentence-initial topic position, double-subject constructions, pragmatically constrained zero anaphora, subject-creating constructions, passives, dummy subjects, and subject–verb agreement. Of these characteristics, the most frequent in occurrence were the sentence-initial position of topics and zero anaphors. These researchers concluded that the IL of all of their subjects, regardless of L1, was intermediate in topic prominence between a topic-prominent language and a non-topic-prominent language, thus offering support to the initial pragmatic topic-prominent stage in L2 acquisition.

In an exploration of the same topic, Jin's (1994) study questioned whether or not the proposed universal early topic-prominent stage is indeed universal; that is, is this stage evident in the L2 acquisition of all learners, and, more specifically, is it evident in the L2 acquisition of a topic-prominent language – Chinese – by speakers of a non-topic-prominent language – English? The topic prominence of Chinese is characterized by the existence of null subjects, topics, and objects; double-subject constructions; zero marking of specificity on previously identified nouns; and word order. Jin investigated the topic prominence of Chinese IL by measuring the learners' use of the first three of these characteristics. The results indicated that with increased proficiency L2 learners of Chinese increased the number and range (i.e. subject, topic, and object) of null elements produced in spoken and written discourse. Closer examination of the null elements revealed that structural factors also played a role. For instance, null subjects were acquired much earlier than were null topics and objects, and the acquisition of these null subjects was influenced by the type of structure in which they occurred – for example, main clauses versus adverbial clauses. Similar proficiency-based findings occurred for double-subject constructions and for the zero specificity marking of nouns. Jin concluded that these English learners of Chinese did not exhibit a universal topic-prominent stage in their L2 acquisition of Chinese and that it was only with increased proficiency that the common topic-prominent characteristics began to emerge in the L2 Chinese. The findings of Polio (1995) discussed earlier for L2 learners of Chinese would seem to support these results.

Jin suggests that L1 transfer is a more appropriate explanation than a universal pragmatic stage of development, given the following evidence. Both Huebner (1983) and Rutherford (1983) found L1 transfer of the topic-comment structures from Hmong and Mandarin Chinese into L2 English. Jin also points out that Fuller and Gundel do not differentiate between null-subject/non-null subject languages and topic-prominent/subject-prominent languages. For example, while Spanish is subject prominent, it is also a null-subject language. Additional evidence of transfer is seen in Green's (1996) preliminary findings of a strong topic-comment influence in the advanced L2 English writings of L1 Cantonese speakers. Jin proposes that L2 learners follow a series of stages in the development from a subject-prominent to a topic-prominent language (adapted from Jin 1994: 115):

(6.36) *Stages of typological transfer*
  (a) Stage A   +subject prominent
  (b) Stage B   +null subject and subject prominent
  (c) Stage C   mixture of subject prominent and topic prominent
  (d) Stage D   topic + comment language realization

This viewpoint supports a stronger influence of the L1 grammatical structures in L2 acquisition, as opposed to an early universal pragmatic stage.

Finally, a study by Pfaff (1992) explored the issue of grammaticalization of pragmatic categories into syntactic markers. Specifically Pfaff questioned whether grammatical case and gender marking on noun phrases in L2 German develop from early pragmatic categories into later syntactic functors and whether or not the L1 grammaticalizations influence the course of L2 acquisition. Historically, the definite articles – for example, *der*, *die*, *das* – developed from lexical items – the demonstrative pronouns – thus representing a shift to more grammatical structures. Pfaff searched for a similar pattern in the language-acquisition process by comparing bilingual Turkish–German child learners of German with monolingual native child learners of German. Although these subjects were quite young, ranging in age from 1;08 to 5;03, the language preference both at home and at school for the Turkish children is Turkish.

The findings demonstrated that there were differences between the bilingual children and the monolingual child. The Turkish children used the Ø article more and longer and the demonstrative pronouns much more frequently than did the monolingual child, as exemplified in (6.37) (Pfaff 1992: 283):

(6.37) *den* hab ich geguck
        'I've looked at *that*' (book).

Pfaff also found some evidence for the dominance of demonstrative pronouns over articles in the L2 German of the Turkish–German bilinguals, leading to the preliminary conclusion that the grammatical markers for definite articles do develop out of the lexical demonstrative pronouns for these L2 learners. However, in examining the case and gender marking of nouns, Pfaff did not find that these children represent semantic meaning – for example, thematic roles – prior to syntactic case marking for subjects, direct objects, and so on, nor did they transfer L1 syntactic rules for case marking onto the L2. The overall results did not support the proposal of an early universal pragmatic stage which precedes a later syntactic stage.

In answer to this final question, early topic-comment structures did not seem to be the result of a universal pragmatic stage of acquisition but rather resulted from the transfer of grammatical structures in the L1.

6.4 Conclusions

How does the functional approach contribute to what we know about the development of L2 grammars and about the constraints on that development? There are three relevant issues: form–function mapping, types of constraints, and movement from pragmatics to syntax. In terms of form–function mapping, L2 learners acquire the functions of the forms gradually over time, even in cases where the form itself is consistent – for example, Ge's form *is(a)*. It is obvious from these studies that a form-only analysis is insufficient to describe and explain IL systems. With detailed, multi-levelled analyses, the multi-levelled system of constraints on L2 production becomes clearer.

The issue of development from pragmatics to syntax is more problematic. The work described in Klein and Perdue (1992b) highlights the pragmatic and semantic constraints of early learner varieties.[10] However, the investigations of topic prominence as evidence of an initial pragmatic stage are not supportive of this notion. Perhaps the focus on topic-prominent grammatical structures as the foundation for this pragmatic stage is incomplete, and other indicators of a pragmatic stage such as those given in (6.11) need to be explored.

The functional approach highlights the interaction of syntax, semantics, and pragmatics within a grammatical system. It is important to note, however, that the types of tasks that learners are asked to perform may tap into one type of constraint more heavily than into others. For example, all of the data collected here takes the form of spoken or written narratives, which require attention to discourse properties – e.g. identifying the topic of the narrative or dealing with conflicting participants – as well as attention to producing language that is comprehensible to the addressee. On the other hand, L2 learners may be able to identify the target grammatical form in another type of task, for instance, a grammaticality judgement task, but may be unable to produce that target form in a target-like context. The interesting question is how these factors interact in a variety of language tasks, or, more specifically, in the variety of language tasks that learners are required to perform. The aspects central to a functional approach emphasize the wide range of language skills that language learners need to develop.

Notes

1. Halliday (1994: xiii) states that there are 'two very general purposes which underlie all uses of language: (i) to understand the environment (ideational), and (ii) to act on the others in it (interpersonal)'.
2. In addition to subject-prominent and topic-prominent languages, Li and Thompson's typology also includes languages which are both subject prominent and topic prominent with 'two equally important distinct sentence constructions', and languages which are neither subject prominent nor topic prominent in which 'the subject and the topic have merged and are no longer distinguishable in all sentence types' (1976: 459).
3. There are various definitions of given and new information. See Chafe (1976), Halliday (1994), and Prince (1981), among others.
4. Prince (1981) offers three major categories of the addressee's Assumed Familiarity with the participants including New entities, Inferrable entities, and Evoked entities. Each major category is broken down further. For example, New entities are either Brand-new or Unused, and Evoked entities can be evoked either textually or situationally.
5. Again, we see differences in terminology. The notions of topic and comment, given and new information, presupposition and focus, and topic and focus have been used to differentiate given, known, presupposed information from new information which is the focus of the statement (see Chafe 1976; Lyons 1977; Prince 1981). The term 'focus' is used here to identify the picking out of alternative candidates in response to an explicit or implicit question – as related to the L2 studies examining oral narratives produced by L2 learners.
6. This is a simplification of Klein and Perdue's (1992a) proposal, which includes foregrounded and backgrounded information within the structure of the narrative.
7. Givón (1979) refers to this process as syntacticization. Here we adopt the term grammaticalization.

8. Huebner credits a personal communication from D. Bickerton for this binary distinction.
9. The film used was the seven-minute *Pear Film* (Chafe 1980).
10. The basic variety is further explored in a collection of articles edited by Jordens (1997).

7

Conclusions: an integrative perspective of second-language acquisition of grammar

7.1 Introduction

When one considers the work in the field of L2 acquisition of syntax, one is struck by three aspects: the wide variety of approaches taken to the question, the different aspects of the acquisition process addressed, and the common threads found throughout the research. We started out with the claim that understanding the field of L2 acquisition of syntax is often difficult for students because of the inundation of seemingly isolated, decontextualized facts. By presenting those facts within the context of a theoretical paradigm, the questions and the answers become more understandable.

Although the research has been presented here in the context of the particular theoretical approaches, it is difficult to summarize the major contributions of each approach without considering those findings within the context of the entire field. In this conclusion, an attempt is made to fit the different approaches into a coherent picture by focusing on the contributions of each approach to the development of L2 grammatical competence and performance. In order to accomplish this, the contributions of each approach will be characterized as theoretical contributions and factual contributions. This two-way classification of contributions has two advantages: the factual findings in each approach become more comparable, and the theoretical issues contribute to the overall picture of what we currently know about L2 acquisition of syntax.

7.2 Major contributions

7.2.1 FIRST-LANGUAGE AND SECOND-LANGUAGE INTERRELATIONS

To begin, we note that the title of Chapter 2, *First-language and second-language interrelations*, attempts to capture the realization that L2 acquisition is a complex process that encompasses aspects of the L1, aspects of the L2, and relates those aspects in complex and interesting ways. On yet another level – the professional level – early L2 research was influenced by research in L1 acquisition, and, at the same time, L2 research began to explore the aspects that were – and are – unique to the L2 acquisition process. Two research issues emerged: the description of the L2 developmental stages of diverse language structures, and an expanded investigation of the influences of the L1 on L2 acquisition.

One of the assumptions guiding this early research was that the L1 and L2 acquisition processes were similar. By examining L2 developmental stages, one could discover both the similarities and the differences between the two processes. A major theoretical concern in this area of research was how to define the end of one stage and the beginning of another. One difficulty in this endeavour is the gradual nature of L2 acquisition; learners do not flawlessly produce a structure from its first occurrence in the IL. In order to account for this gradual process, researchers developed several different definitions for determining what constitutes a distinct stage: the most prominent structural feature in the stage, the first non-imitative use of the structure, and the first emergence of a development-defining structure. With these different definitions of 'stage', researchers who studied longitudinal development were able to describe developmental sequences for negation, question formation, and word order in L2 English and German. What these sequences demonstrated was that the order of the stages for learners of different L1s was similar, although there were some differences that were attributed to either the L1 or the type of input available to the learner.

Work in this area also highlights the systematicity of learner ILs. The ability to characterize a stage of acquisition by learner use of a specific IL grammar rule – for example, the use of non-inverted yes/no and wh-questions for L2 English – demonstrates that the IL is indeed systematic.

Another contribution of this early work is the extended view of how the L1 can influence the L2 acquisition process. These definitions of transfer extended beyond the original notions of transfer by including notions of transferability, markedness, and conditions on transfer. Not only did researchers find that not all structures were transferable; they also found that there were structural and developmental constraints on the 'what, why and when' of transferability. As a result, the complexity of the concept of L1 influence became clearer.

The overall contributions of these early studies can be summarized as follows:

(7.1) L1 and L2 interrelations: theoretical contributions

   (a) definitions of developmental stages (most prominent feature, first non-imitative use, first emergence of development-defining structure);

   (b) initial characterizations of developmental stages for diverse structures;

   (c) recognition and characterization of IL systematicity;

   (d) extended notions of transfer resulting in a clearer picture of L1 influence;

   (e) universal properties of language acquisition.

(7.2) L1 and L2 interrelations: factual contributions
  (a) developmental stages of negation, question formation, and word order;

  (b) difficulty orders of embedded clauses and pronouns;

  (c) conditions on transfer: L1/L2 structure congruity, L2 structure ambiguity;

  (d) interaction between L1 influences and developmental stages: prerequisite developmental stage, length of stage, constraints on the hypotheses about the L2.

This work on developmental stages and on transferability contributed the extended notion of transfer and the assumption that there are universal properties of language acquisition. L2 syntactic research in other theoretical paradigms connected these factors within the confines of the respective theories.

7.2.2 UNIVERSAL GRAMMAR

Within the generative research paradigm, L2 researchers explore L2 syntactic development as constrained by the linguistic principles and parameters of Universal Grammar. This approach to L2-acquisition research has contributed a detailed description of those syntactic constraints proposed to be universal and of the clusters of structures related by these constraints. In addition, these parameters are proposed to be triggered by specific structures in the input. The detailed theoretical basis of this work allows for precise predictions about both what is acquired – clusters of structures – and how it is acquired – triggered by specific input.

L1 influences are also examined. One approach examines whether the UG principles and parameters that guide L1 acquisition are still accessible in L2 acquisition, and, if so, how they are manifested. One possibility is seen in the interactions between the L1 and the L2 parameter settings. L1 parameter settings may be transferred to the L2, or they may have only limited influence. These interactions are predictable, based on the notion of markedness. As applied to parameter setting, markedness measures are used to predict which parameter settings will be easily reset and which will not. A more recent perspective on the influence of the L1 concerns the particular structural aspects of the L1 – all or only some – that form part of the learner's initial state in the L2 acquisition process.

As we have seen in Chapter 3, some of the same syntactic structures that have been described from the perspective of developmental stages and difficulty orders – word order, nouns and pronouns, negation, and questions – are also examined from a UG perspective. One difference between the two approaches is immediately evident: the types of rules that are posited as part of the learner's IL grammar are distinct. For example, the descriptive word order rules for developmental stages of English wh-questions are quite different from the Subjacency constraints on wh-movement in English wh-questions and the verb-movement constraints on English inversion. One consequence of this abstract quality of UG constraints is that a rule may not be readily apparent from the input. As a result, the instructional input to the learner plays a special role in parameter resetting and can be explored in a number of ways. We see that the theory of UG provides a rich basis for developing research questions concerning L2 acquisition and that it has contributed a number of intriguing findings:

(7.3) Universal Grammar: theoretical contributions
  (a) detailed descriptions of abstract syntactic constraints;
  (b) clusters of related syntactic structures;
  (c) predictions of L1 transfer based on abstract UG principles;
  (d) predictions of cross-linguistic variation based on different parameter settings;
  (e) definitions of the initial learning state for L2 acquisition;
  (f) predictions of required input.

(7.4) Universal Grammar: factual contributions
  (a) L1 transfer of UG parameter settings occurs and may be structure dependent (e.g. tensed versus infinitival clauses for binding, referential versus nonreferential subjects for pro-drop).

  (b) L2 resetting of UG parameter settings occurs.

  (c) Clustering of particular structures is constrained by abstract principles (verb movement: adverb and negative placement, question formation; binding: nouns, pronouns, reflexives, morphological structure, and syntactic domains; pro-drop: null subject pronouns, verbal morphological marking, declarative word orders, and topic marking).

  (d) Parameter resetting may be gradual.

  (e) There may be limits on the initial availability of L1 information for L2 acquisition (lexical phrases only versus lexical and functional phrases).

  (f) Instruction for resetting parameters has varied degrees of success (negative and/or explicit instruction may be necessary).

As discussed in Chapter 3, the changing theoretical basis of UG provides a challenge for L2 researchers. It also provides the opportunity for theory building and theory revising based on the findings of L2 research.

7.2.3 TYPOLOGICAL UNIVERSALS

Linguists working within the theory of typological universals are also concerned with predicting L2 acquisition ease and/or difficulty based on universal linguistic properties. These linguistic universals have been determined by examining surface structures in a broad sample of cross-linguistic data. Languages are classified into different types according to the universal properties that they exhibit.

Typological markedness is based on the simplicity/complexity, frequency, and/or distribution of the structure in question. One category of typological universal is an implicational hierarchy (if p, then q; or $q < p$) that predicts the occurrence of one structure in a language (q) based on the occurrence of another related structure in the language (p). The q is the unmarked value because its existence is implied by the existence of p. These implicational universals, then, represent hierarchies of markedness relationships.

These implicational hierarchies are applied to L2 acquisition of syntax as a means of predicting which forms will be easier to acquire – the unmarked forms – and which forms will be more difficult to acquire – the marked forms. The Markedness Differential Hypothesis (Eckman 1977) incorporates the notions of markedness and transfer into a more predictive tool based on implicational universals: it combines the relative typological markedness of a structure and the structural L1/L2 differences to predict the ease/difficulty of acquisition.

The findings in this area of research (7.6) are limited, given the small number of structures examined: relative clauses, pronouns in relative clauses, and questions. However, this work raises interesting questions about the interaction between markedness and the structural analyses used (i.e. typological markedness versus configurational analyses) and between markedness and instruction.

(7.5) Typological universals: theoretical contributions

   (a) implicational hierarchies of related syntactic structures;

   (b) predictions of L1 transfer based on typological universals and markedness;

   (c) predictions of learning ease and/or difficulty based on implicational hierarchies and markedness;

   (d) linguistic phenomena accessible in surface structures.

(7.6) Typological universals: factual contributions

   (a) influence of typological universal markedness: frequency and accuracy of relative clauses, order of acquisition of questions, and avoidance of marked forms;

   (b) interaction between L1 transfer and markedness: pronoun copies in relative clauses;

(c) interaction between markedness and instruction: instructed and uninstructed learners treat marked forms differently;

(d) instruction of marked forms facilitates the learning of uninstructed unmarked forms.

Work in these three research paradigms focusing on developmental stages, Universal Grammar, and typological universals has examined the development of IL grammatical competence. In each of these approaches, the research has delineated the linguistic rules or abstract constraints that determine the form of IL grammars. The next two research approaches focus on different aspects of L2 acquisition of syntax and explore the relationships between language processing, language use, and IL grammatical competence.

7.2.4 PROCESSING APPROACHES

Processing approaches explore the factors that determine language processing – both language comprehension and speech production. In terms of language comprehension, two approaches, the Competition Model and Input Processing, investigate the types of cues that are used to interpret language.

The Competition Model proposes that the cues that are used are determined by the structural properties of the language in question. Research in this area examines the use of animacy, contrastive stress, nominal case marking, subject–verb agreement, subject and object clitic pronouns, topicalization, and word order as cues to sentence interpretation by both native speakers and non-native speakers of a variety of languages. Research in the area of Input Processing focuses on L2-learner use of processing principles for interpreting meaning (content words, lexical items versus grammatical morphemes, and 'more meaningful morphology' versus 'less or non-meaningful morphology') and for assigning semantic roles ('first noun strategy') with minimal stress on the learners' attentional capabilities.

L2 learners' ability to process and interpret L2 input correctly (producing 'comprehensible input') or their inability to do so (resulting in 'incomprehensible input') directly affects their use of the input in grammar building – i.e. L2 acquisition of syntax. These research areas indicate how L2 learners process input, if and how L2 learners can change their processing strategies, and how instruction can influence input processing.

In terms of speech production, Processability Theory and its predecessor, the Multidimensional Model, propose constraints on processing that predict the developmental stages for sentential word order. These approaches differentiate between structural features whose emergence characterizes a change in developmental stage (e.g. the developmental rules for German word order: adverb preposing, particle shift, inversion, and verb-to-end) and structural features whose emergence is independent of developmental stage (e.g. the emergence of the copula verb as a variational feature). In addition, the

Processability Theory proposes a Processability Hierarchy which determines the linguistic hypotheses that the L2 learner can hold at any given stage of L2 development. Research in this area has examined the ability of the models to predict L2 developmental stages accurately and the influence of instruction on these stages. While Processability Theory is not intended to explain how L2 linguistic knowledge is created, the relationship between a learner's output and the learner's ability to attend to and focus on grammatical structure in the input is a topic currently under debate in the L2 acquisition research.

The findings from these three different approaches to processing – the Competition Model, Input Processing, and Processability Theory – are combined in (7.7) and (7.8).

(7.7)　Processing approaches: theoretical contributions
　　(a)　processing influences on L2 comprehension;

　　(b)　processing influences on L2 production: processing constraints as determining L2 hypothesis space;

　　(c)　processing constraints as determining the subset of input data that becomes available for grammar building as intake data;

　　(d)　definitions of stages of L2 production based on speech-processing constraints.

(7.8)　Processing approaches: factual contributions
　　(a)　Use of processing cues depends on the structures of the L1 and of the L2.

　　(b)　Transfer of semantic cues is easier than the transfer of syntactic cues.

　　(c)　L2 processing strategies are acquired gradually.

　　(d)　Instruction can influence learners' processing of input.

　　(e)　Processing constraints are consistent with stages of acquisition of L2 word order for L2 German and Swedish.

　　(f)　Stages of acquisition for L2 German word order are the same in instructed and natural settings.

　　(g)　Instruction affects learner behaviour within a stage: rules are learned more quickly and rules are applied more frequently and in a wider range of contexts.

　　(h)　There are differences in the teachability of structures: developmental structures are teachable once the prerequisite has been learned; variational structures are teachable once they can be produced.

Up to this point, the findings have related to the linguistic and processing constraints at work in the L2-acquisition process. Work within a functional approach to L2 acquisition explores the interaction between linguistic and discourse constraints.

7.2.5 FUNCTIONAL APPROACHES

The functional approach to language, as opposed to the Universal Grammar and Typological Universals approaches, takes the perspective that syntactic constraints are necessarily connected to semantic and pragmatic constraints. Syntactic constraints are seen to have grown out of their communicative functions – i.e. grammar is the way it is because of the communicative functions that it serves within a discourse. As a result, this approach seeks different kinds of explanations for the syntactic phenomena which occur in L2 acquisition. The choice of one syntactic form over another, for instance, is guided by the type of information that the form conveys. Because the focus is not solely on syntactic forms and the syntactic constraints that govern their usage, the focus of a functional analysis is the L2 acquisition of the syntactic form as well as the function that the form has in the IL.

This form/function approach to the analysis of L2-learner data gives a clearer picture of how L2 learners acquire the syntax and how learners' hypotheses about the syntactic forms change throughout the acquisition process. The L2 research in this area does not differ from the research in the other areas from one perspective: the research examines the constraints that account for the L2-learner data, the transfer of L1 constraints into the L2, and the development of IL grammars from one stage to another (in this case, from a pragmatic stage to a syntactic stage). The differences lie in the type of constraints that are explored, for example, topic marking, topic maintenance versus topic shift, or word-order constraints on information focus and on thematic roles. The results show that IL grammars are determined by definable constraints, that form/function analyses reveal the changing meaning and use assigned to given forms in the IL grammar, and that L1 constraints transfer to the L2 under certain conditions.

(7.9) Functional approaches: theoretical contributions
  (a) detailed description of semantic and pragmatic/discourse constraints;

  (b) alternative form-to-function and function-to-form analyses;

  (c) interactions between syntactic, semantic, and pragmatic constraints in IL production;

  (d) predictions of IL structures based on the development from an early pragmatic to a later syntactic stage of development.

(7.10) Functional approaches: factual contributions
  (a) L2 acquisition involves the gradual shifting of form–function mappings: definite articles functioning as topic markers versus as

determiners, or copula verbs functioning as given-new boundary markers versus as verbs.

(b) L2 production follows discourse topic constraints: e.g. definite articles for the first mention of animate agents as subjects versus indefinite articles for first mention of unknown nonprotagonist agents; nouns, zero anaphors, and pronoun copies conform to constraints on ambiguity and referential distance.

(c) Beginning ILs demonstrate discourse functions before grammatical functions: given-new and first-/subsequent-mention functions before grammatical case marking.

(d) Early IL grammars demonstrate interactions between syntactic, semantic, and discourse constraints on structure choice and word order: lexical nouns/zero anaphors, focus, topic maintenance/topic shift, and thematic roles.

(e) L2 learners begin with structurally unmarked forms (e.g. zero anaphors) and with increased proficiency increase their use of structurally marked forms (e.g. left-dislocated definite nouns or existential indefinite nouns).

(f) Early L2 use of topic-comment structures results from L1 transfer rather than from an early universal pragmatic topic-comment stage for all L2 learners.

The functional approach demonstrates that a form–function analysis offers an explanation for IL syntactic phenomena that seem to be unsystematic. This approach also offers insights into the combination of factors which determine L2-learner production.

7.2.6 SIMILARITIES AND DIFFERENCES

Although the approaches described in this book differ, they also have a lot in common. By reviewing the questions asked within each theoretical paradigm, it becomes clear that most of the paradigms discussed here address four essential questions:

(7.11) Common questions
    (a) What are the constraints which operate in the L2 acquisition process?

    (b) How does L2 acquisition proceed (from unmarked to marked, from stage to subsequent stage, from form–function mapping to subsequent form–function mapping)?

    (c) What is the role of the L1 in L2 acquisition?

    (d) How does instruction influence L2 acquisition?

While the questions are essentially the same, they reflect the principles of the different theories, and they address different aspects of the process. In addition, we have seen that the answers to these questions are sometimes inconclusive, sometimes contradictory, and, therefore, thought-provoking. Below we briefly outline how these different issues can fit together in a more complete picture of L2 acquisition.

(7.12) Steps in the L2-acquisition process
   (a) Input
      ● positive and/or negative uninstructed input
      ● positive and/or negative (error correction) instruction
      ● meaning-bearing input (possibly leading to comprehensible input)

   (b) Input Processing
      ● input-processing principles leading to intake
      ● cue strategies for interpretation

   (c) Linguistic constraints and grammar building
      ● developmental stage constraints
      ● discourse constraints
      ● semantic constraints
      ● typological universals
      ● UG constraints
      ● L1 influences
      ● markedness

   (d) Output
      ● speech-processing constraints
      ● noticing of gaps and L1/L2 mismatches in the output feeds back into the input

Although the research in no single approach addresses all of these steps in the acquisition process, the combination of the issues addressed in the approaches highlights the necessity of each approach to an overall understanding of the process – i.e. what is learned and how. Moreover, the examination of a single syntactic structure from all of these perspectives can foreground how these diverse approaches really do contribute to what we know about the L2 acquisition process.

7.3 Comparative analysis of noun phrases: nouns, pronouns, zero anaphors, reflexives

Noun phrases (NPs) were chosen as the focus of this comparative analysis based on their centrality in the research of each approach. This analysis of NPs examines how the NPs are addressed in each research paradigm from the perspective of the types of NPs examined, the constraints on these NP forms, and the input processing and production of these forms.

What we find at the beginning of this comparative analysis is that researchers in each approach select from a wide variety of types of nominal structures for examination:

(7.13) Nominal forms examined
   (a) *Stages*: nouns, pronouns, and zero pronouns in object position

   (b) *Universal Grammar*: nouns, pronouns, and zero pronouns in subject and object positions; reflexive pronouns

   (c) *Typological universals*: nouns and pronoun copies in relative clauses

   (d) *Processing approaches*: nouns, stressed pronouns, and clitic pronouns in subject and object positions

   (e) *Functional approaches*: nouns, stressed pronouns, clitic pronouns, zero pronouns, pronoun copies in subject, object, and topic positions

The selection of the grammatical structures examined is, of course, determined by the theoretical constructs of each approach. Two good examples are reflexive pronouns and pronoun copies. Although reflexive pronouns figure prominently in the UG-based research of Binding Theory, they are not addressed in other research paradigms. Similarly, pronoun copies are examined from a typological perspective in marked positions on the NP Accessibility Hierarchy and from a discourse perspective as markers of continued topics in oral narratives but not in other paradigms. This theory-driven selection results overall in a varied and somewhat incomplete view of L2 acquisition of nominal forms. At the same time, this theory-based approach presents a detailed view of certain select aspects of nominal forms.

We now narrow the focus of the analysis to a subset of the nominal forms, namely pronouns: lexical pronouns, zero pronouns, and pronoun copies. As noted above, each approach to L2 acquisition addresses a different stage in the acquisition process. As a result, at each stage in the L2-acquisition process, different constraints are proposed, either as constraints on processing L2 input or output or as L2 linguistic constraints to be acquired. An overview of these constraints on pronominal forms is given below:

(7.14) Constraints on pronominal forms in L2 acquisition
   (a) Input processing
      1. linguistic cues for sentence interpretation: Syntax: word order; Morphology: subject–verb agreement, nominal case marking, subject and object clitic pronouns; Semantics: animacy; Pragmatics: contrastive stress, topicalization;
      2. constraints on cue use: cue validity (based on cue availability and cue reliability), conflict validity, and cue cost (perceivability and assignability);
      3. input-processing principles for processing meaning: content

words first, lexical items before grammatical items, 'more meaningful' morphology before 'less or non-meaningful morphology', 'first noun strategy'.

(b) Linguistic constraints: syntactic
1. allowance of lexical pronouns or zero pronouns;
2. syntactic structures in which a given pronominal form can occur;
3. the positions of the pronoun (versus the full noun form) relative to the verb;
4. syntactic restrictions on coreference of pronouns;
5. markedness constraints on nominal grammatical devices;
6. markedness constraints on the allowance of pronoun copies.

(c) Linguistic constraints: semantic
1. differences in the semantic information encoded in the pronoun (gender, person, social relationship);
2. semantic constraints on information encoding: controller first, controller of source state outweighs controller of target state.

(d) Linguistic constraints: pragmatic
1. pragmatic constraints on information encoding: given versus new information, informational focus;
2. topic continuity/predictability constraints: referential distance, potential ambiguity, and topical persistence;
3. markedness constraints on discourse contexts.

(e) Output processing
1. constraints on hypothesis space (e.g. main and subordinate clauses, inter-phrasal information exchange, phrasal informational exchange, lexical morphemes, and words).

The constraints that are concentrated on within the UG and the Typological paradigms are mostly syntactic in nature. The stages, processing, and functional research represent a broader view with a focus on syntactic, morphological, semantic, and pragmatic constraints. The inclusion of these approaches in an examination of L2 acquisition helps to present a more comprehensive view of the L2 system that learners are acquiring.

A final review of some of the findings concerning pronominal forms also highlights this claim.

(7.15) Acquisition and Input/Output Processing of Pronominal Forms
(a) Stages
1. L2 learners tend to follow predicted stages of difficulty orders of object nouns/pronouns/zero anaphors based on L2-learner hypotheses from the perspective of L1/L2 comparisons.
2. L2 learners avoid difficult pronominal structures by using nouns instead of pronouns.

(b) Universal Grammar
1. IL grammars show evidence of UG constraints on zero pronouns: pro-drop tied to morphological structure.
2. L1 transfer of UG parameter settings occurs and may be structure dependent (e.g. referential versus nonreferential subjects for pro-drop).
3. Clustering of particular structures is constrained by abstract principles (e.g. binding: nouns, pronouns, reflexives, morphological structure, and syntactic domains; pro-drop: null subject pronouns, verbal morphological marking, declarative word orders, and topic marking).

(c) Typological Universals
1. The interaction between L1 transfer and typological universal markedness is demonstrated by the use of pronoun copies in relative clauses.

(d) Processing
1. Use of processing cues depends on the structures of the L1 and of the L2.
2. Transfer of semantic cues is easier than the transfer of syntactic cues.
3. Instruction can influence learners' processing of input of pronominal forms.

(e) Functions
1. Early IL grammars demonstrate interactions between syntactic, semantic, and discourse constraints on structure choice and word order: lexical nouns/zero anaphors, focus, topic maintenance/ topic shift, and thematic roles.
2. L2 production follows discourse topic constraints: e.g. nouns, zero anaphors, and pronoun copies conform to topic marking constraints on ambiguity and referential distance.
3. Beginning ILs demonstrate discourse functions before grammatical functions: given-new and first-/subsequent-mention functions before grammatical case marking.
4. L2 learners follow markedness constraints by beginning with structurally unmarked forms (e.g. zero anaphors) and subsequently increasing their use of structurally marked forms (e.g. left-dislocated definite nouns or existential indefinite nouns).

Though research in each theoretical paradigm is determined by distinct theoretical constructs, a comparison of the results reveals some interesting facts. First of all, we see that findings in one paradigm may be corroborated in another paradigm. For instance, the avoidance of difficult pronominal forms found in the stages research is also found in the functional research and is seen to conform to constraints on topic ambiguity. In addition, the L2 research shows evidence for the different notions of markedness: simplicity/complexity of nominal grammatical markers and typological frequency and distribution of pronoun copies. A final finding is that L1 influences are evident at different stages of L2 acquisition, for example, during both input processing and grammar building. This comparative analysis of the NP structures illustrates just a few examples of the interconnections that can be made from exploring L2 acquisition from a variety of theoretical approaches and suggests the benefits of a comparison of other grammatical structures from a similarly broad approach.

The issues in L2 acquisition presented in this book – the operative constraints, the sequence of the acquisition process, the role of the L1, and the role of instruction – highlight both the similarities and the differences between the theories guiding the work of L2 researchers. The perspectives that different theoretical approaches offer us add to the richness and complexity of information that we have. At the same time, however, these diverse perspectives also point to the incompleteness of the picture and stress the different routes that are available for arriving at a more complete picture.

7.4 Implications

The final aspect of L2 acquisition to be considered here is its application. There is no denying that there is a connection between language acquisition and language teaching. This connection is evident in a number of ways: the final 'Implications for Language Instruction' section in most L2-acquisition research articles, the required L2 acquisition course in teacher-training programmes, and students' queries concerning what all of this research information means for the L2 teacher. Nevertheless, the research/teaching connection is a controversial issue.

Several researchers have addressed the question of the implications of L2-acquisition research for the classroom, and there are various opinions on this matter, ranging from the belief that there need not be any direct implication for the L2 classroom to the belief that applied linguistics research may offer various implications for classroom instruction (Clarke 1994; Crookes 1997; Ellis 1997; Gass 1993, 1995a, b; Jakobovits 1974; Lightbown 1985; Martohardjono and Flynn 1995). Here we examine several issues raised in the L2 syntactic acquisition research which may be relevant to L2 classroom learning and L2 classroom instruction. However, it is first necessary to discuss a few basic assumptions.

7.4.1 BASIC ASSUMPTIONS

The first common assumption is that L2-acquisition research should be directly applicable to the L2 classroom. This is not necessarily true. Basic research involving theoretical or experimental investigation seeks to gain knowledge about a particular phenomenon, whereas the goal of applied research is to use knowledge towards a practical end. Let us define basic research in this case as research concerned with theories of human language and of human behaviour related to language acquisition and applied research in this case as research concerned with the practice of teaching and learning languages (cf. Newmeyer 1983). Given these definitions, basic L2-acquisition research need not address, and in many cases does not address, questions of immediate concern to language teachers.

Several researchers (Ellis 1997; Gass 1995a; Lightbown 1985; Martohardjono and Flynn 1995; Pica 1994) have suggested ways in which L2-research findings are relevant to L2 pedagogy. For example, Pica (1994) illustrates several ways in which L2 research offers answers to some of teachers' most frequently asked questions. However, two facts become clear: whereas some of the questions asked by L2 teachers are indeed addressed in some form and to some extent by basic L2-acquisition research undertaken within some approaches – e.g. the effect of an L1 on learning an L2 or the role of explicit or negative input on L2 acquisition – other concerns are clearly of a pedagogical nature and have generated less L2-acquisition research – e.g. the encouragement of student participation and the effectiveness of group work. In addition, Ellis (1997: 70) echoes earlier admonitions by Hatch (1978b) when he notes that, in the still young field of L2-acquisition research, 'there are still few certainties. It might be felt, therefore, that "apply with caution" – or not at all – should still be the order of the day.'

Proceeding with caution, we make a second assumption, which is that here we are addressing potential implications of L2-acquisition research for the L2 classroom teacher to consider rather than endorsing direct applications of research findings to the L2 classroom. From a theorist's view, Newmeyer (1983) has argued that much of the disillusionment with early generative linguistic theory was based on the slow emergence of possible applications and the misapplication of theory to language teaching. In an earlier discussion of the topic from the teacher's perspective, Jakobovits (1974) argued that the expectations that language teachers have of 'experts' and their research is unrealistic and that the instructional activities are the responsibility of the teacher. Jakobovits endorsed that teachers have the 'freedom to teach ... freedom from the tyranny of irrelevant expertise, freedom to feel the responsibility that goes with professional integrity' (p. 85). Clarke (1994) similarly maintains that teachers need to evaluate researchers' and theorists' recommendations in the light of their own expertise and teaching situations.

With these cautionary notes in mind, one can still claim that basic L2-acquisition research offers insights into many L2-acquisition issues: what our learners are doing, how the acquisition process proceeds, what our learners can attend to and are attending to, and what effects grammatical, discourse, and processing constraints have on L2 learning and production. While the research findings may answer these questions, the answer is not necessarily directly applicable to the classroom. For example, authentic classroom settings are not the same as classroom research settings; what results from a research study may be very different from what results from similar classroom instruction. Language teachers can benefit by understanding the L2-acquisition process; however, few, if any, L2-acquisition researchers would argue that experimental conditions can or should be adopted in the L2 classroom.

Additionally, it is important to note that in this book we have dealt with the issues involved in L2 acquisition of syntax. This represents only a single aspect of the L2-acquisition process. One must recognize that language acquisition is an extraordinarily complex process including a wide variety of factors: grammatical factors, processing factors, and psychological and sociocultural factors. No research finding will or can address all of these potential learning factors. As Ellis (1997: 74) points out, L2-acquisition researchers have a much more narrow focus than do language teachers – for instance, the description of grammatical competence as opposed to the goal of increased proficiency in communicative settings.

Similarly, language teaching is an extraordinarily complex process. While the learners' L2 acquisition is the long-term goal, teachers are faced with innumerable issues both inside and outside the classroom: establishing long-term and short-term goals; selecting content; selecting, preparing, and organizing activities, materials, and teaching strategies; meeting student prerequisite skills; predicting and avoiding problems; meeting the needs of individual students; motivating all students; managing the class; strengthening teaching skills; evaluating results and re-evaluating teaching practices; and completing administrative tasks, to name but a few. Teachers are constantly making decisions about this wide range of issues. In an analysis of teachers' decisions, Clarke (1994) clearly illustrates the complexity of this decision-making process with an individual teacher's identification of eight different factors contributing to three of her videotaped classroom decisions. Additionally, Richards and Lockhart (1994: 78–89) categorize teachers' decisions into three categories: planning decisions which teachers make before a lesson is taught, interactive decisions which teachers make during the course of the lesson in reaction to the changing dynamics of the lesson, and evaluative decisions which teachers make after a lesson has been taught. Any discussion of the implications of L2 research to teaching must be based on the recognition that an understanding of L2 acquisition, while important, is but one area of expertise that a language teacher has to master.

To summarize these points, the following basic assumptions delineate the limits of the subsequent discussion of classroom implications of L2 research:

(7.16) Basic assumptions
   (a) *language learning assumption*: the recognition that no single research finding nor body of research will or can address all of the relevant learning factors;

(b) *language teaching assumption*: the recognition that an understanding of L2 acquisition is but one of a language teacher's areas of expertise;

(c) *language teacher assumption*: the recognition that language teachers are decision-makers;

(d) *L2-acquisition research assumption*: the belief that L2-acquisition research can offer insights into the language learning process, and that, while authentic classroom settings are not the same as classroom research settings, the results of research can add to the knowledge base from which teachers make decisions.

The perspective taken here is that L2-acquisition research can serve two basic needs: first, it offers valuable information and forms a basis for generating additional questions and research about L2 acquisition. Second, based on the notion that teaching involves a series of decisions, L2-research findings can form one body of information from which teachers re-evaluate what they do in the classroom and why they do it.

7.4.2 TEACHERS AS DECISION-MAKERS

What is the basis of teachers' decisions? From the narrow perspective of language, pedagogical decisions are based on the teacher's knowledge and beliefs about the nature of language, the nature of language learning, and the nature and needs of language learners (see Richards and Lockhart 1994 and Freeman 1989 for a broader focus). These beliefs influence, explicitly or implicitly, the decisions that teachers make regarding instruction. No claim is made that L2-acquisition research translates directly into classroom practice. Simply, the idea to be pursued here is that L2-acquisition research offers results that teachers can use, in addition to other information, to formulate, or reformulate, their notions about language, language learning, and language teaching. In order to pursue this proposal, we will take each area – language, language learning, and language teaching – and outline a few examples from the research that offer insights for teachers.

7.4.2.1 Language

In terms of language, we have seen throughout this work that L2 research into the acquisition of syntax has explored the nature of language from the view of syntactic, semantic, and pragmatic/discourse constraints. While language textbooks may be very good at presenting learners and teachers alike with pedagogical rules, they do not deal with some of the abstract constraints which are proposed to influence learners' L2 acquisition. For instance, textbooks offer detailed explanations of relative-clause formation and the choice of correct relative pronouns. However, textbooks do not take into account the issues of unmarked/marked relative clauses and pronoun copies that we have seen in the typological research that affect the frequency and accuracy of relative clauses, the avoidance of marked forms, and the use of pronoun copies.

L2 research on pronouns also offers other illuminating examples. A list of pronouns with their translations does not comprise all there is to know about pronouns: the syntactic constraints on local or long-distance coreference; the syntactic, semantic, and discourse constraints on zero pronouns; the distinction between structurally marked and unmarked nominal forms (e.g. zero pronouns, clitic pronouns, stressed pronouns, full nouns), and the processing difficulties related to pronouns. This series of findings clearly illustrates that a seemingly simple form that is usually taught quite early is deceptively complex.

A final 'language' example is word order. While the strict nature of English word order is quite straightforward as opposed to the word order in languages such as German, Italian, and Spanish, we have seen in several chapters that the constraints on English word order are somewhat complex. For example, from a typological perspective, English question word order is determined by markedness. The descriptions of the stages of development of negation and questions also demonstrate the complexity of English word order. Moreover, the examples of the possible adverb placements as determined by the verb-movement parameter of UG also demonstrate that the rules for word order are not always clearly evident on the surface. These few examples – relative clauses, pronouns, and word order – show that the linguistic constraints on these structures are both complicated and abstract in nature. Pedagogical rules often mask the abstractness and true complexity of the language rules with which our learners are dealing.

7.4.2.2 Language learning

All experienced language teachers realize that teaching a language form does not entail that the form is learned. In addition, evidence of 'mastery' of a form may be short-lived – until after the unit test, for example. In addition, the acquisition of the form does not necessarily entail the acquisition of the function. Several of the L2-acquisition studies address some of these language-learning issues explicitly, while others may simply hint at possible causes of the learning sequences and reversals.

L2 research into the developmental stages of certain structures – e.g. German word order – provide an approximate map for the developmental sequences. Although most of the developmental stages outlined are the result of L2 acquisition in a natural environment as opposed to an instructed environment, L2 research has shown that the natural sequences are followed to some extent by learners in an instructional setting as well (cf. Lightbown 1985).

Another phenomenon found in natural acquisition is the gradual change from one form–function mapping to another (e.g. the function of definite and indefinite articles). L2 learners do not necessarily acquire the form and the function at the same time. In addition, learners seem to acquire some discourse functions before they acquire the grammatical forms to mark those functions. The gradual development of form–function mapping in instructional settings is suggested in some of the research concerning object pronouns: instructed learners may begin with lexical pronouns to refer to entities in the grammatical object position and then adopt the zero pronoun or the full noun before shifting back to the native-like use of the lexical pronoun.

Language learning is also proposed to be influenced by the clustering of several language structures controlled by a single grammatical constraint. The UG research examining these related structures – e.g. the relation between verbal morphological marking and the restrictions on nouns and pronouns or the movement restrictions on adverbs, negation, and questions – suggests that the L2 acquisition of such structures is also influenced by the L1. Although the effects of these acquisitional interactions are currently unresolved, the abstract connections between seemingly unrelated structures may offer insights into the sometimes puzzling structures that are in evidence in our students' IL systems. However, Gass (1995b) argues that the abstract connection between these clustered structures may in fact be the reason why the parameters do not function as they do in L1 acquisition. That is, L2 learners do not perceive these structures as related. Those structures that are seen as more connected – e.g. subject–verb inversion and subject zero pronouns – may offer a better test case for the L2 acquisition of clustered structures.

Finally, the notion of markedness as related to both the L1 and the L2 structures is discussed throughout this work as a determining factor in L2 acquisition. Just as the notion of markedness is delineated in different ways in the different theoretical paradigms, markedness is seen as having a variety of influences on the language-learning process: determining the ease or difficulty of acquisition and determining the transferability of particular structures.

7.4.2.3 Language teaching

Sometimes the goals of basic research – testing a linguistic theory – and the goals of applied research – testing different kinds of instruction – overlap. From the perspective of language teaching, the most clearly relevant research consists of the studies which have attempted to test the theories with different types of instructional input. The examples of instructional studies are varied, and the results of these studies have been intriguing.

For example, within the typological paradigm some research shows that the teaching of a more marked structure on the Noun Phrase Accessibility Hierarchy results in students learning both the instructed marked forms and the uninstructed unmarked forms. Research comparing the effectiveness of implicit positive, explicit positive, and explicit negative input for changing UG parameter settings highlights the need for explicit instruction and explicit grammar correction in some cases. From the perspective of Input Processing, research examining the effectiveness of processing instruction emphasizes the importance of the necessary linking of form and meaning in language-teaching tasks. Finally, the application of the teachability hypothesis to test the flexibility of developmental stages, which are determined by processing constraints, demonstrates that, although instruction does not change the sequence of stages, instruction can alter learners' movement through the stages with increased speed of learning, and increased frequency of use and distribution of structures.

7.5 Conclusions

Finally, we must ask, 'What are the possible implications of these research findings?' We have seen that L2-acquisition researchers ask questions that are not directly related to the classroom. This basic research into the nature of language can, however, provide teachers with an awareness of grammatical details and intricacies that offer insights into the complexity of the system our learners are attempting to learn. This awareness has several implications. First of all, like the strong and weak versions of the contrastive analysis hypothesis discussed in Chapter 1, the results of this basic research can give teachers a greater understanding of the reasons behind their students' learning difficulties. Take zero subject and object pronouns as an example. The persistence of these forms in learner spoken and written production can be exasperating without some understanding of the causes. These zero forms may be the result of the transfer of the L1 setting of the pro-drop parameter into the L2, or they may be the manifestation of an inappropriate topic-prominent orientation to the L2. If our linguistic analyses are correct, we can explore the cause by looking for other indicative characteristics – for instance, uniform morphological marking for pro-drop or double-subject constructions for topic prominence.

While this 'weak' approach may prove beneficial, a strong predictive position is not yet possible given the contradictory nature of some of the current research results. Nevertheless, the predictions made in the L2 research are testable in the classroom. The effects of typological markedness on the L2 acquisition of relative clauses and wh-questions can be tested by trying different instructional sequences. The 'processing instruction' advocated in the Input Processing approach is another likely candidate for classroom testing (Lee and VanPatten 1995). A goal of such classroom testing – for example, is this instructional approach more effective for *my* students than my current approach to this grammatical structure? – would be better able to take into account the individual educational setting and, as a result, would be much more applicable for that class and that teacher in that setting. This type of teacher-centred approach is advocated by Clarke (1994).

A final implication of this grammatical awareness is outlined by Lightbown (1985), who notes that this knowledge serves to temper teachers' expectations of what they can accomplish given the complex nature of the language-acquisition process. Moreover, teachers will also have more realistic expectations of what their students can accomplish.

In addition to the issue of grammatical awareness, many of the issues raised in the L2 research related to language learning and language teaching do have implications for teachers, if approached with caution. One of the central aspects of teachers' planning concerns the content and the manner of instruction: in other words, what to teach, when to teach it, how to teach it, and how much to teach it. Research into the effects of developmental stages and markedness on language learning suggests possible alternatives concerning what to teach and when to teach it. For example, the 'logical' leap from learning to teaching would be to propose that structures be taught in accordance with the developmental sequence (Pienemann 1985, 1987). This, however, is not always feasible nor always desirable depending on student needs. That is, L2 learners might need to be familiar with late-learned structures early – for example, question inversion – because of the demands of communication (Nunan 1994). The compromise is to teach the structure for comprehension early in the acquisition process and not to expect learner production until much later. This points out the interaction between the linguistic restrictions and the communicative needs that must be taken into account in teaching decisions.

The issues of what to teach, how to teach it, and how much to teach it have been addressed from a UG theoretical perspective by Rutherford and Sharwood Smith (1985). They suggest one implication of UG theory to L2 teaching is in choosing the structure to teach, the explicitness of instruction, and the extent of instruction based on the markedness of particular parameter settings and the availability of the input triggers. Similarly, Martohardjono and Flynn (1995) suggest that UG-based L2 research can influence the development of theory-driven language pedagogy based on an understanding of the complexity of structures. As with the L2 instructional research discussed above, such direct applications of L2 theoretical research would require taking into account the constraints of the real classroom in order to test the effectiveness of the suggested classroom interventions.

The end result is that researchers may identify a number of implications of L2 research for L2 teaching, but researchers cannot address the intricacies of the direct applications of these implications into individual classrooms. The cautious tone adopted here underscores the complexity of the theoretical and pedagogical issues involved. The research–teaching connection may not be as direct or as strong as some would like it to be. The techniques and goals are different. L2 researchers are experts who develop theories and test the questions raised within those theories. L2 teachers are experts who make decisions about the most effective ways to promote language learning by artfully using a variety of techniques, skills, and knowledge. What is needed is a realistic means of translating L2 theory into practice (Clarke 1994; Crookes

1997; Ellis 1997). The moral of this research–teaching story is relatively simple: the more we know about language and language learning, the more informed decisions we make about language teaching. The crucial part of this moral is knowing how to use this knowledge most effectively.

References

Adjemian, C. 1976: On the nature of interlanguage systems. *Language Learning* 26, 297–320.

Agnello, F. 1977: Exploring the pidginization hypothesis: a study of three fossilized negation systems. In Henning, C.A. (ed.), *Proceedings of the Los Angeles Second Language Research Forum*. Los Angeles: Department of English, University of Los Angeles, 224–34.

Andersen, R.W. 1983: Transfer to somewhere. In Gass, S. and Selinker, L. (eds.), *Language Transfer in Language Learning*. Rowley, MA: Newbury House, 177–201.

—— (1984): Discussant. In response to Kellerman. In Davies, A., Criper, C., and Howatt, A.P.R. (eds.), *Interlanguage*. Edinburgh: Edinburgh University Press, 123–9.

Badalamenti, V. and Henner-Stanchina, C. 1993: *Grammar Dimensions: Form, Meaning, and Use*. Boston, MA: Heinle & Heinle.

Baker, C.L. 1979: Syntactic theory and the projection problem. *Linguistic Inquiry* 10, 533–81.

Bailey, N. 1989: Theoretical implications of the acquisition of the English simple past and past progressive: putting together the pieces of the puzzle. In Gass, S.M., Madden, C., Preston, D. and Selinker, L. (eds.), *Variation in Second Language Acquisition. Volume 2: Psycholinguistic Issues*. Clevedon, Avon: Multilingual Matters, 109–24.

—— Madden, C., and Krashen, S. 1974: Is there a 'natural sequence' in adult second language learning? *Language Learning* 21, 235–43.

Bardovi-Harlig, K. 1992a: The relationship of form and meaning: a cross-sectional study of tense and aspect in the interlanguage of learners of English as a second language. *Applied Psycholinguistics* 13, 253–78.

—— 1992b: The use of adverbials and natural order in the development of temporal expression. *International Review of Applied Linguistics* 30, 299–320.

Bates, E. and MacWhinney, B. 1981: Second-language acquisition from a functionalist perspective: pragmatic, semantic, and perceptual strategies. In Winitz, H. (ed.), *Native Language and Foreign Language Acquisition*. New York: Annals of the New York Academy of Sciences 379, 190–214.

—— —— 1982: Functionalist approaches to grammar. In Wanner, E. and Gleitman, L.R. (eds.), *Language Acquisition: The State of The Art*. Cambridge: Cambridge University Press, 173–218.

—— —— 1987: Competition, variation and language learning. In MacWhinney, B. (ed.), *Mechanisms of Language Acquisition*. Hillsdale, NJ: Lawrence Erlbaum, 157–93.

—— —— Caselli, C., Devescovi, A., Natale, F. and Venza, V. 1984: A cross-linguistic study of the development of sentence interpretation strategies. *Child Development* 55, 341–54.

—————— and Smith, S. 1983: Pragmatics and syntax in psycholinguistic research. In Felix, S.W. and Wode, H. (eds.), *Language Development at the Crossroads*. Tübingen: Gunter Narr, 11–30.

Battistella, E. 1989: Chinese reflexivization: a movement to INFL approach. *Linguistics* 27, 987–1012.

Bennett, S. 1994: Interpretation of English reflexives by adolescent speakers of Serbo-Croation. *Second Language Research* 10, 125–56.

Bialystok, E. 1978: A theoretical model of second language learning. *Language Learning* 28, 69–83.

—————— 1981: The role of linguistic knowledge in second language use. *Studies in Second Language Acquisition* 4, 31–45.

—————— 1985: The compatibility of teaching and learning strategies. *Applied Linguistics* 6, 255–61.

—————— 1988: Psycholinguistic dimensions of second language proficiency. In Rutherford, W. and Sharwood Smith, M. (eds.), *Grammar and Second Language Teaching*. Boston MA: Heinle & Heinle, 31–50.

—————— 1990a: The competence of processing: classifying theories of second language acquisition. *TESOL Quarterly* 24, 635–48.

—————— 1990b: The dangers of dichotomy: a reply to Hulstijn. *Applied Linguistics* 11, 46–51.

—————— 1992: Selective attention in cognitive processing: the bilingual edge. In Harris, R.J. (ed.), *Cognitive Processing in Bilinguals*. Amsterdam: North-Holland, 501–13.

—————— 1994: Representation and ways of knowing: three issues in second language acquisition. In Ellis, N.C. (ed.), *Implicit and Explicit Learning of Languages*. London: Academic Press, 549–69.

—————— 1997: The structure of age: in search of barriers to second language acquisition. *Second Language Research* 13, 116–37.

—————— and Ryan, E.B. 1985: A metacognitive framework for the development of first and second language skills. In Forrest-Pressley, D.L. MacKinnon, G.E. and Waller T.G. (eds.), *Metacognition, Cognition and Human Performance. Volume 1: Theoretical Perspectives*. Orlando, FL: Harcourt Brace Jovanovich, 207–52.

—————— and Sharwood Smith, M. 1985: Interlanguage is not a state of mind: an evaluation of the construct for second language acquisition. *Applied Linguistics* 6, 101–17.

Bley-Vroman, R.W. 1983: The comparative fallacy in interlanguage studies: the case of systematicity. *Language Learning* 33, 1–17.

—————— 1989: What is the logical problem of foreign language learning? In Gass, S.M. and Schachter, J. (eds.), *Linguistic Perspectives on Second Language Acquisition*. Cambridge: Cambridge University Press, 41–68.

—————— 1991: Processing, constraints on acquisition, and the parsing of ungrammatical sentences. In Eubank, L. (ed.), *Point Counterpoint: Universal Grammar in the Second Language*. Amsterdam: John Benjamins, 191–7.

—————— Felix, S.W. and Ioup, G.L. 1988: The accessibility of universal grammar in adult language. *Second Language Research* 4, 1–32.

Bowerman, M. 1982: Starting to talk worse: clues to language acquisition from children's late speech errors. In Strauss, S. (ed.), *U-Shaped Behavioral Growth*. New York: Academic Press, 101–45.

Braidi, S.M. 1991a: A theoretical framework for the interaction of input and syntactic principles and parameters in the formation of second language grammars. Doctoral dissertation, University of Delaware, 1990. *Dissertation Abstracts International* 51, 3720A.

—————— 1991b: Reanalyzing universal grammar effects in second language acquisition from an input perspective. Paper presented at the 11th Second Language Research Forum, Los Angeles.

Braidi, S.M. 1995: Reconsidering the role of interaction and input in second language acquisition. *Language Learning* **45**:1, 141–75.

Broselow, E. and Finer, D. 1991: Parameter setting in second language phonology and syntax. *Second Language Research* **7**, 35–59.

Brown, J.D. 1983: An exploration of morpheme-group interactions. In Bailey, K.M., Long, M. and Peck, S. (eds.), *Second Language Acquisition Studies*. Rowley, MA: Newbury House, 25–40.

Brown, R. 1973. *A First Language*. Cambridge, MA: Harvard University Press.

—— and Hanlon, C. 1970: Derivational complexity and order of acquisition in child speech. In Hayes, J.R. (ed.), *Cognition and the Development of Language*. New York: Wiley, 11–52.

Butterworth, G. and Hatch, E. 1978: A Spanish-speaking adolescent's acquisition of English syntax. In Hatch, E. (ed.), *Second Language Acquisition*. Rowley, MA: Newbury House, 231–45.

Cancino, H., Rosansky, E.J. and Schumann, J. 1978: The acquisition of English negatives and interrogatives by native Spanish speakers. In Hatch, E.M. (ed.), *Second Language Acquisition: a Book of Readings*. Rowley, MA: Newbury House, 207–30.

Cazden, C. 1968: The acquisition of noun and verb inflections. *Child Development* **39**, 433–48.

Chafe, W.L. 1976: Givenness, contrastiveness, definiteness, subjects, topics, and point of view. In Li, C.N. (ed.), *Subject and Topic*. New York: Academic Press, 25–55.

—— 1980: *The Pear Stories: Cognitive, Cultural and Linguistic Aspects of Narrative Production*. Norwood, NJ: Ablex.

Chaudron, C. 1988: *Second Language Classrooms: Research on Teaching and Learning*. Cambridge, MA: Cambridge University Press.

—— and Parker, K. 1990: Discourse markedness and structural markedness: the acquisition of English noun phrases. *Studies in Second Language Acquisition* **12**, 43–64.

Chomsky, N. 1965: *Aspects of the Theory of Syntax*. Cambridge, MA: MIT Press.

—— 1981: *Lectures on Government and Binding*. Dordrecht: Foris.

—— 1986a: *Barriers*. Cambridge, MA: MIT Press.

—— 1986b: *Knowledge of Language*. New York: Praeger.

—— 1988: *Language and Problems of Knowledge: the Managua Lectures*. Cambridge, MA: The MIT Press.

—— 1992: *A minimalist Program for Linguistic Theory*. MIT Occasional Papers in Linguistics 1. Cambridge, MA: MIT, Department of Linguistics and Philosophy.

—— 1995: *The Minimalist Program*. Cambridge, MA: MIT Press.

—— and Lasnik, H. 1995: The theory of principles and parameters. In Chomsky, N. *The Minimalist Program*. Cambridge, MA: MIT Press, 13–127.

Clahsen, H. 1980: Psycholinguistic aspects of L2 acquisition: word order phenomena in foreign workers. In Felix, S. (ed.), *Second Language Development: Trends and Issues*. Tübingen: Gunter Narr, 57–79.

—— 1984: The acquisition of German word order: a test case for cognitive approaches to L2 development. In Andersen, R.W. (ed.), *Second Languages: a Cross-linguistic Perspective*. Rowley, MA: Newbury House, 219–42.

—— 1988a: Critical phases of grammar development. A study of the acquisition of negation in children and adults. In Jordens, P. and Lalleman, J. (eds.), *Language Development*. Dordrecht: Foris, 123- 48.

—— 1988b: Parameterized grammatical theory and language acquisition: a study of the acquisition of verb placement and inflection by children and adults. In Flynn, S. and O'Neil, W. (eds.), *Linguistic Theory in Second Language Acquisition*. Dordrecht: Kluwer, 47–75.

—— and Muysken, P. 1986: The availability of universal grammar to adult and child learners – a study of the acquisition of German word order. *Second Language Research* 2, 93–119.

—— —— 1989: The UG paradox in L2 acquisition. *Second Language Research* 5, 1–29.

Clarke, M. 1994: The dysfunctions of theory/practice discourse. *TESOL Quarterly* 28, 9–26.

Cole, P., Hermon, G. and Sung, L.-M. 1990: Principles and parameters of long distance reflexives. *Linguistic Inquiry* 21, 1–22.

Comrie, B. 1981: *Language Universals and Linguistic Typology*. Chicago: University of Chicago Press.

—— 1984: Why linguists need language acquirers. In Rutherford, W.E. (ed.), *Language Universals and Second Language Acquisition*. Philadelphia: John Benjamins, 11–29.

—— and Keenan, E.L. 1979: Noun phrase accessibility revisited. *Language* 55, 649–64.

Corder, S.P. 1967: The significance of learner's errors. *International Review of Applied Linguistics* 5, 161–70.

—— 1983: A role for the mother tongue. In Gass, S. and Selinker, L., *Language Transfer in Language Learning*. Rowley, MA: Newbury House, 85–97.

Croft, W. 1990: *Typology and Universals*. Cambridge: Cambridge University Press.

Crookes, G. 1997: SLA and language pedagogy: a socioeducational perspective. *Studies in Second Language Acquisition* 19, 93–116.

Croteau, K.C. 1995: Second language acquisition of relative clause structures by learners of Italian. In Eckman, F.R., Highland, D., Lee, P.W., Milcham, J. and Weber Rutkowski, R. (eds.), *Second Language Acquisition Theory and Pedagogy*. Mahwah, NJ: Lawrence Erlbaum, 115–28.

Crystal, D. 1991. *A Dictionary of Linguistics and Phonetics*. 3rd edn. Oxford: Basil Blackwell.

DeKeyser, R.M. 1994: Implicit and explicit learning of L2 grammar: a pilot study. *TESOL Quarterly* 28, 188–94.

—— (1995): Learning second language grammar rules an experiment with a miniature linguistic system. *Studies in Second Language Acquisition* 17, 379–410.

—— 1997: Beyond explicit rule learning: automatizing second language morphosyntax. *Studies in Second Language Acquisition* 19, 195–221.

—— and Sokalski, K.J. 1996: The differential role of comprehension and production practice. *Language Learning* 46, 613–42.

De Villiers, J. and De Villiers, P. 1973: A cross-sectional study of the acquisition of grammatical morphemes in child speech. *Journal of Psycholinguistic Research* 2, 267–78.

Dietrich, R., Klein, W. and Noyau, C. 1995: *The Acquisition of Temporality in a Second Language*. Amsterdam: John Benjamins.

Dittmar, N. 1992: Introduction: grammaticalization in second language acquisition. *Studies in Second Language Acquisition* 14, 249–57.

Doughty, C. 1991: Second language instruction does make a difference. *Studies in Second Language Acquisition*, 13, 431–69.

Dulay, H. and Burt, M. 1972: Goofing, an indicator of children's second language strategies. *Language Learning* 22, 235–52.

—— —— 1973: Should we teach children syntax? *Language Learning* 23, 245–58.

—— —— 1974a: Errors and strategies in child second language acquisition. *TESOL Quarterly* 8, 129–36.

—— —— 1974b: Natural sequences in child second language acquisition. *Language Learning* 24, 37–53.

Du Plessis, J., Solan, D., Travis, L. and White, L. 1987: UG or not UG, that is the question: a reply to Clahsen and Muysken. *Second Language Research* 3, 56–75.

Eckman, F.R. 1977: Markedness and the contrastive analysis hypothesis. *Language* 27, 315–30.

—— 1985a: Some theoretical and pedagogical implications of the markedness differential hypothesis. *Studies in Second Language Acquisition* 7, 289–307.

—— 1985b: The markedness differential hypothesis: theory and applications. In Wheatley, B., Hastings, A., Eckman, F.R., Bell, L., Krukar, G. and Rutkowski, R. (eds.), *Current Approaches to Second Language Acquisition: Proceedings of the 1984 University of Wisconsin-Milwaukee Linguistics Symposium*. Bloomington, IN: Indiana University Linguistics Club, 3–21.

—— 1988. Typological and parametric views of universals in second language acquisition. In Flynn, S. and O'Neil, W. (eds.), *Linguistic Theory in Second Language Acquisition*. Dordrecht: Kluwer, 417–29.

—— 1993: Introduction: one approach to the interaction of linguistics, second-language acquisition, and speech-language pathology. In Eckman, F.R. (ed.), *Confluence Linguistics, L2 Acquisition and Speech Pathology*. Philadelphia: John Benjamins, vii–xv.

—— Bell, L. and Nelson, D. 1988: On the generalization of relative clause instruction in the acquisition of English as a second language. *Applied Linguistics* 9, 1–20.

—— Moravcsik, E.A. and Wirth, J.R. 1989: Implicational universals and interrogative structures in the interlanguage of ESL learners. *Language Learning* 39, 173–205.

Ellis, R. 1984: Can syntax be taught? A study of the effects of formal instruction on the acquisition of WH questions by children. *Applied Linguistics* 5, 138–55.

—— 1997: SLA and language pedagogy. An educational perspective. *Studies in Second Language Acquisition* 19, 69–92.

Eubank, L. 1989a: Parameters in L2 learning: Flynn revisited. *Second Language Research* 5, 43–73.

—— 1989b: A look at a new classic. *University of Hawai'i Working Papers in ESL* 8, 129–53.

—— 1992: Verb movement, agreement, and tense in L2 acquisition. In Meisel, J.M. (ed.), *The Acquisition of Verb Placement: Functional Categories and V2 Phenomena in Language Acquisition*. Dordrecht: Kluwer, 225–44.

—— 1994: Optionality and the initial state in L2 development. In Hoekstra, T. and Schwartz, B.D. (eds.), *Language Acquisition Studies in Generative Grammar*. Amsterdam/Philadelphia: John Benjamins, 369–88.

—— 1997: SLA and language pedagogy: an educational perspective. *Studies in Second Language Acquisition* 19, 69–92.

Faerch, C. and Kasper, G. 1986: Cognitive dimensions of language transfer. In Kellerman, E. and Sharwood Smith, M. (eds.), *Crosslinguistic Influence in Second Language Acquisition*. New York: Pergamon, 49–65.

Fakhri, A. 1989: Variation in the use of referential forms within the context of foreign language loss. In Gass, S., Madden, C., Preston, D. and Selinker, L. (eds.), *Variation in Second Language Acquisition. Volume 2: Psycholinguistic Issues*. Clevedon, Avon: Multilingual Matters, 189–201.

Felix, S.W. 1977: Early syntactic development in first and second language acquisition. In Henning, C.A. (ed.), *Proceedings of the Los Angeles Second Language Research Forum*. Los Angeles, 147–59.

—— 1980: Interference, interlanguage and related issues. In Felix, S.W. (ed.), *Second Language Development: Trends and Issues*. Tübingen: Gunter Narr, 93–107.

—— 1988: UG-generated knowledge in adult second language acquisition. In Flynn, S. and O'Neil, W. (eds.), *Linguistic Theory in Second Language Acquisition*. Dordrecht: Kluwer, 277–94.

Fillmore, C.J. 1968. The case for case. In Bach, E. and Harms, R.T. (eds.), *Universals in Linguistic Theory*. New York: Holt, Rinehart and Winston, 1–88.

Finer, D.L. 1991: Binding parameters in second language acquisition. In Eubank, L. (ed.), *Point Counterpoint: Universal Grammar in the Second Language*. Philadelphia: John Benjamins, 351–74.

—— and Broselow, E.I. 1986: Second language acquisition of reflexive binding. In Berman, S. Choe, J.-W. and McDonough, J. (eds.), *NELS 16: Proceedings of the 16th Annual Northeastern Linguistic Society Meeting*. Amherst, MA: GLAS Department of Linguistics, 154–68.

Flynn, S. 1984: A universal in L2 acquisition based on a PBD typology. In Eckman, F.R., Bell, L.H. and Nelson, D. (eds.), *Universals of Second Language Acquisition*. Rowley, MA: Newbury House, 75–87.

—— 1987a: Contrast and construction in a parameter-setting model of L2 acquisition. *Language Learning* 37, 19–62.

—— 1987b: *A Parameter-setting Model of L2 Acquisition: Experimental Studies in Anaphora*. Dordrecht: Reidel Press.

—— 1988: Nature of development in L2 acquisition and implications for theories on language acquisition in general. In Flynn, S. and O'Neil, W. (eds.), *Linguistic Theory in Second Language Acquisition*. Dordrecht: Kluwer, 79–89.

—— 1993b: Interactions between L2 acquisition and linguistic theory. In Eckman, F.R. (ed.), *Confluence: Linguistics, L2 Acquisition, and Speech Pathology*. Philadelphia: John Benjamins, 15–35.

Frawley, W. 1992: *Linguistic Semantics*. Hillsdale, NJ: Lawrence Erlbaum.

Freeman, D. 1989: Teacher training, development, and decisionmaking: a model of teaching and related strategies for language teacher education. *TESOL Quarterly* 23, 27–45.

Fries, C. 1945: *Teaching and Learning English as a Foreign Language*. Ann Arbor, MI: University of Michigan Press.

Fuller, J.W. and Gundel, J.K. 1987: Topic-prominence in interlanguage. *Language Learning* 1, 1–18.

Gass, S.M. 1979: Language transfer and universal grammatical relations. *Language Learning* 29, 327–44.

—— 1980: An investigation of syntactic transfer in adult second language learners. In Scarcella R.C. and Krashen, S.D. (eds.), *Research in Second Language Acquisition*, 132–41.

—— 1982: From theory to practice. In Hines, M. and Rutherford, W. (eds.), *On TESOL '81*. Washington, DC: TESOL, 129–39.

—— 1983: Language transfer and universal grammatical relations. In Gass, S.M. and Selinker, L. (eds.), *Language Transfer in Language Learning*. Rowley, MA: Newbury House, 69–82.

—— 1984: A review of interlanguage syntax: language transfer and language universals. *Language Learning* 34, 115–31.

—— 1987: The resolution of conflicts among competing systems: a bidirectional perspective. *Applied Psycholinguistics* 8, 329–50.

—— 1988a: Integrating research areas: a framework for second language studies. *Applied Linguistics* 9, 198–217.

—— 1988b: Second language acquisition and linguistic theory: The role of language transfer. In Flynn, S. and O'Neil, W. (eds.), *Linguistic Theory in Second Language Acquisition*. Dordrecht: Kluwer, 384–403.

—— 1989a: How do learners resolve linguistic conflicts?. In Gass, S. and Schachter, J. (eds.), *Linguistic Perspectives on Second Language Acquisition*. Cambridge: Cambridge University Press, 183–199.

Gass, S.M. 1989b: Language universals and second-language acquisition. *Language Learning* **39**, 497–534.

—— 1993: Second language acquisition: past, present and future. *Second Language Research* **9**, 99–117.

—— 1994: The reliability of second-language grammaticality judgments. In Tarone, E.E., Gass, S.M. and Cohen, A.D. (eds.), *Research Methodology in Second-Language Acquisition*. Hillsdale, NJ: Lawrence Erlbaum, 303–22.

—— 1995a: Learning and teaching: the necessary intersection. In Eckman, F.R., Highland, D., Lee, P.W., Milcham, J. and Weber Rutkowski, R. (eds.), *Second Language Acquisition Theory and Pedagogy*. Mahwah, NJ.: Lawrence Erlbaum, 3–20.

—— 1995b: Universals, SLA, and language pedagogy: 1984 revisited. In Eubank, L., Selinker, L. and Sharwood Smith, M. (eds.), *The Current State of Interlanguage: Studies in Honor of William E. Rutherford*. Amsterdam: John Benjamins, 31–42.

—— and Ard, J. 1984: Second language acquisition and the ontology of language universal. In Rutherford, W.E. (ed.), *Language Universals and Second Language Acquisition*. Philadelphia: John Benjamins, 33–68.

—— and Selinker, L. 1983: *Language Transfer in Language Learning*. Rowley, MA: Newbury House.

—— —— 1992: Introduction. In Gass, S.M. and Selinker, L. (eds.), *Language Transfer in Language Learning* (rev. edn.). Amsterdam: John Benjamins, 1–17.

—— and Varonis, E. 1989: Incorporated repairs in nonnative discourse. In Eisenstein, M.R. (ed.), *The Dynamic Interlanguage: Empirical Studies in Second Language Acquisition*. New York: Plenum Press, 71–86.

Gibson, E. 1992: On the adequacy of the competition model. *Language* **68**, 812–30.

—— and Wexler, K. 1994: Triggers. *Linguistic Inquiry* **25**, 407–54.

Givón, T. 1979: *On Understanding Grammar*. New York: Academic Press.

—— 1984a: *Syntax: A Functional-typological Introduction*. Volume 1. Philadelphia: John Benjamins.

—— 1984b: Universals of discourse structure and second language acquisition. In Rutherford, W.E. (ed.), *Language Universals and Second Language Acquisition*. Philadelphia: John Benjamins, 109–36.

—— 1990: *Syntax: A Functional-Typological Introduction*. Volume 2. Amsterdam: John Benjamins.

—— 1993: *English Grammar: A Function-based Introduction*. Volume 2. Amsterdam: John Benjamins.

Green, C.F. 1996: The origins and effects of topic-prominence in Chinese–English interlanguage. *IRAL* **34**, 119–34.

Greenberg, J.H. 1966a: *Language Universals, with Special Reference to Feature Hierarchies*. Janua Linguarum, Series minor, 59. The Hague: Mouton.

—— 1966b: Some universals of grammar with particular reference to the order of meaningful elements. In Greenberg, J.H. (ed.), *Universals of Language*. 2nd edn. Cambridge, MA: MIT Press, 73–113.

—— Ferguson, C. and Moravcsik, E.A. (eds.). 1978: *Universals of Human Language*. Volume 2. Stanford, CA: Stanford University Press.

Gregg, K. 1984: Krashen's monitor and Occam's razor. *Applied Linguistics* **5**, 79–100.

—— 1988: Epistemology without knowledge: Schwartz on Chomsky, Fodor and Krashen. *Second Language Research* **4**, 66–80.

Grimshaw, J. and Rosen, S. 1990: Knowledge and obedience: the developmental status of the binding theory. *Linguistic Inquiry* **21**, 187–222.

Grondin, N. and White, L. 1993: Functional categories in child L2 acquisition of French. *McGill Working Papers in Linguistics* **9**:1/2, 121–45.

Gundel, J.K., Hedberg, N. and Zacharski, R. 1993: Cognitive status and the form of referring expressions in discourse. *Language* **69**, 274–307.

—— Stenson, N. and Tarone, E. 1984: Acquiring pronouns in a second language: evidence for hypothesis testing. *Studies in Second Language Acquisition* **6**, 215–25.

—— and Tarone, E.E. 1983: Language transfer and the acquisition of pronominal anaphora. In Gass, S.M. and Selinker, L., *Language Transfer in Language Learning*. Rowley, MA: Newbury House, 281–96.

Halliday, M.A.K. 1994: *An Introduction to Functional Grammar*. 2nd edn. London: Edward Arnold.

Hamilton, R.L. 1994: Is implicational generalization unidirectional and maximal? Evidence from relativization instruction in a second language. *Language Learning* **44**, 123–57.

—— 1995: The noun phrase accessibility hierarchy in SLA: determining the basis for its developmental effects. In Eckman, F.R., Highland, D., Lee, P.W., Milcham, J. and Weber Rutkowski, R. (eds.), *Second Language Acquisition Theory and Pedagogy*. Mahwah, NJ: Lawrence Erlbaum, 101–14.

Harrington, M. 1987: Processing transfer: language-specific processing strategies as a source of interlanguage variation. *Applied Psycholinguistics* **8**, 351–77.

—— 1992: Working memory capacity as a constraint on L2 development. In Harris, R.J. (ed.) *Cognitive Processing in Bilinguals*. Amsterdam: North-Holland, 123–35.

—— and Sawyer, M. 1992: L2 working memory capacity and L2 reading skill. *Studies in Second Language Acquisition* **14**, 25–36.

Hatch, E. 1978a: Acquisition of syntax in a second language. In Richards, J.C. (ed.), *Understanding Second and Foreign Language Learning*. Rowley, MA: Newbury House, 34–69.

—— 1978b: Apply with caution. *Studies in Second Language Acquisition* **2**, 123–43.

—— 1978c: Discourse analysis, speech acts, and second language acquisition. In Ritchie, W.C. (ed.), *Second Language Acquisition Research: Issues and Implication*. New York: Academic Press, 137–55.

—— (ed.). 1978d. *Second Language Acquisition: A Book of Readings*. Rowley, MA: Newbury House.

—— 1983: *Psycholinguistics: A Second Language Perspective*. Rowley, MA: Newbury House.

Hawkins, R. 1989: Do second language learners acquire restrictive relative clauses on the basis of relational or configurational information? The acquisition of French subject, direct object and genitive restrictive relative clauses by second language learners. *Second Language Research* **5**, 141–88.

Heilenman, K. and McDonald, J. 1993: Processing strategies in L2 learners of French: the role of transfer. *Language Learning* **43**, 507–57.

Hermon, G. 1992: Binding theory and parameter setting. *Linguistic Review* **9**, 145–81.

—— 1994: Long-distance reflexives in UG: theoretical approaches and predictions for acquisition. In Lust, B., Hermon, G. and Kornfilt J. (eds.), *Syntactic Theory and First Language Acquisition: A Cross-linguistic Perspectives. Volume 2: Binding, Dependencies, and Learnability*. Hillsdale, NJ: Lawrence Erlbaum, 91–111.

—— and Yoon, J. 1989: The licensing and identification of *pro* and the typology of AGR. In Wiltshire, C., Graczyk, R. and Music, B. (eds.), *Papers from the 25th Regional Meeting of the Chicago Linguistic Society*. Chicago, IL: Chicago Linguistic Society, 174–92.

Hernandez, A., Bates, E. and Avila, L. 1994: On-line sentence interpretation in Spanish-English bilinguals: what does it mean to be 'in between'? *Applied Psycholinguistics* **15**, 417–46.

Hilles, S. 1986: Interlanguage and the pro-drop parameter. *Second Language Research* **2**, 33–52.

—— 1991: Access to Universal Grammar in second language acquisition. In Eubank, L. (ed.), *Point Counterpoint: Universal Grammar in the Second Language*. Philadelphia: John Benjamins, 305–38.

Hirakawa, M. 1990: A study of the L2 acquisition of English reflexives. *Second Language Research* **6**, 60–85.

Hirsh-Pasek, K., Golinkoff, R., Braidi, S. and McNally, L. 1986: 'Daddy throw': on the existence of implicit negative evidence for subcategorization errors. Paper presented in October at the Boston Language Conference, Boston University, Boston.

Hoekstra, T. and Schwartz, B.D. 1994: *Language Acquisition Studies in Generative Grammar*. Amsterdam/Philadelphia: John Benjamins.

Huang, C.–T.J. 1984: On the distribution and reference of empty pronouns. *Linguistic Inquiry* **15**, 531–74.

Huang, J. and Hatch, E. 1978: A Chinese child's acquisition of English. In Hatch, E. (ed.), *Second Language Acquisition*. Rowley, MA: Newbury House, 118–31.

Hudson, T. 1993: Nothing does not equal zero: problems with applying developmental sequence findings to assessment and pedagogy. *Studies in Second Language Acquisition* **15**, 461–93.

Huebner, T. 1983: *A Longitudinal Analysis of the Acquisition of English*. Ann Arbor, MI: Karoma.

Hulstijn, J.H. 1989: A cognitive view on interlanguage variability. In Eisenstein, M.R. (ed.), *The Dynamic Interlanguage: Empirical Studies in Second Language Variation*. New York: Plenum Press, 17–31.

—— 1990: A comparison between the information-processing and the analysis/control approaches to language learning. *Applied Linguistics* **11**, 30–45.

—— and de Graff, R. 1994: Under what conditions does explicit knowledge of a second language facilitate the acquisition of implicit knowledge? A research proposal. *AILA Review* **11**, 97–112.

Hyams, N. 1986: *Language Acquisition and the Theory of Parameters*. Dordrecht: Reidel Press.

—— 1992: A reanalysis of null subjects in child language. In Weissenborn, J., Goodluck, H. and Roeper, T. (eds.), *Theoretical Issues in Language Acquisition (Continuity and Change in Development)*. Hillsdale, NJ: Lawrence Erlbaum, 249–67.

—— 1994: Commentary: null subjects in child language and the implications of cross-linguistic variation. In Lust, B., Hermon, G. and Kornfilt J. (eds.), *Syntactic Theory and First Language Acquisition: A Cross-linguistic Perspectives. Volume 2: Binding, Dependencies, and Learnability*. Hillsdale, NJ: Lawrence Erlbaum, 287–99.

—— and Safir, K. 1991: Evidence, analogy and passive knowledge: comments on Lakshmanan. In Eubank, L. (ed.), *Point Counterpoint: Universal Grammar in the Second Language*. Philadelphia: John Benjamins, 411–18.

—— and Sigurjónsdóttir, S. 1990: The development of 'long-distance anaphora': a cross-linguistic comparison with special reference to Icelandic. *Language Acquisition* **1**, 57–93.

Hyltenstam, K. 1977: Implicational patterns in interlanguage syntax variation. *Language Learning* **27**, 383–411.

—— 1984: The use of typological markedness conditions as predictors in second language acquisition: the case of pronominal copies in relative clauses. In Andersen, R.W. (ed.), *Second Languages: A Cross-Linguistic Perspective*. Rowley, MA: Newbury House, 39–58.

Ioup, G. 1983: Acquiring complex sentences in ESL. In Bailey, K.M., Long, M.H. and Peck, S. (eds.), *Second Language Acquisition Studies*. Rowley, MA: Newbury House, 41–55.

—— and Kruse, A. 1977: Interference versus structural complexity as a predictor of second language relative clause acquisition. In Henning, C. (ed.), *Proceedings of the Second Language Research Forum*. Los Angeles: UCLA, 48–60.

Jackendoff, R. 1987: The status of thematic relations in linguistic theory. *Linguistic Inquiry* 18, 369–411.

Jaeggli, O. and Hyams, N.M. 1988: Morphological uniformity and the setting of the null subject parameter. In Blerins, J. and Carter, J. (eds.), *NELS 18: Proceedings of the 18th Annual North Eastern Linguistic Society Meeting*. Volume 1. Amherst, MA: GLSA, Department of Linguistics, 238–53.

—— and Safir, K.J. 1989: The null subject parameter and parametric theory. In Jaeggli, O.A. and Safir, K.J. (eds.), *The Null Subject Parameter*. Dordrecht: Kluwer, 1–44.

Jakobovits, L.A. 1974: Freedom to teach and freedom to learn. In Jakobovits, L.A. and Gordon, B. (eds.), *The Context of Foreign Language Teaching*. Rowley, MA: Newbury House, 79–105.

Jin, H.G. 1994: Topic-prominence and subject-prominence in L2 acquisition: evidence of English-to-Chinese typological transfer. *Language Learning* 44, 101–22.

Johnson, J.S. and Newport, E.L. 1991: Critical period effects on universal properties of language: the status of subjacency in the acquisition of a second language. *Cognition* 39, 215–58.

Jordens, P. 1997. Introducing the basic variety. *Second Language Research* 13, 289–300.

Kail, M. 1989: Cue validity, cue cost, and processing types in sentence comprehension in French and Spanish. In MacWhinney, B. and Bates, E. (eds.), *The Cross-linguistic Study of Sentence Processing*. New York: Cambridge University Press, 77–117.

Kaplan, R. and Bresnan, J. 1982: Lexical-functional grammar: a formal system for grammatical representation. In Bresnan, J. (ed.), *The Mental Representation of Grammatical Relations*. Cambridge, MA: MIT Press, 173–281.

Katada, F. 1991: The LF representation of anaphors. *Linguistic Inquiry* 22, 287–313.

Kayne, R.S. 1994: *The Antisymmetry of Syntax*. Cambridge, MA: MIT Press.

Keenan, E.L. and Comrie, B. 1977: Noun phrase accessibility and universal grammar. *Linguistic Inquiry* 8, 63–99.

Kellerman, E. 1978: Giving learners a break: native language institutions as a source of implications about transferability. *Working Papers on Bilingualism* 15, 59–92.

—— 1979: Transfer and non-transfer: where we are now. *Studies in Second Language Acquisition* 2, 37–57.

—— 1983: Now you see it, now you don't. In Gass, S. and Selinker, L. (eds.), *Language Transfer in Language Learning*. Rowley, MA: Newbury House, 112–34.

—— 1984: The empirical evidence for the influence of the L1 in interlanguage. In Davies, A., Criper, C., and Howatt, A.P.R. (eds.), *Interlanguage*. Edinburgh: Edinburgh University Press, 98–122.

—— 1985: If at first you *do* succeed. In Gass, S.M. and Madden, C.G. (eds.), *Input in Second Language Acquisition*, Rowley, MA: Newbury House, 345–53.

Kempen, G. and Hoenkamp, E. 1987: An incremental procedural grammar for sentence formulation. *Cognitive Science* 11, 201–58.

Kilborn, K. 1989: Sentence processing in a second language: the timing of transfer. *Language and Speech* 32:1, 1–23.

—— and Cooreman, A. 1987: Sentence interpretation strategies in adult Dutch–English Bilinguals. *Applied Psycholinguistics* 8, 415–31.

—— and Ito, T. 1989: Sentence processing strategies in adult bilinguals. In Bates, E. and MacWhinney, B. (eds.), *The Crosslinguistic Study of Sentence Processing*. Cambridge: Cambridge University Press, 257–91.

Klein, W. and Perdue, C. 1989: The learner's problem of arranging words. In Bates, E. and MacWhinney, B. (eds.), *The Crosslinguistic Study of Sentence Processing*. Cambridge: Cambridge University Press, 292–327.

—— —— 1992a: Framework. In Klein, W. and Perdue, C. (eds.), *Utterance Structure: Developing Grammars Again*. Amsterdam: John Benjamins, 11–59.

—— —— 1992b: *Utterance Structure: Developing Grammars Again*. Amsterdam: John Benjamins.

Kleinmann, H.H. 1977: Avoidance behavior in adult second language acquisition. *Language Learning* 27, 93–107.

Krashen, S. 1981: *Second Language Acquisition and Second Language Learning*. Oxford: Pergamon Press.

—— 1982. *Principles and Practice in Second Language Acquisition*. New York: Pergamon Press.

—— 1985: *The Input Hypothesis: Issues and Implications*. London: Longman.

Kumpf, L. 1984: Temporal systems and universality in interlanguage. In Eckman, F.R., Bell, L.H. and Nelson, D. (eds.), *Universals of Second Language Acquisition*. Rowley, MA: Newbury House, 132–43.

—— 1992: Preferred argument in second language discourse: a preliminary study. *Studies in Second Language* 16, 369–403.

Lado, R. 1957: *Linguistics Across Cultures*. Ann Arbor, MI: University of Michigan Press.

Lakshmanan, U. 1991: Morphological uniformity and null subjects in child second language acquisition. In Eubank, L. (ed.), *Point Counterpoint: Universal Grammar in the Second Language*. Philadelphia: John Benjamins, 389–410.

—— 1993–94: 'The boy for the cookie' – some evidence for the nonviolation of the case filter in child second language acquisition. *Language Acquisition* 3, 55–91.

Lantolf, J.P. 1990: Reassessing the null-subject parameter in second language acquisition. In Burmeister, H. and Rounds, P.L. (eds.), *Variability in Second Language Acquisition. Proceedings of the Tenth Meeting of the Second Language Research Forum*. Eugene, OR: University of Oregon, 429–51.

Larsen-Freeman, D. 1975: The acquisition of grammatical morphemes by adult learners of English as a second language. *TESOL Quarterly* 9, 409–30.

—— 1976: An explanation for the morpheme acquisition order of second language learners. *Language Learning* 26, 125–34.

—— and Long, M. 1991: *An Introduction to Second Language Acquisition Research*. London: Longman.

Lee, J.F. and VanPatten, B. 1995. *Making Communicative Language Teaching Happen*. New York: McGraw-Hill.

Levelt, W.J.M. 1989: *Speaking*. Cambridge, MA: MIT Press.

Levinson, S.C. 1983: *Pragmatics*. Cambridge: Cambridge University Press.

Li, C.N. and Thompson, S. 1976: Subject and topic: a new typology of language. In Li, C.N. (ed.), *Subject and Topic*. New York: Academic Press, 457–89.

—— ——1990: Chinese. In Comrie, B. (ed.), *The World's Major Languages*. Oxford: Oxford University Press, 811–33.

Li, P., Bates, E., Liu, H. and MacWhinney, B. 1992: Cues as Functional Constraints on sentence processing in Chinese. In Chen, H.C. and Tzeng, O.J.L (eds.), *Language Processing in Chinese*. Amsterdam: North-Holland, 207–34.

—— —— and MacWhinney, B. 1993: Processing a language without inflections: a reaction time study of sentence interpretation in Chinese. *Journal of Memory and Language* 32, 169–92.

Liceras, J.M. 1988: Syntax and stylistics: more on the 'pro-drop' parameter. In Pankhurst, J., Sharwood Smith, M. and Van Buren, P. (eds.), *Learnability and Second Languages*. Dordrecht, Holland: Foris Publications, 71–93.

—— 1989: On some properties of the 'pro-drop' parameter: looking for missing subjects in non-native Spanish. In Gass, S.M. and Schachter, J. (eds.), *Linguistic Perspectives on Second Language Acquisition*. Cambridge: Cambridge University Press, 109–33.

Lightbown, P.M. 1985: Input and acquisition for second-language learners in and out of classrooms. *Applied Linguistics* 6, 263–73.

—— 1992: Getting quality input in the second/foreign language classroom. In Kramsch, C. and McConnell-Ginet, S. (eds.), *Text and Context. Disciplinary Perspectives on Language Study*. Lexington, MA: D.C. Heath and Company, 18–197.

Lightfoot, D. 1989: The child's trigger experience: degree–0 learnability. *Behavioral and Brain Sciences* 12, 321–75.

—— 1991: *How to Set Parameters: Arguments from Language Change*. Cambridge, MA: MIT Press.

Liu, H., Bates, E. and Li, P. 1992: Sentence interpretation in bilingual speakers of English and Chinese. *Applied Psycholinguistics* 13, 451–84.

Long, M.H. 1983a: Linguistic and conversational adjustments to non-native speakers. *Studies in Second Language Acquisition* 5, 177–93.

—— 1983b: Native speaker/non-native speaker conversation and the negotiation of comprehensible input. *Applied Linguistics* 4, 126–41.

—— 1983c: Native speaker/non-native speaker conversation in the second language classroom. In Clarke, M.A. and Handscombe, J. (eds.), *On TESOL '82: Pacific Perspectives on Language Learning and Teaching*. Washington, DC: TESOL, 207–25.

—— 1990: The least a second language acquisition theory needs to explain. *TESOL Quarterly* 24, 649–66.

—— 1991. Focus on form: a design feature in language teaching methodology. In de Bot, K., Ginsberg R.B. and Kramsch, C. (eds.), *Foreign Language Research in Cross-cultural Perspective*. Philadelphia: John Benjamins, 39–52.

—— and Sato, C. 1984: Methodological issues in interlanguage studies: an interactionist perspective. In Davies, A., Criper, C. and Howatt, A.P.R. (eds.), *Interlanguage*. Edinburgh: Edinburgh University Press, 253–79.

Lust, B. Hermon, G. and Kornfilt, J. (eds.). 1994a. *Syntactic Theory and First Language Acquisition: Cross-linguistic Perspectives. Volume 2: Binding, Dependencies, and Learnability*. Hillsdale, NJ: Lawrence Erlbaum.

—— Kornfilt, J., Hermon, G., Foley, C., Nuñez del Prado, Z. and Kapur, S. 1994: Introduction. In Lust, B., Hermon, G. and Kornfilt J. (eds.), *Syntactic Theory and First Language Acquisition: Cross-linguistic Perspectives. Volume 2: Binding, Dependencies, and Learnability*. Hillsdale, NJ: Lawrence Erlbaum, 1–37.

Lyons, J. 1977: *Semantics*. Vol. 2. Cambridge: Cambridge University Press.

McDaniel, D. and Maxfield, T.L. 1992: Principle B and contrastive stress. *Language Acquisition* 2, 337–58.

McDonald, J.L. 1986: The development of sentence comprehension strategies in English and Dutch. *Journal of Experimental Child Psychology* 41, 317–35.

—— 1987a: Assigning linguistic roles: the influence of conflicting cues. *Journal of Memory and Language* 26, 100–17.

—— 1987b: Sentence interpretation in bilingual speakers of English and Dutch. *Applied Psycholinguistics* 8, 379–413.

—— and Heilenman, L.K. 1991: Determinants of cue strength in adult first and second language speakers of French. *Applied Psycholinguistics* 12, 313–48.

—— —— 1992: Changes in sentence processing as second language proficiency increases. In Harris, R.J. (ed.), *Cognitive Processing in Bilinguals*. Amsterdam: Elsevier Science Publishers, 325–36.

McLaughlin, B. 1987: *Theories of Second-language Learning*. London: Edward Arnold.
—— 1990: Restructuring. *Applied Linguistics* 11, 113–28.
—— 1995: Aptitude from an information-processing perspective. *Studies in Second Language Research* 11, 370–87.
—— Rossman, T. and McLeod, B. 1983: Second language learning: an information-processing perspective. *Language Learning* 33, 135–58.
McLeod, B. and McLaughlin, B. 1986: Restructuring or automaticity? Reading in a second language. *Language Learning* 36, 109–23.
MacWhinney, B. 1987: Applying the competition model to bilingualism. *Applied Psycholinguistics* 8, 315–27.
—— Bates, E. and Kliegel, R. 1984: Cue validity and sentence interpretation in English, German, and Italian. *Journal of Verbal Learning and Verbal Behavior* 23, 127–50.
—— Pléh, C. and Bates, E. 1985: The development of sentence interpretation in Hungarian. *Cognitive Psychology* 17, 178–209.
Martohardjono, G. and Flynn, S. 1995: Language transfer: What do we really mean? In Eubank, L., Selinker, L. and Sharwood Smith, M. (eds.), *The Current State of Interlanguage: Studies in Honor of William E. Rutherford*. Amsterdam/Philadelphia: John Benjamins, 205–18.
—— and Gair, J.W. 1993. Apparent UG inaccessibility in second language acquisition: misapplied principles or principled misapplication? In Eckman, F.R. (ed.), *Confluence: Linguistics, L2 Acquisition, and Speech Pathology*. Philadelphia: John Benjamins, 79–103.
Meisel, J.M., Clahsen, H. and Pienemann, M. 1981: On determining developmental stages in natural second language acquisition. *Studies in Second Language Acquisition* 3, 109–35.
Mellow, D.J. 1996: On the primacy theory in applied studies: a critique of Pienemann and Johnston (1987). *Second Language Research* 12, 304–18.
Miao, X. 1981: Word order and semantic strategies in Chinese sentence comprehension. *International Journal of Psycholinguistics* 8, 109–22.
Moravcsik, E. and Wirth, J. 1983: Markedness – an overview. In Eckman, F.R., Morvavcsik, E. and Wirth, J. (eds.), *Markedness*. New York: Plenum Press, 1–11.
Nation, R. and McLaughlin, B. 1986: Language learning in multilingual subjects: an information-processing point of view. In Cook, V.J. (ed.), *Experimental Approaches to Second Language Learning*. Oxford: Pergamon, 41–53.
Nayak, N., Hansen, N., Krueger, N. and McLaughlin, B. 1990: Language learning strategies in monolingual and multilingual subjects. *Language Learning* 40, 221–44.
Nemser, W. 1971: Approximative systems of foreign language learners. *International Review of Applied Linguistics* 9, 115–24.
Newmeyer, F.J. 1983: *Grammatical Theory: Its Limits and Its Possibilities*. Chicago: University of Chicago Press.
Newport, E., Gleitman, H. and Gleitman L.R. 1977: Mother, I'd rather do it myself: some effects and non-effects of maternal speech style. In Snow, C.E. and Ferguson C.E. (eds.), *Talking to Children: Language Input and Acquisition*. Cambridge: Cambridge University Press, 109–49.
Nunan, D. 1994: Linguistic theory and pedagogic practice. In Odlin, T. (ed.), *Perspectives on Pedagogical Grammar*. Cambridge: Cambridge University Press, 253–70.
Odlin, T. 1989: *Language Transfer: Cross-linguistic Influence in Language Learning*. Cambridge: Cambridge University.
—— 1994: *Perspectives on Pedagogical Grammar*. Cambridge: Cambridge University Press.

O'Grady, W. 1987: *Principles of Grammar and Learning*. Chicago: University of Chicago Press.

Pavesi, M. 1986: Markedness, discoursal modes, and relative clause formation in a formal and an informal context. *Studies in Second Language Acquisition* 8, 38–55.

Perdue, C. 1990: Complexification of the simple clause in the narrative discourse of adult language learners. *Linguistics* 28, 983–1000.

—— 1993: *Adult Language Acquisition: Cross-linguistic Perspectives. Volume 1. Field Methods.* Cambridge: Cambridge University Press.

—— Deulofeu, J. and Trévise, A. 1992: The acquisition of French. In Klein, W. and Perdue, C. (eds.), *Utterance Structure: Developing Grammars Again.* Amsterdam: John Benjamins, 225–300.

—— and Klein, W. 1992a: Conclusions. In Klein, W. and Perdue, C. (eds.), *Utterance Structure: Developing Grammars Again.* Amsterdam: John Benjamins, 301–37.

—— —— 1992b: Introduction. In Klein, W. and Perdue, C. (eds.), *Utterance Structure: Developing Grammars Again.* Amsterdam: John Benjamins, 1–10.

—— —— 1992c: Why does the production of some learners not grammaticalize? *Studies in Second Language Acquisition* 14, 259–72.

Pfaff, C.W. 1987. Functional approaches to interlanguage. In Pfaff, C.W. (ed.), *First and Second Language Acquisition Processes.* Cambridge, MA: Newbury House, 81–102.

—— 1992: The issue of grammaticalization in early German second language. *Studies in Second Language Acquisition* 14, 273–96.

Phinney, M. 1987: The pro-drop parameter in second language acquisition. In Roeper, T. and Williams, E. (eds.), *Parameter Setting.* Dordrecht: Reidel, 221–38.

Pica, P. 1991. On the interaction between antecedent-government and binding: the case of long-distance reflexivization. In Koster, J. and Reuland, E. (eds.), *Long-Distance Anaphora.* Cambridge: Cambridge University Press, 119–35.

Pica, T. 1988: Interlanguage adjustments as an outcome of NS–NNS negotiated interaction. *Language Learning* 38, 45–73.

—— 1994: Questions from the language classroom: research perspectives. *TESOL Quarterly* 28, 49–79.

—— and Doughty, C. 1985: Input and interaction in the communicative language classroom: a comparison of teacher-fronted and group activities. In Gass, S.M. and Madden, C.G. (eds.), *Input in Second Language Acquisition.* Rowley, MA: Newbury House, 115–32.

Pienemann, M. 1980. The second language acquisition of immigrant children. In Felix, S.W. (ed.), *Second Language Development: Trends and Issues.* Tübingen: Gunter Narr, 41–56.

—— 1984. Psychological constraints on the teachability of languages. *Studies in Second Language Acquisition* 6, 186–214.

—— 1985: Learnability and syllabus construction. In Hyltenstam, K. and Pienemann, M. (eds.), *Second Language Acquisition.* Clevedon, Avon: Multilingual Matters, 23–75.

—— 1987: Determining the influence of instruction on L2 speech processing. MS.

—— 1989: Is language teachable? Psycholinguistic experiments and hypotheses. *Applied Linguistics* 10, 52–79.

—— 1997: A unified framework for the study of dynamics in language development – applied to L1, L2, 2L1 and SLI. MS.

—— and Håkansson, G. 1996: Towards a theory of L2 processability: Swedish as a test case. MS.

—— and Johnston, M. 1986: An acquisition based procedure for second language assessment (ESL). *Australian Review of Applied Linguistics* 9, 92–122.

Pienemann, M. and Johnston, M. 1987: Factors influencing the development of language proficiency. In Nunan, D. (ed.), *Applying Second Language Acquisition Research*. Adelaide: National Curriculum Resource Centre, 45–141.

—— —— 1996: A brief history of processing approaches to SLA: reply to Mellow. *Second Language Research* 12, 319–34.

—— —— and Meisel, J. 1993: The multidimensional model, linguistic profiling, and related issues: a reply to Hudson. *Studies in Second Language Acquisition* 15, 495–503.

Pinker, S. 1984: *Language Learnability and Language Development*. Cambridge, MA: Harvard University Press.

—— 1989: Resolving a learnability paradox on the acquisition of the verb lexicon. In Rice, M.L. and Schiefelbusch, R.L. (eds.) *The Teachability of Language*. Baltimore: Paul H. Brookes Publishing, 13–61.

Polio, C. 1995: Acquiring nothing?: the use of zero pronouns by nonnative speakers of Chinese and the implications for the acquisition of nominal reference. *Studies in Second Language Acquisition* 17, 353–77.

Pollock, J. 1989: Verb movement, universal grammar and the structure of IP. *Linguistic Inquiry* 20, 365–424.

Prince, E. 1981: Toward a taxonomy of given-new information. In Cole, P. (ed.), *Radical Pragmatics*. New York: Academic Press, 223–55.

Ravem, R. 1974: The development of wh-questions in first and second language learners. In Richards, J.C. (ed.) *Error Analysis: Perspectives on Second Language Acquisition*. London: Longman, 134–55.

Richards, J.C. 1974: A non-contrastive approach to error analysis. In Richards, J.C. (ed.), *Error Analysis*. London: Longman, 172–88. Reprinted from *English Language Teaching* 25.

—— and Lockhart. 1994: *Reflective Teaching in Second Language Classrooms*. Cambridge: Cambridge University Press.

—— Platt, J. and Platt, H. 1992: *Dictionary of Language Teaching and Applied Linguistics*. 2nd edn. London: Longman.

Rizzi, L. 1982: *Issues in Italian Syntax*. Dordrecht: Foris.

Robinson, P. 1996: *Consciousness, Rules and Instructed Second Language Acquisition*. New York: Peter Lang.

—— 1997: Generalizability and automaticity of second language learning under implicit, incidental enhanced, and instructed conditions. *Studies in Second Languge Acquisition* 19, 223–47.

Rosansky, E. 1976: Methods and morphemes in second language acquisition research. *Language Learning* 26, 409–25.

Rutherford, W. 1983: Language typology and language transfer. In Gass, S.M. and Selinker, L. (eds.), *Language Transfer in Language Learning*. Rowley, MA: Newbury House, 358–70.

—— 1988: Grammatical theory and L2 acquisition: a brief overview. In Flynn, S. and O'Neil, W. (eds.), *Linguistic Theory in Second Language Acquisition*. Dordrecht: Kluwer, 404–16.

—— and Sharwood Smith, M. 1985: Consciousness raising and Universal Grammar. *Applied Linguistics* 6, 274–82.

—— —— 1988: Introduction. In Rutherford, W. and Sharwood Smith, M. (eds.), *Grammar and Second Language Teaching: A Book of Readings*. New York: Newbury House, 1–8.

Sasaki, Y. 1991: English and Japanese interlanguage comprehension strategies: an analysis based on the competition model. *Applied Psycholinguistics* 12, 47–73.

—— 1994: Paths of processing strategy transfers in learning Japanese and English as foreign languages: a competition model approach. *Studies in Second Language Acquisition* **16**, 43–72.

—— 1997: Material and presentation condition effects on sentence interpretation task performance: methodological examinations of the competition experiment. *Second Language Research* **13**, 66–91.

Sato, C.J. 1988: Origins of complex syntax in interlanguage development. *Studies in Second Language Acquisition* **10**, 371–95.

—— 1990: *The Syntax of Conversation in Interlanguage Development*. Tübingen: Gunter Narr.

Schachter, J. 1974: An error in error analysis. *Language Learning* **27**, 205–14.

—— 1983: A new account of language transfer. In Gass, S.M. and Selinker, L. (eds.), *Language Transfer in Language Learning*. Rowley, MA: Newbury House, 98–111.

—— 1989a: A new look at an old classic. *Second Language Research* **5**, 30–42.

—— 1989b: Testing a proposed universal. In Gass, S.M. and Schachter, J. (eds.), *Linguistic Perspectives on Second Language Acquisition*. Cambridge: Cambridge University Press, 73–88.

—— 1990: On the issue of completeness in second language acquisition. *Second Language Research* **6**, 93–124.

—— and Celce-Murcia, H. 1977: Some reservations concerning error analysis. *TESOL Quarterly* **11**, 441–51.

—— and Rutherford, W. 1979: Discourse function and language transfer. *Working Papers on Bilingualism* **19**, 3–12.

Schmidt, M. 1980: Coordinate structures and language universals in interlanguage. *Language Learning* **30**, 397–416.

Schmidt, R.W. 1990: The role of consciousness in second language learning. *Applied Linguistics* **11**, 129–58.

—— 1993: Consciousness, learning and interlanguage pragmatics. In Kasper, G. and Blum-Kulke, S. (eds.), *Interlanguage Pragmatics*. Oxford: Oxford University Press, 1–43.

—— 1994: Deconstructing consciousness in search of useful definitions for applied linguistics. *AILA Review* **11**, 11–26.

—— 1995: Consciousness and foreign language learning: a tutorial on the role of attention and awareness in learning. In Schmidt, R. (ed.), *Attention and Awareness*. Honolulu: University of Hawai'i, Second Language Teaching and Curriculum Center, 1–63.

—— and Frota, S. 1986: Developing basic conversational ability in a second language: a case study of an adult learner of Portuguese. In Day, R. (ed.), *Talking to Learn*. Rowley, MA: Newbury House, 237–326.

Schumann, J.H. 1979: The acquisition of English negation by speakers of Spanish: a review of the literature. In Andersen, R.W. (ed.), *The Acquisition and Use of Spanish and English as First and Second Languages*. Washington, DC: TESOL, 3–32.

—— 1980: The acquisition of English relative clauses by second language learners. In Scarcella, R. and Krashen, S.D. (eds.), *Research in Second Language Acquisition*. Rowley, MA: Newbury House, 118–31.

—— 1987: The expression of temporality in basilang speech. *Studies in Second Language Acquisition* **9**, 21–41.

Schwartz, B.D. 1986: The epistemological status of second language acquisition. *Second Language Research* **2**, 120–59.

—— 1990: Un-motivating the motivation for the fundamental difference hypothesis. In Burmeister, H. and Rounds, P.L. (eds.), *Variability in Second Language Acquisition. Proceedings of the Tenth Meeting of the Second Language Research Forum*. Eugene, OR: University of Oregon, 667–84.

Schwartz, B.D. 1992: Testing between UG-based and problem-solving models of L2A: Developmental sequence data. *Language Acquisition* 2, 1–19.

—— 1993: On explicit and negative data effecting and affecting competence and linguistic behavior. *Studies in Second Language Acquisition* 15, 147–63.

—— and Gubala-Ryzak, M. 1992: Learnability and grammar reorganization in L2A: against negative evidence causing the unlearning of verb movement. *Second Language Research* 8, 1–38.

—— and Sprouse, R. 1994: Word order and nominative case in non-native language acquisition: a longitudinal study of (L1 Turkish) German interlanguage. In Hoekstra, T. and Schwartz, B.D. (eds.), *Language Acquisition Studies in Generative Grammar.* Amsterdam: John Benjamins, 317–68.

Selinker, L. 1972: Interlanguage. *International Review of Applied Linguistics* 10, 209–31.

—— 1992: *Rediscovering Interlanguage.* London: Longman.

Sharwood Smith, M. 1986: The competence/control model, crosslinguistic influence and the creation of new grammars. In Kellerman, E. and Sharwood Smith, M. (eds.), *Crosslinguistic Influence in Second Language Acquisition.* New York: Pergamon, 10–20.

—— 1991: Speaking to many minds: on the relevance of different types of language information for the L2 learner. *Second Language Research* 7, 118–32.

—— 1993: Input enhancement in instructed SLA: theoretical bases. *Studies in Second Language Acquisition* 15, 165–79.

—— and Kellerman, E. 1986: Crosslinguistic influence in second language acquisition: an introduction. In Kellerman, E. and Sharwood Smith, M. (eds.), *Crosslinguistic Influence in Second Language Acquisition.* New York: Pergamon Institute of English, 1–9.

Sheldon, A. 1974: The role of parallel function in the acquisition of relative clauses in English. *Journal of Verbal Learning and Verbal Behavior* 13, 272–81.

Shook, D.J. 1994: Fl/L2 reading, grammatical information, and the input-to-intake phenomenon. *Applied Language Learning* 5, 57–93.

Spolsky, B. 1989: *Conditions for Second Language Learning.* Oxford: Oxford University Press.

Sportiche, D. 1981: Bounding nodes in French. *Linguistic Review* 1, 219–46.

Stauble, A.-M. 1978: The process of decreolization: A model for second language development. *Language Learning* 28, 29–54.

Swain, M. 1985: Communicative competence: Some roles of comprehensible input and comprehensible output in its development. In Gass, S.M. and Madden, C.G. (eds.), *Input in Second Language Acquisition.* Rowley, MA: Newbury House, 235–53.

—— 1995: Three functions of output in second language learning. In Cook, G. and Seidlhofer, B. (eds.), *Principles and Practice in Applied Linguistics.* Oxford: Oxford University Press, 125–44.

Tarallo, F. and Myhill, J. 1983: Interference and natural language processing in second language acquisition. *Language Learning* 33, 55–76.

Thomas, M. 1989: The interpretation of English reflexive pronouns by non-native speakers. *Studies in Second Language Acquisition* 11, 281–303.

—— 1991: Do second language learners have 'rogue' grammars of anaphora? In Eubank, L. (ed.), *Point Counterpoint: Universal Grammar in the Second Language.* Philadelphia: John Benjamins, 375–88.

—— 1993: *Knowledge of Reflexives in a Second Language.* Amsterdam: John Benjamins.

—— 1995: Acquisition of the Japanese reflexive *zibun* and movement of anaphors in logical form. *Second Language Research* 11, 206–34.

Tomaselli, A. and Schwartz, B.D. 1990: Analysing the acquisition of negation in German: support for UG in adult SLA. *Second Language Research* 6, 11–38.

Tomlin, R.S. 1984: The treatment of foreground–background information in the on-line descriptive discourse of second language learners. *Studies in Second Language Acquisition* 6, 115–42.

—— 1990: Functionalism in second language acquisition. *Studies in Second Language Acquisition* 12, 155–77.

—— and Villa, V. 1994: Attention in cognitive science and second language acquisition. *Studies in Second Language Acquisition* 16, 183–204.

Trahey, M. and White, L. 1993: Positive evidence and preemption in the second language classroom. *Studies in Second Language Acquisition* 15, 181–204.

Trévise, A., Perdue, C. and Deulofeu, J. 1991: Word order and discursive coherence in L2. In Appel, G. and Dechert, H.W. (eds.), *A Case for Psycholinguistic Cases*. Philadelphia: John Benjamins, 163–76.

Uziel, S. 1993: Resetting universal grammar parameters: evidence from second language acquisition of subjacency and the empty category principle. *Second Language Research* 9, 49–83.

Vainikka, A. and Young-Scholten, M. 1994: The early stages in adult L2 syntax: additional evidence from Romance speakers. MS.

—— —— 1998: The initial state in the L2 acquisition of phrase structure. In Flynn, S., Martohardjono, G. and O'Neil, W. (eds.), *The Generative Study of Second Language Acquisition*. Hillsdale, NJ: Lawrence Erlbaum, 17–34.

Valian, V. 1994: Children's postulation of null subjects: parameter setting and language acquisition. In Lust, B., Hermon, G. and Kornfilt J. (eds.), *Syntactic Theory and First Language Acquisition: A Cross-linguistic Perspectives. Volume 2: Binding, Dependencies, and Learnability*. Hillsdale, NJ: Lawrence Erlbaum, 273–86.

VanPatten, B. 1990: Attending to content and form in the input: An experiment in consciousness. *Studies in Second Language Acquisition* 12, 287–301.

—— 1994: Evaluating the role of consciousness in second language acquisition: terms, linguistic features and research methodology. *AILA Review* 11, 27–36.

—— 1995: Cognitive aspects of input processing in second language acquisition. In Heshemipour, P., Maldonado, I. and van Naerssen, M. (eds.), *Festschrift for Tracy David Terrel*. New York: McGraw-Hill, 170–83.

—— 1996: *Input Processing and Grammar Instruction in Second Language Acquisition*. Norwood, NJ: Ablex.

—— and Cadierno, T. 1993a: Explicit instruction and input processing. *Studies in Second Language Acquisition* 15, 225–43.

—— 1993b: Input processing and second language acquisition: a role for instruction. *The Modern Language Journal* 77, 45–57.

—— and Oikkenon, S. 1996: Explanation versus structured input in processing instruction. *Studies in Second Language Acquisition* 18, 495–510.

—— and Sanz, C. 1995: From input to output: Processing instruction and communication tasks. In Eckman, F., Highland, D., Lee, P.W., Mileham, J. and Weber, R.R. (eds.), *Second Language Acquisition and Pedagogy*. Mahwah, NJ: Lawrence Erlbaum, 169–85.

Van Valin, R.D., Jr. 1996: Functional relations. In Brown, K. and Miller, J. *Concise Encyclopedia of Syntactic Theories*. Pergamon: Oxford, 98–110.

Wagner-Gough. J. 1978: Comparative studies in second language acquisition. In Marcussen-Hatch, E. (ed.), *Second Language Acquisition: A Book of Readings*. Rowley, MA: Newbury House, 155–71.

Wardhaugh, R. 1970: The contrastive analysis hypothesis. *TESOL Quarterly* 4, 123–30.

Wesche, M.B. 1994: Input and interaction in second language acquisition. In Callaway, C.

and Richards, B.J. (eds.) *Input and Interaction in Language Acquisition*. Cambridge: Cambridge University Press, 219–49.

Westney, P. 1994: Rules and pedagogical grammar. In Odlin, T. (ed.), *Perspectives on Pedagogical Grammar*. Cambridge: Cambridge University Press, 72–96.

Wexler, K. and Manzini, M.R. 1987: Parameters and learnability in binding theory. In Roeper, T. and Williams, E. (eds.), *Parameter Setting*. Dordrecht: Reidel, 41–76.

White, L. 1985a: The acquisition of parameterized grammars: subjacency in second language acquisition. *Second Language Research* 1, 1–17.

—— 1985b: The 'pro-drop' parameter in adult second language acquisition. *Language Learning* 35, 47–61.

—— 1986: Implications of parametric variation for adult second language acquisition: an investigation of the pro-drop parameter. In Cook, V.J. (ed.), *Experimental Approaches to Second Language Learning*. Oxford: Pergamon Press, 55–72.

—— 1987a: Against comprehensible input: the input hypothesis and the development of L2 competence. *Applied Linguistics* 8, 95–110.

—— 1987b: Markedness and second language acquisition: the question of transfer. *Studies in Second Language Acquisition* 9, 261–86.

—— 1987c: Universal Grammar: is it just a new name for old problems? Paper presented at Second Language Research Forum, Los Angeles, CA.

—— 1988: Island effects in second language acquisition. In Flynn, S. and O'Neil, W. (eds.), *Linguistic Theory in Second Language Acquisition*. Dordrecht, The Netherlands: Kluwer, 144–72.

—— 1989: *Universal Grammar and Second Language Acquisition*. Philadelphia: John Benjamins.

—— 1990–1: The verb-movement parameter in second language acquisition. *Language Acquisition* 1, 337–60.

—— 1991a: Adverb placement in second language acquisition: some effects of positive and negative evidence in the classroom. *Second Language Research* 7, 133–61.

—— 1991b: Second language competence versus second language performance: UG or processing strategies? In Eubank, L. (ed.), *Point Counterpoint: Universal Grammar in the Second Language*. Philadelphia: John Benjamins, 167–89.

—— 1991c: The verb-movement parameter in second language acquisition. *Language Acquisition* 1, 337–60.

—— 1992a: Long and short verb movement in second language acquisition. *Canadian Journal of Linguistics* 37, 273–86.

—— 1992b: On triggering data in L2 acquisition: a reply to Schwartz and Gubala-Ryzak. *Second Language Research* 8, 120–37.

—— 1992c: Subjacency violations and empty categories in L2 acquisition. In Goodluck, H. and Rochemont, M. (eds.), *Island Constraints*. Dordrecht: Kluwer, 445–64.

—— 1995: Chasing after linguistic theory. How minimal should we be? In Eubank, L., Selinker, L. and Sharwood Smith, M. (eds.), *The Current State of Interlanguage*. Philadelphia: John Benjamins, 63–71.

—— Spada, N., Lightbown, P.M., and Ranta, L. 1991: Input enhancement and L2 question formation. *Applied Linguistics* 12, 416–32.

—— Travis, L. and MacLachlan, A. 1992: The acquisition of wh-question formation by Malagasy learners of English: evidence for Universal Grammar. *Canadian Journal of Linguistics* 37, 341–68.

Williams, J. 1988: Zero anaphora in second language acquisition. *Studies in Second Language Acquisition* 10, 339–70.

—— 1989: Pronoun copies, pronominal anaphora and zero anaphora in second language production. In Gass, S.M., Madden, C., Preston, D. and Selinker, L. (eds.), *Variation in Second Language Acquisition. Volume 1: Discourse and Pragmatics.* Clevedon, Avon: Multilingual Matters, 153–89.

Wode, H. 1978a: Developmental sequences in naturalistic L2 acquisition. In Hatch, E. (ed.), *Second Language Acquisition: A Book of Readings.* Rowley, MA: Newbury House, 101–17.

—— 1978b: The L1 vs. L2 acquisition of English interrogation. *Working Papers on Bilingualism* 15, 37–57.

—— 1980: Operating principles and 'universals' in L1, L2, and FLT. In Nehls, D. (ed.), *Studies in Language Acquisition.* Heidelberg: Julius Groos Verlag, 53–67.

—— 1981: *Learning a Second Language.* Tübingen: Gunter Narr.

—— 1984: Some theoretical implications of L2 acquisition research and the grammar of interlanguages. In Davies, A., Criper, C. and Howatt, A.P.R. (eds.), *Interlanguage.* Edinburgh: Edinburgh University Press, 162–84.

—— 1986: Language transfer: a cognitive functional and developmental view. In Kellerman, E. and Sharwood Smith, M. (eds.), *Crosslinguistic Influence in Second Language Acquisition.* New York: Pergamon Institute of English, 173–85.

Wolfe-Quintero, K. 1992: Learnability and the acquisition of extraction in relative clauses and wh-questions. *Studies in Second Language Acquisition* 14, 39–70.

Wulfeck, B.B., Juarez, L., Bates, E. and Kilborn, K. 1986: Sentence interpretation strategies in healthy and aphasic bilingual adults. In Vaid, J. (ed.), *Language Processing in Bilinguals: Psycholinguistic and Neurological Perspectives.* Hillsdale, NJ: Lawrence Erlbaum, 199–219.

Young-Scholten, M. and Vainikka, A. 1992: The development of functional projections in L2 syntax. Paper presented in January at the LSA annual meeting, Philadelphia.

Zobl, H. 1980a: Developmental and transfer errors: their common bases and (possibly) differential effects on subsequent learning. *TESOL Quarterly* 14, 469–79.

—— 1980b: The formal and developmental selectivity of L1 influence on L2 acquisition. *Language Learning* 30, 43–57.

—— 1983: L1 acquisition, age of L2 acquisition, and the learning of word order. In Gass, S. M. and Selinker, L. (eds.), *Language Transfer in Language Learning.* Rowley, MA: Newbury House, 205–21.

—— 1995: Converging evidence for the 'acquisition-learning' distinction. *Applied Linguistics* 16, 35–56.

Author index

Language index

Subject index